# VIROID

'This volume offers a trenchant account of the transhuman condition. The author thoughtfully considers the extent to which humankind is poised on the threshold of a transhuman future, and demands that we radically rethink our assumptions about the human animal in order that biology and philosophy might join forces in order to rid Western thought of its pernicious anthropocentric prejudices.'

Daniel W. Conway, Pennsylvania State University

'A post-critical tour de force which leads the reader to reconsider the boundary between the human and the inhuman. An essay which ranks alongside those of Deleuze and Baudrillard.'

Mike Gane, University of Loughborough

*Viroid Life* presents a bold challenge to existing conceptions of biotechnology and artificial life through Nietzsche's thinking of the 'overman'. Arguing that current debates are lodged in a historical and insufficiently machinic framework, Keith Ansell Pearson insists that artifice must be seen as an integral feature of nature. Far from being able to stand outside and control developments in bio-technology, the human being is bound up in a very becoming that is implicated in the inventions of technics and machines. Resisting uncritical contemporary interpretations in thrall to biotechnology, *Viroid Life* reinstates Nietzsche's thinking on life – and death – to make us confront the nature of the human and move beyond the anthropocentrism of technics and acknowledge the more complicated conceptions of evolution.

Offering insights into Darwinism, neo-Darwinism, the new paradigms of contemporary biology and the thought of Gilles Deleuze and Félix Guatarri, Keith Ansell Pearson shows how viral developments in science can create new, rhizomatic ways of thinking in philosophy.

Essential reading for anyone concerned with the future of philosophy, *Viroid Life: Perspectives on Nietzsche and the Transhuman Condition* provides a fascinating new starting point for any discussion on the future of evolution and will interest students of continental philosophy, social theory and cultural studies.

**Keith Ansell Pearson** is Senior Lecturer and Director of Graduate Research at the University of Warwick. He is the author of *Nietzsche contra Rousseau* and *An Introduction to Nietzsche as a Political Thinker*.

# VIROID LIFE

Perspectives on Nietzsche and the Transhuman Condition

**KEITH ANSELL PEARSON**

LONDON AND NEW YORK

First published 1997
by Routledge
11 New Fetter Lane, London EC4P 4EE

Simultaneously published in the USA and Canada
by Routledge
29 West 35th Street, New York, NY 10001

© 1997 Keith Ansell Pearson

Typeset in Perpetua by Keystroke, Jacaranda Lodge, Wolverhampton
Printed and bound in Great Britain by Creative Print and Design (Wales), Ebbw Vale

All rights reserved. No part of this book may be reprinted or
reproduced or utilized in any form or by any electronic,
mechanical, or other means, now known or hereafter
invented, including photocopying and recording, or in any
information storage retrieval system, without permission in
writing from the publishers.

*British Library Cataloguing in Publication Data*
A catalogue record for this book is available from the British Library

*Library of Congress Cataloging in Publication Data*
Ansell Pearson, Keith
Viroid life: perspectives on Nietzsche and the transhuman condition / Keith Ansell Pearson.
p.   cm.
Includes bibliographical references and index.
1. Nietzsche, Friedrich Wilhelm, 1844–1900.  2. Superman.  3. Philosophical anthropology.
I. Title.
B3318.S8A57   1997
128—dc21      96–49700

ISBN 0–415–15434–0 (hbk)
0–415–15435–9 (pbk)

For friends down under

To open us up to the inhuman and superhuman . . . to go beyond the human condition is the meaning of philosophy, in so far as our condition condemns us to live among badly analyzed composites, and to be badly analyzed composites ourselves.

(Gilles Deleuze, *Bergsonism*, 1966)


Sometimes he wondered what zone of transit he himself was entering, sure that his own withdrawal was symptomatic not of a dormant schizophrenia, but of a careful preparation for a radically new environment, with its own internal landscape and logic, where old categories of thought would merely be an encumbrance.

(J. G. Ballard, *The Drowned World*, 1962)


Man is such a hive and swarm of parasites that it is doubtful whether his body is not more theirs than his, and whether he is anything but another kind of ant-heap after all. May not man himself become another sort of parasite upon the machines? An affectionate machine-tickling aphid?

(Samuel Butler, *Erewhon*, 1872)

# CONTENTS

Acknowledgements xi
Introduction 1

**1 Loving the Poison**
The memory of the human and the promise of the overhuman  9

**2 Towards the Overhuman**
On the art and artifice of Nietzsche's selection  37

**3 Dead or Alive**
On the death of eternal return  57

**4 Nietzsche contra Darwin**  85

**5 Viroid Life**
On machines, technics, and evolution  123

**6 Timely Meditations on the Transhuman Condition**
Nihilism, entropy, and beyond  151

Bibliography 191
Index 199

# ACKNOWLEDGEMENTS

Five of the chapters which make up this volume have appeared, or will appear, in a number of publishing projects. I am grateful to the editors and publishers listed below for their permission to reproduce this material.

Chapter 1 is an extended version of a chapter due to appear in John Lippitt (ed.), *Nietzsche and the Future of the Human*, Macmillan.

Chapter 2 is a modified version of an essay that first appeared as 'Toward the Übermensch: Reflections on the Year of Nietzsche's Daybreak', in *Nietzsche-Studien* 23 (1994), Walter de Gruyter.

Chapter 3 is a modified and extended version of an essay entitled 'The Return of Death' that will appear in *Journal of Nietzsche Studies*, 1997 in a special issue devoted to the eternal return edited by David Owen.

Chapter 4 will appear in modified form in D. W. Conway (ed.), *Nietzsche: Critical Assessments*, Routledge.

Chapter 5 is a modified and shortened version of a chapter that will appear in Keith Ansell Pearson (ed.), *Deleuze and Philosophy*, Routledge.

This book might never have reached this stage were it not for the encouragement, provocation, and critical intervention of several people. Serious thanks are due to Daniel W. Conway, Adrian Driscoll, Mike Gane, Graham Parkes, Paul Patton, and John Protevi. My debt to Dan Conway in particular for his support for what I am trying to accomplish in this book is incalculable. Catherine Dale played a seminal role in the book's final consummation, inspiring the end, and continues to play a 'minor' role in the involution of my thinking and writing.

# INTRODUCTION

'All truth is simple' — is that not a compound lie?

'There are more idols in this world than realities: that is *my* 'evil eye' for this world, that is also my 'evil ear'.

(Nietzsche, *Twilight of the Idols*)

In this volume of essays I question, problematize, overturn, revalue, announce, renounce, advocate, interrogate, affirm, deny, celebrate, critique, the 'transhuman condition', exploring the human as a site of contamination and abduction by alien forces and rendering, in the process, the phenomenon polyvalent and polysemous. I resist attempts to foreclose the condition by those who would claim to have defined it and demonstrated it once and for all. In recent years the 'transhuman' has assumed a viral life, becoming a cultural meme. But this condition does not spread naturally; it requires critical and careful cultivation if it is to possess any genuine sense or 'meaning'. By treating this condition I realize I place myself on perilous and treacherous ground, opening myself up to contamination by strange forces of various kinds and guises. But philosophy is not simply a tribunal of reason; it is also a battleground of infections and sicknesses. My response to the predicament I find myself in has been to adopt a 'perspectival' position on the phenomenon. Virtually all of the essays in this volume confront the same 'problem', namely that of the future of the human, with the result that some repetition is inevitable. However, it is my genuine hope that the more eyes, various eyes, that are employed to treat the transhuman condition, the more complete and objective will the treatment be.

It is important to resist attempts to reduce the 'transhuman condition' to anything obviously empirical, such as a 'biological' condition or a 'technological' one (neither of these are, in fact, simply 'empirical'). Current techno-theorizing contends that evolution – not *human* evolution but evolution in- and for-itself – is now entering a bio-technological phase, with biological life becoming more and more technological and technological life becoming more and more biological. But the rise of this dubious neo-Lamarckism, which demands that we give ourselves 'over' to the future as an act of blind faith and in terms of a quasi-Heideggerian destiny (only a machine can save us), rests on a highly anthropomorphic conception of life's becoming, positing a straightforwardly linear and perfectionist model of evolution. The promise of a genetic take-over by machines that is predicted by many, a threat that goes back to Samuel Butler and his writing in the 1860s in the wake of Darwin, must be treated with suspicion, if not derision. It would not be difficult to expose the anthropocentric conceits informing much of the discussion and celebration of the coming of intelligent robots and machines. In fact, Baudrillard has already done so – in his *The Illusion of the End* (1994) and now in *The Perfect Crime* (1996). In this conception of life's evolution leading in the direction of non-affective machines, in which thought exists without a body, there is no future of, or for, invention, since all is given. The future is no longer virtual: indeed it no longer exists; it no longer 'is'. Instead what we are being presented with is a paranoid and phobic anthropocentrism that is bent on imperialistically and entropically colonizing the entire known and unknown universe, all for the sake of immortal life. This is the ultimate Platonic fantasy. So today we find that it is no longer Christianity that is fulfilling the role of a Platonism for the people, but rather a cyberspace cult. In the age of irresistible, endo-colonistic capitalism never has such an unintelligent hybrid – that of 'bio-technological' vitalism – been more suspect and in need of 'critique'. We find ourselves in an ironical situation – what other situation would we expect to find ourselves in at the end of the millennium? – in which cyber-celebrations of the transhuman, or even more dubiously, of the posthuman, condition, can ultimately be shown to rest on a (non-dialectical) cancellation of this condition. It is not a question of 'self-overcoming' since there is nothing to overcome. The process of evolution is naturalized and reified, a new theology of capital emerges to cavalierly justify and legitimize the inanities of the commodified postmodern present, a legitimization which rests on the vicious return of outmoded grand narratives, and there is a complete lack of any appreciation of what it is that has made, and continues to make, the human such an interesting animal, an animal and a machine still in need of revaluation and transvaluation. The human and its genealogical past are simply not being taken 'seriously'. The result, it seems to me, is a vacuous, pernicious, and politically naive conception of our condition and of our 'fate' at the end of the twentieth century. Affirming the inhuman and demonic powers of the future is not equivalent to a biological or technological manipulation of the future: it is not to arrive at a radical conception of the time of the future but to nullify its demonic becoming. The writing in this volume can be interpreted as offering a resistance to the postmodern/posthuman if these are taken to imply what Fredric Jameson has described as a systematic effacement of all the supposed anachronistic traces of our recent historical past.

The reader of this volume, however, should be forewarned that my advocacy and problematizing of a genuinely 'Nietzschean' conception of the transhuman condition do not desire to preserve anything about the human in terms of notions of its integrity, inviolability, or supremacy. The reading is decidedly 'supra-moral' in this regard. Neither do I adhere to fantasies of historical revolution in which we humans will reclaim our rightful control and mastery over nature and society. This desire for complete historical immanence, which has inspired the major critical theorists of this century from Marcuse to Debord and Vaneigem, and continues to inspire major contemporary theorists like Fredric Jameson, fills me with as much dread and loathing as do the articles of faith promulgated by our contemporary cyberspace gurus. It is perhaps no wonder, then, that these days I find myself out on a limb.

In 1979 Lyotard defined the 'postmodern condition' as 'incredulity' in the face of those grand or meta-narratives which have served to provide human existence with teleological meaning and significance, so that the lament of the loss of meaning in postmodernity boils down to mourning the fact that knowledge is now no longer principally narrative. The 'stories' the West has told of itself to itself and to 'others' – such as that of emancipation through rational enlightenment and progress – turn out to have been a great conceit and deceit. Now that myth has come to waste and ruin, and, so Lyotard wanted us to believe, the period of mourning is over. Little did Lyotard know at the time of his writing that the grand narrative of the Enlightenment would soon become replaced by another one, equally insidious in its vapid generalized character and undemonstrable universalization. Although Lyotard acknowledged that he was 'simplifying to the extreme', his definition and summation proved highly influential, giving rise to a whole series of lamenting, and lamentable, crisis-reflections on the end of history, the end of politics, the end of time, and so on. A genuine crisis of 'critical theory' was perceived as taking place, since if the subject of critique was dead (the proletariat, man as the purpose of history, and a self-transformative humanity as the goal of history), what remained of the force and purchase of the critical intent? However, Lyotard's declaration of the end of grand narratives has proved premature since today we see their return taking place within a variety of contemporary discourses. Within postmodernity a belated 'return' to the question of technology is taking place in which philosophy is getting infected by its own perplexity in the face of the sheer monstrous otherness of the question and the confusion it generates, displacing all normal questioning and corroding many human self-certainties. But is there anything really radically new in this requestioning? The shock of the future was analysed incisively by a postwar generation of leading critical theorists such as Jacques Ellul, Lewis Mumford, and Herbert Marcuse, all of whom addressed the question of technology in terms of a concern with the future of time and the time of the future, as well as in terms of a political perspicacity that is often lacking in current discourse. What appears to be different in the return to the question today is recognition of the scale of disorientation and displacement created by the impact of computerization, the rise of new forms of engineering and new modes of knowledge, the creation of artificial life, etc. However, these new realities demand not an impetuous abandonment of a thinking and valuing of the 'human' condition, but rather a radical re-examination and revaluation, in which one would show the extent to which this condition has always been a matter of invention and reinvention, that is, always a matter of the transhuman. The grand narrative today is likely to take the form of a facile quasi-Hegelianism in which the rise of the machine is construed in linear and perfectionist terms: the ever-growing inhuman character of 'technology' resides in the 'simple' fact that it is machines that are proving to be more successful in creating an adequate response to the tasks laid down by evolution than the creatures whose existence first gave rise to it. This new narrative rests on a curious amalgam of Darwinian and Lamarckian elements. On the one hand, it is claimed that machines are proving to be 'fitter' in the task of life's survival against the dissipative forces of entropy, so enjoying a high adaptive value that is far superior to the limited capacities which the human being has for further adaptation; on the other hand, it is also being claimed by some that the rise of 'intelligent' computerized machines signifies a goal-oriented desire on the part of 'evolution' itself to attain a trans-human condition (conceived literally and linearly).

Clearly, given the techno-phobic nature of the philosophical tradition, thought today needs to embark on a new negotiation with technology. This can be cultivated in a number of ways. Firstly, one can recognize that from its 'origins' the human has been constituted by technical evolution. It is the mediation afforded by technics which makes it impossible simply to describe evolution in terms of a self-contained, or monadic, subject that passively 'adapts' to an object-like environment. Although technics is not peculiar to the human form of evolution, what is distinctive about it is the extent to which it drastically alters the meaning of 'adaptation' and 'evolution' in the case of the human animal. It is both the sign or mark of human distinctive futurity and the source of the *artificial* character of human inventions and 'evolutions'. The question of what we are becoming and what 'adaptation' might mean in an artificially created world (an environment not simply created by us since such creation always exceeds what we 'are') is badly treated if technology is read in terms of an extension of natural history. The human being is the greatest freak of nature and the only futures we can be certain of are monstrous ones characterized by perpetual mutation and morphing. The 'meaning' of 'technics' and of 'technology' is deliberately left open-ended in these essays in order to provoke, rather than de-limit or foreclose, reflection. Both notions are clearly caught up in a philosophical tradition of metaphysics, but their determination for the greater part of the history of philosophy has been that of an anthropocentric kind: technics/techniques are simply tools and devices employed as means to the furtherance of human ends. However, an anti-humanist reading of their meaning reveals its own cavalier aspects, and easy celebrations of the arrival of the posthuman – which is how the postmodern condition is now being treated – are far too unreflective about their historical conditioning and genealogical (in-)formation. Reification of the most obfuscatory kind takes place when the contingent nature of human becoming and its inventions of technology are taken to denote a desire for runaway adaptation and greater and greater complexity on the part of evolution. I am not denying that such complexity has taken place; what I take issue with in this study is the anthropomorphic claim that the process of complexification is 'inhuman' and the expression of 'life'. To declare that technology amounts to 'the pursuit of life by means other than life' is not to provide insight into the past and future condition of evolution but to encourage blindness regarding matters of life and death within late-capital. Such a claim deprives us of any genuinely interesting and critical in-humanity.

The second, and more innovative, way in which a new negotiation with our technical natures and artificial becomings can be forged is by granting primacy to the question concerning the machine (which is molecular, dealing solely with virtual realities) over the question concerning technology (which is perhaps always molar, all too molar, and lacking an appreciation of the virtual character of 'evolution'). Typically the machine is construed as a deficient form of life, lacking in autopoietic formative power, in contrast to organismic life, which is regarded as enjoying a monopoly over formative power and self-generative evolution. In the work of Deleuze and Guattari we find an innovative and far-reaching revaluation of the machine/organism distinction in which the 'machinic' is pitted against both the mechanical and the organic in order to account for novel and complex becomings within evolution. As a point of fact, however, these machinic or rhizomatic becomings do not so much take place 'in' evolution as create or invent it, so marking the 'of' evolution as an event of a genuine becoming (or what Bergson called 'creative evolution'). When things evolve machinically they do so immanently and pragmatically, by means of contagion and contamination, following laws neither of resemblance nor of utility (see Massumi 1992: 192–3). A machinic conception of evolution is based on a radical pluralism, in which one can speak of a diverse range of alterior becomings to do with technical machines, social machines, semiotic machines, axiological machines, animal machines, existential machines, and so on. Inquiry into their nature and becoming is not governed by a reified (humanized) notion of what constitutes their vital autonomy based on an abstract animal model, but in terms of their specific enunciative consistencies (Guattari 1992/1995). Moreover, it is not a question of humanizing this universe of machines so that everywhere one sees only the mirror image of our own desire for control, influence, design, and mastery. Human thought clearly plays a major role in the evolution of a machinic phylogenesis, but it is hubris which leads to the positing of the human, all too human as the meaning and telos of this machinism. For the greater part of evolution human thought has relied on the mediation of technical machines – an originary mnemotechnics is constitutive of human thinking – but this cannot mean that the thought that is generated can be characterized as solely or strictly 'human' in terms of some ethic of possessive individualism. Thought is 'transhuman' in all the senses of the word one cares to think of. The music which these machines speak does not provide access to a single, univocal truth 'of' Being, as if *techne* possessed an essence available only to humans as part of their supposed unique and privileged residency in the cosmos; rather, machines provide pathic and cartographic access to a plurality of beings and of worlds. As Guattari noted, within the machinic universe beings have only the status of virtual entities; that is, they are sites of becoming in which what becomes is always something alien.

In terms of its fundamental preoccupations – searching the meaning of time, of history, of life, of evolution, of humanity, and so on – this book is a continuation of problems posed in my earlier study *Nietzsche contra Rousseau* (1991). I am seeking a radical inhuman philosophy that would serve to 'destroy' the immature and imperious claims made upon life by all forms of philosophical anthropocentrism. I see the 'critical' task of excessive thinking, which is utilized by the untimely meditator, as one of disentangling the lines which cut across, machincally, the 'recent' past and the 'near' future. The critical thinker uses history excessively for the sake of the 'beyond', acting contra time, on time, through time, out of time, *for the sake of time*, which amounts to becoming-other than what history has made us and wishes to make of us. Moreover, this process of becoming also involves overcoming what we make of ourselves since emancipation from the idols of one's time must necessarily entail emancipating oneself from one's suffering of one's time, a time that the self is deeply implicated in as its peculiar sickness. The task of working-through the transhuman condition thus involves the task of thinking beyond the 'beyond'.

The task of tracking the 'reality of the creative', which is not to be confused with identifying with the merely 'fashionable', involves an exposition of a variety of transcendent(al) illusions, connected to, for example, nihilism (which is only a sign or symptom of decay and the arrival of the new), to entropy, to the death-drive, to 'evolution' as classically conceived, and to the alleged autonomous theo-logic of capital. Transcendent(al) illusions concerning the human condition arise out of an ingrained resistance to fluxes of becoming. As the quotation from Deleuze at the start of this book says, it is not simply the case that we dwell among badly analysed composites, but that we ourselves are badly analysed composites. As Deleuze and Guattari state it in their *What is Philosophy?*, these illusions emanate from an inability to tolerate infinite movements and from a desire to master and tame the infinite speeds of time and the future which crush what we are. The illusions of 'transcendence', of 'universals', and of 'eternal verities' can all be explained in this way. The problem that remains is how to think *trans*humanly the future, a mode of thinking of the future that will inevitably appear as 'inhuman' when it comes into contact, and conflict, with all earthly seriousness to date. But this transhuman praxis of thought nevertheless enjoys its own seriousness. To 'access' such a mode of thinking one must be inspired by Bergson's contention that the function of philosophy is to do violence to the mind by breaking with both the natural bent of the intellect and with scientific habits. At the same time, one must recognize and acknowledge one's involvement with anthropomorphism, with its straitjacket, without conceding that thinking and its task must remain, and must restrict themselves to, human-all-too-human. This would be, and is, to betray the human. This somewhat elevated conception of philosophy is out of sync with the timidity that currently infects and afflicts the postmodern *Stimmung*. Postmodernism often strikes me as the culminating point of Western narcissisim and humanism. Theoretical postmodernism is thus how a redundant species of intellectuals grant themselves a spurious self-importance in the face of a phase-space transition to inhuman futures and the birth, evident all around us, of new 'alien' intelligences and becomings. The task today is no longer to seek God, dead or alive (though there are caves in which his shadow continues not only to flicker but to burn brightly), but to be drawn to the land of the future where human impotence no longer makes us mad and where it is possible to decode the signs of alien life within and without us. For this we do not so much require new truths; rather it becomes necessary to remember and relearn some ancient ones. One will then discover them as if for the first time, for there is only the 'first' time that is repeated again and again. The future, for example, has always been 'out there'. It does not simply lie ahead of us. It is the place of the 'outside'.

In writing as an 'advocate' of Nietzsche I write as someone who necessarily reads Nietzsche contra himself. In its conceptions of the will-to-power and the eternal return, through which it endeavours to articulate an alternative biological model of selection to prevailing Darwinian ones, Nietzsche's thinking reveals itself to be as ensnared in anthropomorphism as any philosophy of life of the modern epoch. It is not simply a question of criticizing Nietzsche for replacing the prejudices of morality with prejudices of his own; rather, the task is to show how his attempt to go beyond the human is implicated in the becoming of the human. Fortunately, there are resources in Nietzsche's texts for demonstrating the force of this insight. My relationship to Nietzsche, therefore, is decidedly, and undecidably, 'complex'.

The essays which make up this volume do not explore these questions either systematically or exhaustively. They are best read as perspectival essays-in-progress – on or towards the transhuman condition – which pursue modest ambitions of exploring, critically and affirmatively, the phenomenon of the transhuman, and which seek to make a contribution to, and a critical intervention in, some of the key questions of the present. As Nietzsche notes, one climbs up the steps of thought to pass 'over' them, not to remain settled on them.

Full details of my source material can be found in the bibliography. It should be noted that I have modified the translations of Nietzsche used without explicitly signalling this.

# 1

# LOVING THE POISON

## The memory of the human and the promise of the overhuman

I

Read from a distant planet, the majuscule-script of our earthly existence would perhaps seduce the reader to the conclusion that the earth was the ascetic planet *par excellence*, an outpost of discontented, arrogant, and nasty creatures who harboured a deep distrust for themselves, for the world, for all life and hurt themselves as much as possible out of pleasure in hurting.

(Nietzsche 1994: 90)

Probably we, too, are still 'too good' for our trade, probably we, too, are still the victims, the prey, the sick of this contemporary taste for moralization, much as we feel contempt towards it, – it probably infects *us* as well.

(Nietzsche 1994: 109)

The Age of Postbiological Man would reveal the human condition for what it actually is, which is to say, *a condition to be gotten out of*. Friedrich Nietzsche, the philosopher, had already seen the truth of this back in the nineteenth century: 'Man is something that should be overcome', he had written in 1883. 'What have you done to overcome him?' Back then, of course, the question was only rhetorical, but now in *fin-de-siècle* twentieth century, we had all the necessary means in front of us . . . for turning ourselves into the most advanced transhumans imaginable.

(Regis 1992: 175)

Nothing in biology in general, or in our own human life in particular, makes sense except in the context of memory, of history.

(Rose 1992: 327).

The question of the future of the human opens up a zone of monstrous thought, calling into being the necessity of a thinking of the transhuman condition. One thinks of Nietzsche's 'great' question: 'what may still become of "man"?', in which 'man' only becomes such at a certain juncture in historical evolution, his name presupposing a transcendence of race and nation (Nietzsche 1968: section 957).[1] Critical questions proliferate: is the overhuman not the peculiar and unique configuration of the future? Can new origins be created for humans, other than those which are canonically handed down to those children of the future who patiently seafare their way to a land that is far away from fatherlands and Oedipal complexes? In discovering 'for the first time' the country of 'man' do we not also at the same time discover the 'human future' (Nietzsche 1969: 'Old and New Law-Tables' section 28)? Is not the future our un-natural birth-right? Is the future at all intelligible to the human? Perhaps the unintelligibility of the future applies only to the common sense of humanity and the good sense of philosophic reason. Nietzsche claimed to be able to decipher the hieroglyphs of the future, but for this task there is required an extra-human – and inhuman – sense and sensibility.

Several crucial and complex questions are implicated in the problematic of the future of the human as they relate to Nietzsche, including the following:

- The figuration of the future in Nietzsche, in which Nietzsche portrays himself as a posthumous destiny belonging to another history; his is a philosophy 'of' the future which claims to speak not only 'of' the future but 'from' the future.

---

1 This section runs: 'Inexorably, hesitantly, terrible as fate, the great task and question is approaching: how shall the earth as a whole be governed? And to what end shall "man" as a whole – and no longer as a people, a race – be raised and trained?' For the German see Nietzsche 1987, volume 11: 581ff. It is interesting to note that one of the major studies of 'technics' of this century, Jacques Ellul's *The Technological Society*, poses the question of 'la technique ou l'enjeu du siècle' in very Nietzschean terms, in which the question of the 'wherefore' of evolution is replaced by the triumph of the last man. For Ellul, though, it is no longer a question of the last man blinking when he finds 'happiness'. 'It is apparently our fate', he writes concerning speculations about a genetically designed future, 'to be facing a "golden age" in the power of sorcerers who are totally blind to the meaning of the human adventure. When they speak of preserving the seed of outstanding men, whom pray, do they mean to be the judges? It is hardly likely that they will deem a Rimbaud or a Nietzsche worthy of posterity . . . None of our wise men ever pose the question of the end of all their marvels. The "wherefore" is resolutely passed by. The response which would occur to our contemporaries is: for the sake of happiness. Unfortunately, there is no longer any question of that.' To approach the question of *la technique* on the level of genetic design is simply to enclose it within the restricted – human, all too human – economy of technology: 'The last meager motive we could possibly ascribe to the technical adventure thus vanishes into thin air through the very existence of technique itself' (Ellul 1965: 435–6).

'The future speaks in a hundred signs even now' (Nietzsche 1968: preface), and 'It is the future which regulates our today' (Nietzsche 1986: preface). What is the 'appeal' to the future which informs Nietzsche's writing? What would it mean to give the earth a 'purpose'? To redeem reality from the curse which the ascetic ideal had placed upon it (Nietzsche 1994: II, section 24)? Is Nietzsche entitled to draw upon notions of purpose and meaning in the wake of his critique of metaphysics, of its anthropocentrism and anthropomorphism, as well as his taking on board the impact of Darwin?[2]

- The question of time, which has barely been thought in relation to the question of the time of the overhuman. On the contrary, its actuality has been conceived either in conventional linear terms, as that which comes 'after' humans, or eschatologically and apocalyptically as marking a new beginning. Derrida sought to problematize radically the various moves to think of the human 'and' the overhuman in his now classic essay of the late 1960s on 'The Ends of Man', noting that what is most difficult to think is an 'end' 'of' 'man' that would not be organized by a 'dialectics of truth' and 'be a teleology in the first person plural' (Derrida 1982: 121). Within metaphysics the 'name of man' has meaning only in an 'eschato-teleological situation'. Derrida selects Nietzsche as the key post-metaphysical thinker – over and above Heidegger – on account of his pluralization of style and meaning. Within Nietzsche's styles we can locate a 'laughter' and a 'dance' that come from 'outside', which neither 'repeat' in the same old fashion of metaphysical humanism nor pursue the 'beyond' in the form of a 'memorial' of the meaning of 'Being'. However, Derrida's attempt to think the 'beyond' of metaphysics in a way that is attentive to the paradoxes involved in such a move remains entirely with the 'idealism' of metaphysics. Thus his invocation at the end of the essay of the notions of 'active forgetting' and festivals of cruelty strike us as merely gestural and solely writerly, with no regard for the matter of life and its deviant becoming in either biology, technics, or material history. Heidegger's postwar reading of Nietzsche completely historicized the figure of the overhuman, subjecting it to a reading of technology by linking it to a 'future master of the earth' who wields to higher purposes and powers what 'falls' to the human of the future with the dawning of the

---

2 The opening sections of *Human, All Too Human* strike me as offering a post-Darwinian conception of philosophical culture, so that Darwin has to be seen as an essential part of Nietzsche's call for a new Enlightenment in an age of nihilism. In the opening sections he calls for a new style of 'historical philosophizing' whose most important virtue will be that of 'modesty' (Nietzsche 1986: sections 1, 2).

'technological transformation of the earth and of human activity' (Heidegger 1968: 59). The only philosopher of postwar times to connect the overhuman with questions of form and forces in terms of a complex becoming is Deleuze: 'The question that continually returns is therefore the following: if the forces within man compose a form only by entering into a relation with forms from the outside, with what new forms do they now risk entering into a relation, and what new form will emerge that is neither God nor man? This is the correct place for the problem which Nietzsche called the "superman"' (Deleuze 1988b: 130). Nietzsche does speak of man belonging to a 'higher history' in the aftermath of the death of God, but this higher history is implicated in a still formative 'pre-history' and is bound up with history itself in complicated ways. It is a question of 'evolution' as a question of foldings and of 'life' conceived as the great fold: 'Man hitherto — as it were, an embryo of the man of the future; — all the form-shaping forces directed toward the latter are present in the former; and because they are tremendous, the more a present-day individual determines the future. This is the profoundest conception of suffering: the form-shaping forces are in painful collision. — The isolation of the individual ought not to deceive us: something flows on *underneath* individuals' (Nietzsche 1968: section 686).

- The question of Nietzsche's relation to modern biology and theories of evolution, notably Darwinism. Why does Nietzsche utilize embryology to articulate his theory of will-to-power, and the primacy it accords to spontaneous and expansive form-shaping forces, in *On the Genealogy of Morality*? Why does he appeal to biology at certain crucial points in his argument on a genealogy of morals (for example, appraising 'states of legality' from 'the highest biological point of view', 1994: 54)? To what extent is Nietzsche's genealogy of *morals* based on a necessary revaluation of Darwinian 'biological' values? Heidegger's point contra biologism and a biologistic reading of Nietzsche — namely, that biology is also 'metaphysics' — remains important and apposite, but it does not exhaust the question (Heidegger 1961: I, 517ff.; trans. 1987: 39ff.). Moreover, why after a hundred years and more do we need to be told again and again of the ultimate truth of Darwin's theory of natural selection by biologists (Dawkins 1976) and philosophers (Dennett 1995b) alike as if it were an uncomplicated 'truth' for humans?[3] It is here that 'we' may sound strangest. The lesson of

---

3 In his *The Selfish Gene* Dawkins seeks to advance a new cultural Darwinism by interpreting the evolution of culture in terms of a memetics. He argues that concentration on the gene as the unit

Nietzsche's genealogy of morality is perhaps more apposite now than ever before. It is not accidental that Nietzsche's genealogy should 'select' humans as it focus. It does this while eschewing anthropocentric naivety. His genealogy shows the extent to which the human animal has been subject to an 'evolution' characterized by un-natural selection. In saying this we are not positing a dubious metaphysical division between the art and artifice of humans over the blind and dumb mechanical workings of nature, for 'nature' too has its technics of invention. However, and paradoxically, it is the refusal to acknowledge the distinctive character of human artificial and technical evolution that leads to a reinstatement of anthropocentrism and that fails to come to terms with 'the real problem regarding man'. It is thus necessary to demonstrate that through the invention of techniques of the self (the invention of the 'soul', the formation and deformation

---

of selection is unhelpful when it comes to understanding the 'evolution of modern man' (1989: 191). However, he simply fails to appreciate the immense complications which the notion of 'memes' raises for a theory of human 'evolution'. To replace 'genes' with 'memes' as a basis for understanding 'culture' is to remain on the level of naturalism (as opposed to artificiality). Memetics completely reifies the processes of cultural evolution since it has no insight into how such processes involve technical and social mediation. The idea that culture develops in terms of a process of self-replication analogous to genetic evolution is an assertion at best and completely unfounded.

In spite of his efforts to distance himself from philosophy, Dawkins's influential theory of the selfish gene is a 'replication' of a recognizable philosophical position, that of a distinctly Schopenhauerean kind. Brian Goodwin has noted how Dawkins' argument breaks down into an essentially religio-metaphysical doctrine, along the following lines: (a) Organisms are composed of groups of genes whose 'goal' is 'selfishly' to leave more copies of themselves (in other words, life is born in sin and our inheritance is a 'base' one); (b) the inherently selfish qualities of this hereditary material find expression in the competitive interactions between epiphenomenal organisms which result in the survival of the fitter variants that are generated by the more 'successful' genes; (c) the struggle for life is endless on account of the fact that the 'fitness landscape', in which organisms evolve and compete with one another, keeps changing (for which we can read: we are condemned to a life of conflict and perpetual toil); (d) paradoxically, human beings are able to develop altruistic behaviour that works against their selfish endowment through the training of education and culture (that is, by faith and moral effort humanity can be saved from its fallen, selfish state). See Goodwin 1995: 29–30. Dennett's consideration of the impact of Darwin's dangerous idea on our moral endowment – which he expresses as the idea that 'An impersonal, robotic, mindless, little scrap of molecular machinery is the ultimate basis of all the agency, and hence meaning, and hence consciousness, in the universe' (1995b: 203) – leads him to the conclusion that Darwinism is unable to provide answers to our deepest dilemmas, though it does, he maintains, help us to see why the long-standing ambition of discovering an algorithmic ethics is forlorn (1995b: 511ff.). One wonders why we need Darwinism to instruct us on this issue.

of memory, and so on), which Nietzsche makes central to his conception of the human animal, humans have created for themselves an environment in which artificial excess reigns and governs both their 'memory' and 'promise'. Shorn of its fatal association with Nazi eugenics, a breeding programme designed to produce and reproduce the eternal return of the *same* entropically, the figure of the *Übermensch* is once again prominent within techno-discourses on the fate and future of evolution. These discourses speak of a new emerging 'biotechnological' civilization in which technology becomes more and more biological, while biology becomes more and more technological (see Kelly 1994: chapter 1, 'The Made and the Born'). The 'superman' of Nietzsche legend has become the emblem of this brave new world of meat–metal symbiosis. However, what is forgotten and erased in this contemporary use and abuse of Nietzsche is that Nietzsche's repeated invocation of the overhuman calls us back to the human. The promise of the overhuman is bound up in ways yet barely explored, and in ways little understood, with the memory of the human. Contemporary techno-theorizing blinds us to the 'real problem regarding man'.

For Nietzsche, man is the temporal and futural animal par excellence. The real 'problem' of humankind is the breeding of an animal which has the capacity or ability to make promises, and this requires a certain training and cultivation. This is a paradoxical task that nature has set *itself* in the case of man. The labour of overcoming denotes the essence of man; his being has always involved a becoming and a birth from the future. Man has been constituted by the over-man from the 'point' of his 'origin'.[4] This is why attempts to cite Nietzsche's declared goal of translating man back into nature, so as to be able to read the 'eternal basic text of *homo natura*', in support of a Nietzschean naturalism or philosophical ecology, are so problematic (Nietzsche 1966: section 230). It suggests erroneously that the question of man's origin is straightforward, that man simply and unambiguously 'belongs' among the animals.[5] But we know that for Nietzsche man is a sick

---

4 It is misleading to refer to a 'point' of origin since in carrying out a complex rendition of genealogy, Nietzsche does not seek to trace the evolution of man in terms of a punctual system. On the significance of distinguishing between the line (the rhizome as 'becoming') and the point (genealogy as 'memory') see Deleuze and Guattari 1988: 294. Whilst recognizing the novelty of their conception of 'evolution' as a rhizomatic becoming, a form of 'creative evolution', I am keen to deconstruct the unmediated opposition Deleuze and Guattari end up positing between becoming and memory (becoming is an 'antimemory of man', they maintain).
5 Such a profound misreading of Nietzsche has inspired some commentators to argue that Nietzsche's fidelity to the earth presages a new ecologism or 'green' politics. For one example of this new trend in Nietzscheanism see Lampert's excellent study (1993: 432).

animal, a strange animal, and that he calls upon us always to aim our vision and riddles 'beyond' man. Moreover, man's becoming has never been a question of harmony or balance; on the contrary, it has been characterized by extreme discord and positive feedback. The evolution of 'nature' could also be viewed in such non-equilibrial terms, but the difference in the case of man, as Nietzsche's genealogy so spectacularly shows, is that he has internalized this discord in terms of an 'inner evolution', pursuing an experimental praxis of life that transcends any alleged natural laws of being and becoming. A genealogy of morals as a genealogy of man has a different, more complex and difficult, lesson to teach us than simply placing man amongst the animals. Man is a bridge, not a goal, but the the bridge (man) and the goal (overman) are one, related immanently, as in the 'lightning-flash' that emerges from out of the 'dark cloud' that is 'man'. A note from the *Nachlass* informs us that not only does man return eternally, but so does the overman (Nietzsche 1987, volume 11: 281). In other words, the overman would not be possible without the becoming of man, and this 'becoming' refers to a ceaseless labour and play of 'self-overcoming'. The 'goal' is immanent, and hence man's 'being' *is* a becoming, nothing other than becoming, becoming as invention.[6] How else is it possible to comprehend Nietzsche's statement in *Ecce Homo* that 'man is overcome at every moment' (Nietzsche 1979a: 107)?

A careful reading of Nietzsche's genealogy of morals demonstrates the extent to which for him the human is the site of a perpetual overcoming. The question concerning origins, and the concomitant desire for self-transparency, is displaced at the outset of the book. 'We' humans must remain strangers to ourselves 'out of necessity'; we cannot be knowers, especially when it comes to ourselves. Equally it is important to appreciate that Nietzsche's critical question of a genealogy of morals – to what extent are moral values signs of exuberant life or degenerating life? – is also subject to a derangement. In his uncovering of the history of morality Nietzsche discovers that it is in his becoming-sick, in his 'blood-poisoning', that human promise is to be found. It thus becomes possible to show that any attempt to locate the overhuman outside the human, including outside of history, and to give the overhuman different origins, is fundamentally misguided.[7] The positing

---

6 See Nietzsche 1968: section 617: 'Becoming as invention (*Erfinden*), willing self-denial, overcoming of self (*Sich-selbst Überwinden*): no subject but an action, a positing, creative, no "causes and effects"'. For the German see Nietzsche 1987, volume 12: 313.
7 Deleuze's reading of Nietzsche (1983) is often interpreted in these terms, as positing history as nothing more than a story of decline. But this is to miss the 'subtle' and 'sophisticated' character of his reading of Nietzsche. Deleuze makes the experiment of eternal return central and pivotal

of a pure and purely active overhumanity is out of tune with the spirit of Nietzsche's music in the genealogy of morals, in which all the so-called 'reactive' values can be subjected to revaluation if one considers them as tools (techniques) for the further cultivation and enhancement of the human animal. Then one discovers that they conceal an essential *activity*. Humans' only justification does indeed lie 'outside' – outside themselves, outside nature – but this outside is immanent in their becoming.

Nietzsche's articulation of the need for a 'critique' of moral values can easily be interpreted as solely a form of *negative* critique. Such a critique, however, Nietzsche designs in positive terms as the development of a new kind of understanding and knowledge concerning the conditions and circumstances under which particular values evolved and changed, and in which morality acts as a symptom and a sickness, but also as a stimulant and poison. Nietzsche insists that an inquiry into the 'origin' of values and into our tables of good and evil is no way identical with a 'critique' of them.[8] Revelations of the shameful origin of values may result in a feeling of diminution, but it only prepares the way to a critical attitude towards them (Nietzsche 1968: section 254). In this new general economy of values and morals the question of the problem of 'man' can be posed in a way that leads us through and 'beyond' morality. The attempt to cultivate a critique of morality and go beyond it also entails 'discovering' this hitherto uncharted land for the first time. As the 'danger of dangers' morality is fundamentally ambiguous: it has led to the poisoning of man, to the darkening of the skies over him, culminating in our feeling nausea and pity at the sight of his

---

to his reading of 'transformation', and it is here that his argument is at its most convoluted. He does not simply argue that eternal return annihilates the reactive forces; rather, his delicate thesis is that when subjected to the test of return the 'reactive' can only come back as 'active': 'It is no longer a question of the simple thought of the eternal return eliminating from willing everything that falls outside this thought, but rather, of the eternal return making something come into being which cannot do so without changing nature. It is no longer a question of selective thought but of selective "being"' (Deleuze 1983: 71). 'Selection' is a motif that runs throughout Deleuze's writings, and demands careful investigation. One initial attempt is made in chapter 2.

8 Heidegger is thus wrong to claim that in Nietzsche critique of the highest values hitherto 'properly means illumination of the dubious origins of the valuations that yield them, and thereby demonstration of the questionableness of these values themselves' (1961: I, 35; trans. 1979: 26). For Nietzsche the question of 'origins' is not irrelevant to the formation of a critique of morals, but it is no way the decisive question concerning their 'value'. The same 'genetic fallacy' is committed by Foucault in his now classic, but deficient, essay on 'Nietzsche, Genealogy, History' (1977).

domestication; but it has also cultivated a strange and fascinating breeding ground for his extra-moral self-overcoming. In section 6 to the preface to the genealogy, Nietzsche speaks of morality being 'responsible' — the accusation of blame by Nietzsche is an indication of his, and our, implication in the evolution of morality — for the human species never reaching its 'highest potential and splendour'. Nietzsche informs us that he writes for a species that does not yet exist (Nietzsche 1968: section 958), but in truth the 'ones' he writes for will not constitute a 'species'. In a note of 1883, in which he writes of the rapport between the human and the overhuman, morality is placed within a restricted economy of life conceived as an economy of the 'species'. If all moralities have hitherto been utilized so as to maximize the 'unconditional durability' of the species, then once this has been attained the goals can be set much 'higher' (Nietzsche 1987, volume 10: 244). This openness to the future which is open to the risk and dangers of experimentation is part of Nietzsche's promise — which is, as he tells us, a promise to write for the *barbarians of the twentieth century*' (Nietzsche 1968: section 868).

Nietzsche claims that his 'distinction' is to read 'critically' the long, hard-to-decipher hieroglyphic script of our moral past and to take this past seriously. He separates himself from Rée, the author of *The Origin of our Moral Sensations*, on this point. Although Rée had read Darwin, Nietzsche contends that he had produced a merely 'entertaining' account of the confrontation between the 'Darwinian beast' and the 'ultra-modern, humble moral weakling who no longer bites' (Nietzsche 1994: preface, section 7). In other words, Rée has simply not taken 'seriously' what is at stake in the return to the question of man's origins (the 'real problem' regarding man). He then speaks of the 'reward' one can expect from undertaking a serious inquiry into the origin of morality, turning the tragedy of human history into a comedy of existence, so that history becomes subject to a higher 'eternal' becoming, and a new twist and outcome unfolds for the Dionysian drama on the 'fate of the soul'. The preface concludes by appealing to a new memory of man, one that becomes attainable once we overcome that mode of forgetting which plagues 'modern man', namely, a forgetting of the 'art of reading'. Until this art — an art involving a certain praxis of memory — is relearned, it will be 'some time' before Nietzsche's script on our moral past and extra-moral future can become readable. This remembrance of reading has to be incorporated and inscribed upon our bodies as a writing 'of' the flesh.

What drives the psychologist? The question becomes acute in the case of man when historical and pyschological inquiry has degenerated into the task of belittling him. How can Nietzsche fight the poison so as to resist the temptation of arriving at a pessimistic suspicion in the face of man, which would be no more reliable than the mistrust of the disillusioned and of surly idealists who have turned poisonous and green? The aim of Nietzsche's genealogist is not to cut man down to size, to allow oneself to be bitten by the tarantula of revenge, but rather to be brave and generous in the face of bitter and ugly, unchristian, post-Darwinian truths.

What is the value of the priest? The priest is a bizarre creature of 'life' that has turned against itself and who makes everything dangerous. It is on the 'foundation' of this dangerous form of human existence that man becomes an 'interesting animal'. Contra Rousseau, Nietzsche conceives this profound transformation which the human animal undergoes in the hands of morality in extra- or supra-moral terms. Thus he can write – as a 'contra Rousseau' position – that the problem of civilization is not that it has corrupted man but rather that it has failed to corrupt him sufficiently (Nietzsche 1968: sections 98–100). The two basic forms of human superiority over animals – its depth and its capacity for evil – both owe their emergence to the priestly form of existence. It is the slaves' revolt in morality which introduces intelligence – *Geist* – into human history (Nietzsche 1994: I, section 7). By 'intelligence' Nietzsche means phenomena such as cunning, mimicry, patience, dissimulation, self-control, and so on (Nietzsche 1979a: 76). The noble man is really quite stupid and limited in intelligence. While the noble is confident and frank with himself, being both 'upright' and 'naive', the man of *ressentiment* is neither, being neither honest nor straight with himself, and hence his potentialities for self-overcoming are that much greater (Nietzsche 1994: I, section 10).

Nietzsche goes on to construct an imaginary discourse with a democrat. For the democrat it is superfluous to speculate about what is noble since the morality of the common people, and its intoxication, has conquered through blood-poisoning (*Blutvergiftung*) (it has mixed up the races). The secular democrat recognizes that the passage of the poison of the slaves' revolt through the whole body of the human is irreversible. The problem he has with the 'Church', which professes to be the saviour of the 'poison', is that it alienates when it should seduce. It is committed to slowing down and blocking its passage when creative energies should be devoted to 'accelerating' it. The democrat then confesses that he loathes the Church but '*not* its poison . . . Apart from the Church, we too love the poison (*Gift*)' (1994: 1, section 9).

Nietzsche offers this passage as the 'epilogue' of a 'free-thinker' and an honest animal. It is the speech of someone who has listened to Nietzsche 'up to a certain point' but who cannot 'stand listening' to his silence. How ought we to interpret

Nietzsche's telling silence? I would suggest that Nietzsche is concealing the 'truth' of his own confession within that of the democrat, for as a genealogist he too must learn to love the poison. Unlike the democrat, however, who can see only a development (an 'evolution') moving in the direction of an increasing equalization and homogenization, the genealogist is able to decode the signs of a different kind of becoming, an involution of forms and forces, in which novel kinds of self-overcoming can be cultivated.

Man is the caged animal enclosed in the 'walls of society and peace', subject to an 'internalization' process, and notable not only for his experiments on nature, but for his self-experimentation. Originally man's inner world was stretched ever so thinly as though 'between two layers of skin'. However, once internalized it quickly expanded and extended itself, reaching the point where it becomes distinctive of man's 'being'. Impatiently man rips himself apart, gnawing at himself, subjecting himself to self-abuse, so 'full of emptiness' in his natural state – his genetic make-up bestows little – that he had to create for himself a torture-chamber, a 'hazardous wilderness' entirely within. The invention of a 'bad conscience' represents man's 'forcible breach with his animal past'; it is both a leap and a fall into new situations and conditions of existence (Nietzsche 1994: II, section 16). Nietzsche describes this 'evolution' in terms of a 'positive' critique, speaking of the prospect of an animal turning against itself as something profound and new, as something puzzling, contradictory, and as an event on earth that can only be understood as 'momentous' (*Zukunftsvolles*), that has changed the 'whole character of the world' in an 'essential way'. This becoming of man is a spectacle too subtle and wonderful, too paradoxical, to be 'allowed to be played senselessly unobserved on some ridiculous planet'. And yet, again, there is no hint of anthropocentric naivety on Nietzsche's part in speaking of the animal 'man' in such privileged terms. Rather, he construes the mark of man in terms of an 'announcement', as if through him something other were being prepared, 'as though man were not an end but just a path, an episode, a bridge, a great promise' (ibid.).[9] Although the spectacle of man necessarily strikes us as one almost too ugly and painful to behold, it would be a mistake to adopt a disparaging attitude towards it. Moreover, even though the internalization of man gives way to the breeding of all sorts of reactive values and to the danger of morality, it is also possible to locate an essential activity within the formation of the bad conscience. 'Fundamentally', Nietzsche writes, 'it is the same active force as the one that is at

---

9 Compare Bergson 1983: 265, for whom it is only in a 'quite special sense that man is the "term" and "end" of evolution'.

work on a grand scale' in artists of violence who create and build 'negative ideals'. He can thus contend:

> This secret self-violation, this artist's cruelty, this desire to give form to oneself as a piece of difficult, resisting, suffering matter, to brand it with a will, a critique, a contradiction, a contempt, a 'no', this uncanny, terrible but joyous labour of a soul voluntarily split within itself, which makes itself suffer out of the pleasure of making suffer, this whole *active* 'bad conscience' has finally — we have already guessed — as true womb of ideal and imaginative events, brought a wealth of novel, disconcerting beauty and affirmation to light.
>
> (ibid.: II, section 18)

Nietzsche can only have belief in man to the extent that it is possible to identify in his evolution the 'time' and 'space' of the overhuman. The promise of the overhuman forces us to return to man, to re-collect his memory, while the discovery, or invention, of that memory reveals to us this promise of overhuman futures.[10] The genealogy of morals constantly folds back upon itself in its unfolding of man's identity and being, an identity that can only be conceived in terms of an essential difference and a being that can only treated as a becoming. We return to the memory 'of' man — return in terms of a positive critique of the present — on account of the promise of the overman. The task is to examine the 'accumulation and increase of forces' so as to know 'what might yet *be made of man*' and to learn that man 'is still unexhausted for the greatest possibilities'. The genealogist of man knows from the 'most painful memories what wretched things have so far usually broken a being of the highest rank that was in the process of becoming, so that it broke, sank, and became contemptible' (Nietzsche 1966: section 203). Nietzsche thus calls for a new willing and cultivation of the human that will prevent its degeneration into a herd-animal by 'putting an end to that gruesome dominion of nonsense and accident that has so far been called "history"' (ibid.). In other places, Nietzsche recognizes the futile and counter-productive nature of this deluded quest for control over evolution and history. The most promising possibilities

---

10 One of the earliest, and still few, attempts to approach Nietzsche in the terms of this chapter can be found in Arendt's *The Human Condition*. However, whereas Arendt restricts the promise of the overhuman to the faculty of promises itself, I wish to enlarge it by taking into account human cultivation of cruelty, of pain and suffering, of self-experimentation through technical engineering, in short the whole rich panoply of human culture and civilization. Arendt reads the cultivation of promise-making as signalling in Nietzsche's analysis a transcendence of the notion of will-to-power, a fact, she says, 'frequently overlooked by Nietzsche scholars' (Arendt 1958: 245, n. 83).

for 'higher' evolution arise unpredictably and incalculably from a new and spontaneous amalgamation of disparate forces and desires. As he notes, at points of punctuated equilibrium 'variation' suddenly appears on the scene in the greatest abundance as 'deviation' and as 'degeneration and monstrosity'. With these non-calculable 'turning points of history' it is possible to observe a mutual involvement and entanglement of diverse and opposite values and desires, denoting a 'manifold, junglelike growth and upward striving', a 'tremendous ruin and self-ruination' that breaks the discipline of the old morality and renders superfluous the preaching of moral philosophers, including any pretensions Nietzsche might himself have in this field (ibid.: 262).

The attempt to 'save' activity from the 'contamination' of morality results in a highly idealistic, quasi-apocalyptic reading of Nietzsche and his figuration of the beyond of man. We should not be surprised at the extent to which, for example, Deleuze's reading in *Nietzsche and Philosophy* concludes by placing all the emphasis on a conversion of thought in order to reactivate active forces and move from the negative dialectic to the positivity of the overman (Deleuze 1983: 175).[11] This reading, however, produces little more than a new idealism of man and encourages us to practise the most shallow of inversions: 'For the speculative element of negation, opposition, or contradiction Nietzsche substitutes the practical element of *difference* . . . Nietzsche's "yes" is opposed to the dialectical "no"; affirmation to dialectical negation; difference to dialectical negation; joy, enjoyment to dialectical labour; lightness, dance to dialectical responsibilities' (ibid.: 9). Deleuze's 'Nietzschean empricism' offers nothing more than an empty formalism and remains stuck within an idealism of the overman.

In working through the 'real problem' of man, Nietzsche insists on making a distinction between the 'actual instruments' of culture and the 'virtual bearers' of culture. 'Culture' simply means the breeding and taming of the beast of prey 'man' into a civilized animal. The techniques of culture are to be cultivated without culminating in a will-to-power that wills only 'nothingness', that is, a passive nihilism in which the process of the internalization of the will-to-power has gone so far that culture produces an animal that is no longer able to produce anything

---

11 Deleuze cites Nietzsche's reference to man as the 'skin disease' of the earth and poses the question whether another sensibility and another becoming would still be those of 'man'. For Deleuze the 'human condition' would compromise or 'contaminate' the selection of eternal return – making it an object of anguish and repulsion – only if it was the case that the return of active forces took place in terms of the eternally reactive, so rendering transmutation impossible (1983: 65).

out of its sickness other than self-loathing and contempt. On account of what man has become today, history results in the paradoxical situation in which we can only identify in the instruments of culture deformation, so that an attitude of suspicion towards the discipline of culture becomes manifest and acute, resulting in our peculiarly modern *misarchism*. One wants the poison not in order to turn against man but in order to overcome him. Hence Nietzsche can write that what constitutes our aversion to man today is that we suffer from him because we have nothing to fear from him, for he has become 'a teeming mass of worms'. History results in the 'unedifying' spectacle of the 'end of history', an end in which the 'incurably mediocre' have learned to regard themselves as the aim and pinnacle, as the very meaning, of history (Nietzsche 1994: I, section 11). We have grown tired of man, for not only have we lost our fear of him, but we have also lost our love and respect for him, our hope in him, and 'even our will to be man' (ibid.: 12). We can no longer *digest* him (see Nietzsche 1994: III, section 16 on digestion and indigestion).

Out of this confrontation and reckoning with man and the history of culture, Nietzsche will endeavour to argue that man remains constituted by his futurity and by his inventions of the future. Man, he says, is more uncertain, unstable, and changeable than any other animal. He can be defined generically as the sick animal on account of the fact that he has dared, innovated, and braved more 'than all the rest of the animals taken together'. As the great experimenter with himself and insatiable struggler for control over 'animals, nature, and gods' – *through the aid of machines* and 'the completely unscrupulous inventiveness of technicians and engineers' (ibid.: 9) – man remains 'the still-unconquered eternal futurist' whose 'future mercilessly digs into the flesh of every present like a spur' (ibid.: 13). The promise of man lies in the fact that even the 'No' which he says to life brings with it a 'wealth of tender "yeses"'. Although he is the animal who deliberately wounds himself, it is these wounds – and the memory of them – which forces this self-vivisector and master of destruction and self-destruction *to live*.

II

The phenomenon of memory is multiple: one can speak of molecular memories, social memories, short-term and long-term memories, relative and absolute memories, sick memories and healthy memories, of a technics of memory and of an excessive invention of memory, and so on. In *A Thousand Plateaus* Deleuze and

Guattari oppose 'becoming' to 'memory' in their attempt to construct a non-genealogical model of evolution (that is, one which does not restrict evolution to the linear schema presupposed in trees of life). While conceding that molecular or minor memories exist (such as anti-colonial memory), they nevertheless insist that such memories always exist as a factor that is integrated into a molar, or majoritarian, system (Deleuze and Guattari 1988: 294). Deleuze and Guattari's negative appraisal of the creative, and subversive, power of memory rests on their association of it with a mnemotechnics (ibid.: 295). Memory is viewed as functioning in terms of a punctual organization in which the present refers simultaneously to a horizontal line that captures the *flow* of time, moving from an old present to an actual present, and to a vertical line that captures the *order* of time, going from the present to the past, or to the 'representation' of the old present. They oppose 'multilinear systems' to punctual ones, arguing that these kind of open, complex systems, so evident in the work of musicians and painters, free the line from the vertical and the horizontal, making it diagonal. It is in this sense of the line over the point that they argue that every act of creation is, ultimately, 'transhistorical': 'Creations', they write, 'are like mutant abstract lines that have detached themselves from the task of representing a world, precisely because they assemble a new type of reality that history can only recontain or relocate in punctual systems' (ibid.: 296). On this model 'becomings' take place 'in' history but are never reducible to it: 'When this is done [the freeing of the line] it always goes down in History but never comes from it' (ibid.). History, for Deleuze and Guattari, is molar by definition. The only history there can possibly be, has ever been and ever will be is the history of man (although it should be noted that they do allow for 'many becomings of man, but no becoming-man'). The technics of memory has been cultivated in order to serve the molarization of history. But where memory fixes, codes, and assigns functions, the activity of becomings liberates by calling into play *transversal* communication between heterogeneous phenomena, and so they create the genuinely new and different.[12]

---

12 Perhaps the most powerful statement by Deleuze and Guattari on the invention of becoming is to be found in their thinking of the monument in *What is Philosophy?*, where they seek an immanent meaning to the becoming of 'revolution'. See Deleuze and Guattari 1994: 168–9 and 176–7. On 'becoming-revolutionary', which is to be indifferent to questions of past and future, see also Deleuze and Guattari 1988: 292. The innovations made by Deleuze and Guattari in their remapping of 'evolution' through 'becomings' are utilized in 1988: chapter 5. The point I am seeking to make here is that, while I concede that the molecular/molar distinction in their work does not function as a metaphysical opposition, even less a machinic one, it nevertheless remains the case that the critical genealogist (in Nietzsche's sense) cannot completely abandon

It has to be noted that Nietzsche will employ a reading of culture, of mnemotechnics, to quite different effect in his *Genealogy of Morality*. A recent study of memory confirms the impression that Deleuze and Guattari's opposition between memory and becoming simplifies and distorts the actual history of mnemotechnics in which memory was seen to offer an artifice of resistance to established powers (Rose 1992: 67–8; see also Yates 1966). In the time of the Renaissance 'theatres of memory' were constructed as theatres of magic. For Giordano Bruno, a contemporary of Galileo's, who was burned by the Inquisition, these theatres of memory formed an essential feature of occult, hermetic philosophy, that is, of ways of classifying the universe and penetrating its mystery.[13] The opposition drawn between 'memory' and 'becoming' not only rests on an unmediated privileging of becoming, but also ignores the illumination that Deleuze's earlier work brings to bear on the source of the tremendous power of memory. Becoming is inconceivable without memory, including a technics of memory, in which the 'product' always exceeds the law of production (as in the example of Nietzsche's sovereign individual in which the 'tree' of the social straitjacket – the morality of custom – gives rise to a 'fruit' that enjoys the supra-ethical power of 'living beyond'). So we ask: what is the work peculiar to memory? What is being worked-through and worked-out in memory? Can there be a 'historical memory' that is not at the same time an invention of history, an invention of itself (Benjamin)?

In *Nietzsche and Philosophy* Deleuze employs Freud's notion of 'mnemonic traces', in which consciousness is born at the site of a memory-trace, to illuminate the movement of memory in Nietzsche's *Genealogy of Morality*. In *Moses and*

---

the territory of history and concede defeat. In the instance of 'historical memory' it is a question of not taking the molar as given and treating it as a kind of historical *a priori*. The formation of 'the human' as the molar category par excellence, in which anthropocentrism gets constructed in terms of a 'gigantic Memory' that serves to capture nature and technics by filtering their rhizomatic becomings through a centre-point, establishing the one 'frequency' and the one 'resonance', requires an overhuman – or molecular – demonstration (a different history) (Deleuze and Guattari 1988: 293). In this way history is opened up to other becomings and the illusions of the molar exposed. This is what I see Nietzsche providing in his *Genealogy*. In this respect, Deleuze and Guattari are quite right to point out that wherever they use the word 'memories' they meant to say, and were saying, 'becomings' (ibid.: 294). But this is to speak of becomings that are complicated in 'memories', but which are never reducible to, or identifiable with, them.

13 Bruno is, in fact, discussed by Deleuze in his study of Leibniz and the baroque (Deleuze 1993: 23–4).

*Monotheism*, in fact, Freud employs the notion to lend support to his predilection for a Lamarckian schema of evolution. The idea is that memory-traces operate not only ontogenetically but also phylogenetically, constituting an 'archaic heritage of human beings' equivalent to Lamarck's notorious doctrine of the inheritance of acquired characteristics (Freud 1990: 345ff.). Freud insists that he cannot do without this notion as a key factor in the explanation of biological evolution. His position, however, appears to rest on a conflation of human 'technical' evolution and animal 'biological' evolution, evident in his contention that the transmission of ancestral life – the phenomenon of tradition – takes place independently of direct communication and education (in other words, he biologizes the question of heredity).[14] If there is one mode of evolution which would seem to lend itself to a Lamarckian intepretation, it is human culture. But here one is not dealing with 'biology' but with 'technology'.[15]

Let us return, however, to the question of Nietzsche and memory. As in Freud, Deleuze contends, so in Nietzsche we find a theory of two memories (Deleuze 1983: 115). The first is a memory specific to the man of *ressentiment* in whom the traces of memory become so indelibly stamped on his consciousness that he is no longer capable of action (which requires forgetting). It is not simply the case that his only action is reaction; rather, he is unable even to act out reaction since he *feels* his reaction, making it endless (indigestible) in the process. The second is an 'active memory' that no longer rests on traces (Deleuze 1983: 112–15). Here memory is no longer simply a function of the past, an inability to let go, but has become transformed into an activity of the future, a 'memory of the future itself' (ibid.: 134). Reinterpreting the memory of the human, one might suggest, involves tracing an evolution or becoming that has failed to enter contemporary consciousness in which what one is looking for are the traces of 'signs' of the overhuman, and in which a memory of the human would liberate us from our festering wounds, from the contempt and pity we experience in the face of mankind. An inquiry into 'origins' is thus always an inquiry into future becomings and the becoming of the future.

---

14 For an excellent study of heredity and memory in the context of an analysis of Victorian biology and letters, and a nascent anti-Darwinism, see Morton 1984, in which the focus is on the likes of Butler, Thomas Hardy, and Wallace.

15 As Stephen Jay Gould has argued, cultural evolution can proceed faster by orders of magnitude than biological change at its maximal Darwinian rate. Secondly, whereas biological evolution is 'indirect' and largely Darwinian, cultural evolution is 'direct', translineal, and Lamarckian. See 'The Panda's Thumb in Technology' in Gould 1991: 65–7.

As Deleuze maintains in his study of Proust, memory works as a 'tool' — one not simply subject to a wilful manipulation and exploitation of the human, all too human kind that can be placed in the service of an overcoming. The subject 'of' memory is nothing other than this self-overcoming. Thus, he can contend that the orientation of Proust's work is not the past and the discoveries of memory, but rather the future and the progress of learning (Deleuze 1973: 25). The philosopher is neither a physicist nor a metaphysician but an Egyptologist, that is, a figure of truth who is devoted to life as a task of learning how to read signs that are necessarily complicated and implicated in equivocal meaning (Deleuze 1973: 90–1). This is to dwell in the 'obscure zone' of the monstrous. Again, what is being critiqued here is a passive model of memory, as if recollection were simply an act of discovering what was already there as a kind of timeless secret or truth (the transcendent illusions of voluntary memory). This model pays insufficient attention to the interpretive, inventive, virtual, and machinic character of memory and its construction.[16] If Proust revives the Platonic equivalence of creating and remembering, he also shows in the process that memory and creation are but two aspects of the same production — that is, interpreting and deciphering are the 'process of production itself' (Deleuze 1973: 130). 'Remembrance' can be conceived as the working through of memory (Deleuze 1994: 14). We repeat the past not simply to work through it, however, but to discharge and create beyond (beyond ourselves). The aim is not to conserve the past but to lighten its load, so as to make it bearable by making it light. The 'creative evolution' peculiar to memory resides in its 'destructive' character.[17] The construction of the future requires the activity of a profound memory, as Deleuze brings out clearly in his study of Foucault, in which he seeks to illuminate how the process of 'folding' takes place in terms of a memory, namely:

---

16 It is on this point that Deleuze connects Proust's immersion in the 'being of the past in itself' with Bergson's emphasis on the virtual character of memory in *Matter and Memory* (Deleuze 1973: 57ff.). On the 'machinic' see the chapter entitled 'Antilogos, or the Literary Machine' which Deleuze added to the later edition of his Proust book (1973: 93–159). On Proust and Bergson see also Benjamin 1979: 159–60. Benjamin is astute in arguing that the 'eternity' to which Proust opens up time is not 'boundless time' but rather 'convoluted time'. The heart of Proust's universe is 'convolution' (ibid.: 213).

17 Benjamin cites a remark by the American psychologist Theodor Reik: 'Remembrance (*Gedächtnis*) is essentially conservative, memory (*Erinnerung*) is destructive' (Benjamin 1979: 162). Needless to say the two are mutually implicated in a more complicated process of 'becoming what one is'.

the 'absolute memory' or memory of the outside, beyond the brief memory inscribed in strata and archives. . . . Memory is the real name of the relation to oneself, of the affect of self by self . . . time as subject, or rather subjectivation, is called memory. Not that brief memory that comes afterwards and is the opposite of forgetting, but the 'absolute memory' which doubles the present and the outside and is one with forgetting, since it is endlessly forgotten and reconstituted: its fold, in fact, merges with the unfolding because the latter remains present within the former as the thing that is folded. Only forgetting (the unfolding) recovers what is folded in memory (and in the fold itself.)
(Deleuze 1988b: 107)

If it is 'habit' that constitutes the 'foundation' of time (Deleuze follows Butler on this point, 1994: 75), that is, as that which secures the continuity of life and its survival, then it is 'memory' which can be posited as the 'ground' of time, acting as that which causes the present to pass. Whereas the foundation represents the 'moving soil' of time, of the passing present, the ground in fact comes from the sky, challenging the proprietorship of becoming by depriving time of an active subject (Deleuze refers to the 'profound passive synthesis of memory', 1994: 79).[18] Memory is the 'fundamental synthesis' of time since it constitutes the being of the past (namely, that which allows the present to pass).[19]

The story of the human animal provides evidence of both a technics of memory *and* a technics of forgetting (forgetting is also subject to molar operations, such as

---

18  Deleuze argues this position through a rereading of Kant's teaching on time, in which he maintains that Bergson, far from being the great critic of Kant he considered himself to be, was much closer to him than he ever realized. In short, Deleuze reads the 'subjectivity' not as a property of us ourselves but as belonging to time itself, as 'the soul or the spirit, the virtual' (Deleuze 1989a: 82–3). Duration is not subjective in any simple-minded sense, as an illusion of the self. Rather, it is the case that the fold of time resides in its own complex unfolding. Time is not internal to us; we are internal to 'it'. For Deleuze on Kant see also 1984: preface. For Bergson on Kant see Bergson1960: esp. 232ff.

19  See Deleuze 1994: 81, on the significance of Bergson: 'If *Matter and Memory* is a great book, it is perhaps because Bergson profoundly explored the domain of the transcendental synthesis of a pure past and discovered all its constitutive paradoxes.' One of these paradoxes is that the past needs to be construed not as a dimension of time but as the synthesis 'of all time' in which the present and the future constitute the dimensions of time. We cannot say of the past 'it was' but only that it *insists* and *consists* (Deleuze 1994: 82). Compare Nietzsche 1969: 'On Redemption'. See also Deleuze 1989a: 78ff. For Bergson see 1990: 133ff., and 1983: 4–5: 'Memory . . . is not a faculty of putting away recollections in a drawer, of inscribing them in a register. There is no register, no drawer; there is not even, properly speaking, a faculty, for a faculty works intermittently. . . . In reality, the past is preserved by itself, automatically.' For further insight into the character of the profound passive syntheses of time and memory see Williams 1996: 47–61.

we see in commemorative rituals and social disciplines in which collective remembrance also involves collective amnesia).[20] The breeding of memory is a condition of promise-making and gives rise to a control of the future. But there is also present in memory another becoming. A conception of the memory of humans and promise of the overhuman is possible in which the future is not an event of control or prediction, but in which the technics of memory and of promise-keeping gives way to a supra-technics of invention that always exceeds the desire for control of the future through the imposition of forces of blockage. Nietzsche notes that man experiments on himself in ways that he would never tolerate on animals: 'we merrily vivisect our souls out of curiosity' (Nietzsche 1994: III, section 9). This self-experimentation on the part of man does not so much reveal a desire for 'salvation' (of the soul, for example), Nietzsche notes, as a fascination with the infectious character of human sickness and suffering: 'being ill is instructive, we do not doubt, more instructive then being well, – *people who make us ill* seem even more necessary for us today than any medicine men and "saviours"' (Nietzsche 1994: III, section 9). While 'hubris' may well be the distinctive character of our attitude towards nature and machines, such self-experimentation ultimately takes us beyond ourselves and puts to the test our self-certainties and fixed estimations of the value and worth of life.

The attempt to confront the human being with the ultimate truth of Darwinian selection, and then hopelessly to erect on its base a naturalistic ethics 'fit for man', is pernicious since 'man' is a dangerous animal who has not been subject to its laws,

---

20 A point well brought out by Marcuse in his discussion of the education of memory and forgetting in Marcuse 1987: 232ff. Forgetting is both an indispensable requirement of mental and physical health, and the mental faculty that sustains submissiveness and renunciation. In a discussion of Proust's great novel, Benjamin notes that the rituals of experience with their ceremonies and festivals are quite properly nowhere recalled in Proust's work (1979: 161). One of the earliest accounts of the power of 'involuntary memory' can be found in Ewald Hering's lecture of 1870, 'On Memory as a Universal Function of Organized Matter', an English translation of which appears in Butler 1880, reissued 1922: 63ff.: 'The word "memory" is often understood as though it meant nothing more than our faculty of intentionally reproducing ideas. . . . But when the figures and events of bygone days rise up again unbidden in our minds, is this not also an act of recollection or memory? We have a perfect right to extend our conception of memory so as to make it embrace involuntary reproductions of sensations, ideas, perceptions, and efforts; but we find on having done so, that we have so far enlarged her boundaries that she proves to be an ultimate and original power, the source, and at the same time the unifying bond, of our whole conscious life' (68). Hering, as Freud was to do later, utilizes this notion of a powerful unconscious memory to support Lamarck's thesis on the inheritance of acquired characteristics. See also, in this regard, Diderot 1963: 55.

such as 'survival of the fittest' and the competitive struggle for existence, since 'pre-historic' times. Nietzsche's critique of Strauss's attempt to found a genuine Darwinian ethics remains apposite; namely, that any natural scientist who attempts to derive ethical and intellectual values from the 'laws of nature' is guilty of an 'extreme anthropomorphism', and, Nietzsche adds, in the spirit of Kant, of an employment of reason that oversteps the bounds of the permitted (Nietzsche 1983: 31). Human history cannot be modelled on natural history, since its mechanisms of selection have always been unnatural. It is thus risible of Baudrillard to lament the new forces of artificial evolution in which he can only identify the desire of a species to remove itself from the laws of natural selection (one should, however, consult the context in which Baudrillard provokes this claim) (Baudrillard 1994: 84). Human becoming has always involved a reliance on art and artifices of self-preservation and self-enhancement.[21] There is no natural harmony or balance with nature to be striven for, only non-equilibrial self-overcoming, with the 'genius of the species overflowing from all cornucopias of good and bad', and in which the 'highest desires' get 'gruesomely entangled' (Nietzsche 1966: section 262).

Is it a case of nature selecting technics or of technics selecting 'nature'? Today, palaeoanthropologists speak of our accelerated 'evolution' taking place in terms of a series of positive feedback loops between 'learned behaviour' and biology in which the main feature of this evolution is its 'techno-organic' nature (Schick and Toth 1993: 316). Leroi-Gourhan's meditations on the distinctive features of human evolution pointed to the fact that man accesses technology but then technology becomes the criterion of selection: the evolution of an erect posture, a short face, a free hand for locomotion, the absence of fangs, all lend themselves

---

21 One of the few issues on which Darwin and Wallace, the other major inventor of the 'laws' of natural selection, differed was over the problem of mankind. Wallace argued that through tools and techniques mankind has 'taken away from nature that power of slowly but permanently changing the external form and structure in accordance with changes in the external world'. Wallace even went so far as to claim that 'all force is will-force', and adopted a philosophy of life in which the universe exhibits 'intelligence and will-power' (1891: 175ff.). In his most recent untimely meditation, Baudrillard develops a more incisive appreciation of human selection and refers, in fact, to the debate between Darwin and Wallace (1996: 56–7): 'The human race has already gone beyond its potential. Excess of potential intelligence. . . . If the law of natural selection were true, our brains would have to shrink, for their capacities exceed all natural purposes and endanger the species. This is the same question Darwin and Wallace debated, the latter resolving it by the intervention of God. . . . But if God is responsible for this biological extravagance, then he is in collusion with the spirit of Evil, whose specific peculiarity is to drive the universe to excess. Are there not signs of the aberrancy of the divine will in the catastrophic success of man?'

to the use of artificial organs and implements (Leroi-Gourhan 1993: 9). Thus, the uniquely organized mammalian body of the human 'is enclosed and extended by a social body whose properties are such that zoology no longer plays any part in its material development' (ibid.: 21).

The history of technics involves a post-evolutionary 'evolution': 'Our techniques, which have been an extension of our bodies since the first Australanthropian made the first chopper, have reenacted at dizzying speed the events of millions of years of geological evolution until, today, we can already make an artificial nervous system and an electronic intelligence' (ibid.: 173). The history of human memory is graphic in both senses of the word: the first involves an inscription of the body as graphically depicted by Nietzsche; the other, still genealogical, is to do with the invention of writing techniques: 'The first genealogies were written at the precise moment when social hierachization began to affirm itself' (ibid.: 179). Early instruments from the Upper Palaeolithic are symbolic instruments designed as a reckoning tool which very rapidly turned into an instrument of historical memory. We can ask: what kind of a reckoning tool, in the service of a differential 'historical' memory, is Nietzsche's 'genealogy of morals'?

Leroi-Gourhan drew a decisive conclusion from his analyses: 'The whole of our evolution has been oriented toward placing outside ourselves what in the rest of the animal world is achieved *inside* by species adaptation' (ibid.: 235). The freeing of tools, and a freeing of the word through the ability to transfer our memory to a social organism outside ourselves, are both essential aspects of this technical invention of 'man'. However, it would be a parochialism to suggest that technics must be limited to humans, since technical action is found in invertebrates. The main difference lies in the extent to which the human being has exteriorized its memory in machines and apparatuses of all kinds. Our 'organs' are extraneous to us – the plough, the windmill, and the sailing ship can be viewed as 'biological' mutations 'of that external organism which, in the human, substitutes itself for the physiological body' (ibid.: 246). Thus, the significant genetic trait of the human is 'physical (and mental) nonadaptation' (ibid.). Evolution has now entered a new phase with the exteriorization of the human brain, so that 'the distance between ourselves – the descendants of reindeer hunters – and the intelligent machines we have created is greater than ever' (ibid.: 252). The question then arises of our physical compatibility with the artificial environment we now inhabit. Is the human now compelled to withdraw into the palaeontological twilight with the rise of the machine?

The environment is an artificial world. There can be no return to a naive nature, and attempts to establish 'once and for all' a natural order or balance on which to base an ethics or politics of technology is utterly foolish. There is only the excess of technics. This is why one must question the wisdom of Leroi-Gourhan's own final conclusion, in which he invited his readers to envisage a human of the near future who wills to remain sapiens: 'we must stop miming the behaviour of a microbic culture and come to grips with the management of our planet in terms other than those of of a game of chance. . . . Our species is still too closely bound to its origins not to strive spontaneously for the balance that made it human in the first place' (ibid.: 408). The appeal to an originary 'balance' as a constitutive feature of the human being enjoys no more than a mythical status.

Where Nietzsche lays stress on the 'internal' aspects of human evolution, such as the creation of a 'soul', Leroi-Gourhan's analysis would appear to single out the 'externalization' of memory and of organs as the distinctive feature of the human. However Nietzsche is perceptive in showing that the externalization of human memory and organs through the supplement of technics serves only to complicate further the significance of human internalization, so that it becomes possible to see in human involvement with machines and technics an expression and an intensification of human becoming-sick.

Technics is driven by an evolutionary force that places it outside human control and regulation. But the idea that humans are outstripped by their technology is commonplace, and current celebrations of evolution getting 'out of control' offer little more than platitudes lacking in historical acuity (see Winner 1977). A biology of technics is as 'metaphysical' as a biology of nature. There is only a technics of mankind and of nature that demands a critical and supra-moral reading. The task is to render the concepts of soul, life, value, and memory genealogical in Nietzsche's (uncommon) sense, not metaphysical, which requires, in part, removing them from the techno-sciences and their complicity with a metaphysical humanism. This is tantamount to losing humans in the act of finding them. Humans are forgotten in the praxis of making a memory of them.[22]

In contemporary discourse the question concerning the machine is being posed in unequivocal linear terms as that which comes after and supersedes the human. At present we can witness a revival of the 'cosmic evolutionism' associated with the dubious spiritualism of Teilhard de Chardin, in which machine intelligence is construed in terms of a global cerebralization that leads 'inexorably to the emergence of the "noospheric brain"' (Stonier 1992: 190). What is disturbing about this revival of cosmic evolutionism is the attempt to explain the alleged phase-space transition in 'intelligent' evolution in biological terms, which results

---

22 Compare Derrida on the necessity of reinventing invention (1992: 339).

in gross anthropomorphisms. Evolution, we are told, has been 'searching' the planet to find ways of 'speeding itself up', not because it is anthropomorphic but because 'the speeding up of adaptation is the runaway circuit it rides on' (Kelly 1994: 361). The excess of contingent evolution in the domain of technology is treated as if it revealed a necessary and conscious 'desire' on the part of evolution (it 'wants' to become metal). Kelly speaks of 'what evolution really wants' as if evolution wanted anything. In the following claim the entire process of culture and society is made subject to a purely biological reading, in which questions of teleology and technics – understood in Kant's sense[23] – are treated as purely determinant judgements: 'Life, having evolved a being that internalizes the process of natural selection, has finally transcended that process' (Stock 1993: 215). Not only is this statement guilty of what Nietzsche called 'anthropocentric naivety', but it naively depoliticizes questions of evolution. 'Through Metaman' (the name given to the new global super-organism), we are told, 'trial and error are giving way to conscious design. Thus, the future will be ever more directed by the present' (ibid.).

From a 'Nietzschean' perspective, in the sense in which the term possesses 'meaning', recent reports on the transhuman condition ironically amount to an annulment of that condition, to an erasure of the 'memory' of man out of which the promise of the overman can be thought. A recent popular account of 'post-biological man', for example, treats the human condition as an affliction which shouldn't happen to a dog. Humans, we are told, are beings with 'cheap bodies' subject to disease and disability, with 'erratic emotions' and 'feeble mentalities', and 'battlegrounds of warring impulses, drives, and emotions', with only a limited capacity for memory and intelligence (Regis 1992: 145).[24] All that which

---

23 In his critique of teleological judgement Kant seeks to legitimize a 'technical' understanding of nature in terms of the reflective judgement which enjoys a purely regulative status. To treat nature as a system of 'technics' is to consider it as operating intelligently – as opposed to functioning as a blind mechanism – but not to credit it with acting 'designedly', which would be tantamount to basing teleology on a constitutive principle. See Kant 1982: introduction. Nietzsche's justification of the notion of will-to-power in *Beyond Good and Evil* in terms of the 'conscience of method' comes close to Kant's position (1966: section 36).

24 It should be noted that there is nothing particularly of 'now' about Regis's depiction of the transhuman condition. In the 1960s Arthur C. Clarke speculated on the 'progress' of evolution 'from a biological level to a technological one', and, like Regis, even cited Nietzsche on man as the rope stretched between animal and superman to lend some philosophical 'authority' to his claims (Clarke 1964: 212–27). See also, in this regard, McHale's *The Future of the Future* (1969).

Nietzsche regarded as providing fertile soil for an immanent process of continual self-overcoming is here treated as a condition that is to be escaped from. The transhuman condition has become transformed into a classic expression of an ancient ideal – the *ascetic ideal*.[25] As Hans Moravec, one of the chief engineers of this profoundly un-Nietzschean vision of the transhuman condition, has openly confessed, this is 'a sort of a Christian fantasy' in 'how to become pure spirit' (ibid.: 176). Indeed, this flight into 'machine intelligence' resembles a hi-tech Hegelianism much more than it does the inhuman futures envisaged by Nietzsche.[26] Downloading the brain into a computer, in order to attain the transhuman condition (read: to become 'immortal'), would involve 'losing the body' and all that goes with it: 'the world, flesh', and, most revealing of all, 'the devil' (ibid.: 5). The gains would be 'freedom from physical constraints, faster thinking speed, a bigger memory'. Why is the attainment of the 'faster' and the 'bigger' to be regarded as a gain? Is it simply a question of adaptation to a technological environment (the danger here is that of *naturalizing* such a process of adaptation)? As Heidegger noted, with reference to the dawning of the age of information ('IT'), one must hear the 'basic words' for capturing the demeanour of contemporary existence with an American pronunciation. Only young Americans are able to attain the realm of the superficial out of superficiality. In point of fact, however, we do the fantasy of cyberspace too much honour in defining it as the latest expression of the ascetic ideal since it does not even wish to work through its own paradoxical and paralogical concepts; it simply begs for belief and wants believers.[27]

A new fiction (who's telling lies? ooh aah visionary!) is being promulgated within so-called 'posthuman' postmodernity (to coin an ugly phrase for an ugly phenomenon). It is contended, by people who should know better, including the cyber-gurus of our deranged times, that with the emergence of a biotechnological

---

25 See Nietzsche 1994: III, section 28: 'It is absolutely impossible for us to conceal what was actually expressed by that whole willing, which was given its direction by the ascetic ideal: this hatred of the human, and even more of the animalistic, even more of the material, this horror of the senses, of reason itself . . . this longing to get away from appearance, transience, growth, death, wishing, longing itself'.
26 On the rise of 'hi-tech Hegelianism' see Stallabrass 1995: 3–33.
27 See Jameson (1995: 28–9), who, in reference to current collective fantasies of DNA recombination through the artificial hybridization of 'domesticated' species – the word 'domestication' says little given that humans have domesticated not only themselves but the entire planet – speaks perspicaciously of 'our quasi-religious longing for social transubstantiation into another flesh and another reality'. On this reading much of what passes for the posthuman condition amounts to nothing more than the inevitable mutations of a repressed history.

vitalism, the rise of artificial life-forms and intelligences, and developments in genetic engineering, we are now moving into a historical future in which life will exist 'beyond' natural selection. Baudrillard, for example, who *does* know better, has argued that as a result of its conquest of mortality the human race is now putting an end to natural selection (that which guarantees the death of each species 'in accordance with the laws of evolution'). He writes:

In ending evolution (of all species including his own), he is contravening the symbolic rule and hence truly deserves to disappear . . . in his arrogant desire to end evolution, man is ushering in *involution* and the revival of inhuman, biogenetic forms.

(Baudrillard 1994: 84)

He even contemplates the idea that it may be evolution's own destiny to create for itself a species that escapes its own 'laws' of selection, chiefly death. However, while I find myself sympathizing with many of the sentiments which inform Baudrillard's appraisal of new developments in genetic engineering – let us hope, he says, that a random universe will smash the glass coffin which posthumanity is building for itself, so rescuing us from the facile scientific euphoria that is being sustained by drip-feed – at the same time I want to take issue with his claim that only now with the rise of new computerized technologies and new forms of engineering is mankind leaving behind and learning to live beyond natural selection. This is a far too historical reading of the perversity of the human. As Nietzsche never tired of insisting, evolution, human and non-human, has never been solely about survival or preservation (only 'mediocre Englishmen' such as Darwin, Herbert Spencer, and John Stuart Mill believed this); rather, 'evolution' – and human evolution has always enjoyed an originary *involution* (this is the meaning of its skinning of the earth) – is about the spontaneous and expansive growth of gratuitous desire. In the case of the human animal the 'law of selection' was *crossed* some time ago.

Baudrillard goes badly wrong when he suggests that as soon as the human is no longer defined in the terms of 'freedom' and 'transcendence', but solely in terms of 'genes', then the definition of the human, and hence that of humanism, is 'wiped away' (ibid.: 97). On the contrary, freedom and transcendence have always involved the experimentation of sublimely inhuman practices (also consisting of tremendous humaneness). It is gene-ism, in fact, that rests on a supreme humanism, just as Nazi eugenics amounted to a *Vollendung* of narcissistic currents within European humanism. There is nothing 'inhuman' about a Nazi.

Baudrillard is correct in my view, however, to insist that this quest for complete omnipotence and the 'gaining' of control over evolution through biological manipulation – this lazy mode of thinking simply fails to appreciate that 'evolution' is nothing other than an 'invention' of man – amounts to a caricature of the transvaluation of values (Baudrillard 1994: 94). This desire for the 'beyond' of man no longer assumes the form of the old religion but remains entirely within the human, 'humanity reaching beyond its own condition, achieving a transcendence which arises out of its own capacities – an illusion perhaps, but a superior illusion' (ibid.). In the face of this clean and tidy conception of the transhuman, which reeks of antiseptic post-humanism, it becomes necessary to advocate once again Nietzsche's philosophy of the future conceived as a complex teaching of 'evil'. 'Man', Baudrillard writes, 'is the scorpion.' What binds living things together is not 'ecological, biospherical solidarity', a homoeostatic equilibrium that is another term for death. Rather, in liberating the good we also liberate the evil, and it is their inseparability that constitutes 'our true equilibrium' and balance (ibid.: 82) (see also Baudrillard 1996: 78 and 139). Rather than reconciling ourselves to nature we need to recognize that promising futures reside only in the affirmation of a *maleficent* ecology: 'Good and evil . . . should be weapons and ringing symbols that life must overcome itself again and again! . . . the greatest evil belongs with the greatest good: this, however, is the creative good' (Nietzsche 1969: 125, 139). Or, as Baudrillard points out, nature is made up not simply of well-adjusted and harmonious, stable ecosystems; it also includes germs, viruses, bacteria, chaos, and scorpions.[28]

For Nietzsche the only condition to be 'perfected' is nihilism. When he speaks of the 'arrival' of nihilism – a wisdom which comes from an ancient time – in terms of a 'pathological *transitional* stage', not only is it important to 'hear' the reference to *Übergang* in this formulation; it is equally important to remember that the transition is *without end*. To acclaim the arrival of postbiological mankind is not to announce the 'end of mankind' but to return us to the 'real problem' regarding mankind, since the problem has never been a biological one. This is the filthy lesson of Nietzsche's 'genealogy of morals'. This is a 'genealogy' that can only

---

28 This is in the context of a discussion of the 'Biosphere 2' project, which Baudrillard points out is notable for its exclusion of such phenomena from its artificial re-creation of nature. But as he also astutely notes, the project is not an experiment but an 'experimental attraction' along the lines of Disneyland (1994: 85–6). The 'Bio 2 project is treated at length in Kevin Kelly's *Out of Control* (1994: 150ff.) as a 'fine example of ecotech, the symbiosis of nature and technology' (162). For Kelly the 'lesson' to be learned from the 'experiment' of the project is that 'Life is the ultimate technology' (165). Such a baldly stated declaration amounts to a reification since what Kelly is referring to is not 'life' at all – certainly not *viroid* life as we know it – but a *particular* form of technologically engineered life motivated by specific humanist fantasies.

promise inhuman futures to the extent that a monstrous memory of humans is perpetually cultivated and overcome. To speak of the memory 'of' man is to speak double, of the memory which belongs to man as constitutive of his being, and of the human becoming which belongs to a memory which may not be its, but which heralds something other and 'over'. If 'all forgetting is a reification' (Adorno), the reification we have identified in accounts of the transhuman condition consists in a forgetting of 'man' – not of his 'identity' but of the 'difference' in his *making*. I suppose the question that remains now is are we *wanting* too much in this genealogical remembrance of humans – and of the overhuman?

# 2

# TOWARDS THE OVERHUMAN

## On the art and artifice of Nietzsche's selection

In this book you will discover a 'subterranean man' at work, one who tunnels, mines, and undermines. . . .Does it not seem as though some faith were leading him on, some consolation offering some compensation? As though he perhaps desires this prolonged obscurity, desires to be incomprehensible, concealed, enigmatic, because he knows that he will thereby also acquire: his own morning, his own redemption, his own *daybreak*? . . . He will return, that is certain . . . as soon as he has 'become man' again.

(Nietzsche 1982: preface)

As always, it costs me the greatest effort to come to a decision to *accept* life. I have much ahead of me, upon me, behind me. . . . Forward my dear Lou, and upward!

(Nietzsche, letter to Lou Salomé 8 September 1882)

*Ja! Über das Dasein hinlaufen! Das ist es! Das wäre es!*

(Nietzsche 1974: section 60)

## OF VISIONS, RIDDLES, AND ASCETIC IDEALS

It would seem abundantly clear that the notion of the overman is a deeply problematic one, sitting uncomfortably in Nietzsche's work when placed beside his critical exposition of the meaning of ascetic ideals (ideals of escape). If God is dead, if all gods should now be laid to rest, and if we are to venture forth to explore distant lands across expansive new seas, is it credible for Nietzsche to invent the figure of Zarathustra as his closest companion in order to teach that God is dead and the overman should now be the sole meaning and purpose of the earth? Is the overman, in an act of incomplete nihilism, simply to occupy the vacant residence of God? One solution to the problem, adopted by a number of commentators in recent years, is to abandon the notion altogether and discount it for its lack of coherence as a futural ideal. It has been contended that it is necessary to read the story of Zarathustra's *Untergang* (to the land of the human) in terms of a narration in which the initial teaching of the book – that of the overman – is progressively and decisively abandoned in favour of the teaching of eternal return. Laurence Lampert, for example, is opposed to any reading which would place the overman (he prefers the translation 'superman') at the centre of Nietzsche's teaching since this, he argues, would be to impose on the story of Zarathustra's 'descent' a notion of the eschatological fulfilment of time that is out of sync with the deepest core of Nietzsche's critique of metaphysics. Nietzsche's prefiguration, in the dénouement to the second essay of the *Genealogy of Morality*, of 'the one who must come one day', shows all the hallmarks of a theological day of judgement, but one from which the beautiful (not sublime) teaching of the eternal return liberates us (Lampert 1987: 258). Similarly, Daniel Conway has argued that the proclamation of the imminent arrival of the reign of the overman in passages of Nietzsche betrays a nihilistic commitment to the deficiency of the human condition and is a perfect illustration of the ascetic ideal which entropically reduces the desiring-becoming of life to the one goal (Conway 1989: 212). Finally, Robert Pippin has argued, following Heidegger's lead, that the demand to create the overman is motivated, like the ideals of Christian-moral culture, by a revenge against time and a resentment towards reality (Pippin 1988: 55).

Furthermore, is it not the case that the notion of the overman disappears from Nietzsche's writing after the publication of *Thus Spoke Zarathustra*, making only a brief and inconsequential appearance in section 4 of *The Anti-Christ*? Is nothing easier, therefore, than to recognize the overman as a paradoxical and incoherent fantasy which Nietzsche himself never took seriously? Elsewhere I have sought to show that the notion of the overman is inseparable from the experience of *Untergang* contained in the eternal return since it is the thought-experiment of the latter which is able to disclose the experience of time out of which 'we' are to become those 'who we are', the ones who are new, unique, and incomparable, existing and creating beyond the measure of man (Nietzsche 1974: section 335) (Ansell Pearson 1992: 309–33). When situated in the riddle of return, the vision of the overman becomes transformed into a conception impossible to conceive either along fantastical lines of superhuman strength or in spatial terms as that which simply comes 'after' man; rather, the overman is born in acts of repetition, in which repetition constitutes an original creation (an immaculate conception), owing everything to the past but giving itself completely at the same time only to the future. The overman remains faithful to the earth, that is, to man's promise. One can only restore man to time if one is situated outside or beyond him. But the question, as we shall see, is precisely how one is to get 'over' there. It cannot be simply a question of explicating ascetic ideals; rather, the task is to reveal one's *implication* in them. The journey of the overman becoming 'man' again consists in revealing the *meaning* of ascetic ideals. *He* will 'return' once he has *become* man again (and again).

In the middle of the 1880s, a decade of breaks and breakdowns, it dawned on Nietzsche that, owing to the deformed character of modern humans, it would be the fate of his philosophy beyond good and evil to be a philosophy 'of' the future. He would find himself forever on the way 'towards' the overman, and so would his readers. He designed his writings as an exemplification of this way, of the suffering, torment, torture and cruelty experienced in following it. One does not explore the paradoxical and the paralogical – part of the meaning of the ascetic ideal – without becoming paradoxical and paralogical 'in return'. Nietzsche openly wants to know whether his traversing of the 'way', and his execution of the task, is merely the reflection of a personal odyssey or whether it contains a more universal significance. In what follows I want to show, largely through a consideration of the year of Nietzsche's 'daybreak' in 1886, the year in which Nietzsche added new prefaces to editions of his texts, that readings which urge us to abandon the notion of the overman as a contradictory and incoherent ideal rest on a deep misunderstanding of the import of his exploration of the meaning of the ascetic ideal. To abandon the notion of the overman is to give up on *reading* Nietzsche 'well'. For readers of Nietzsche, and inheritors of the self-overcoming of morality, it is necessary to recognize that there is no escaping the fate of the human and its suffering. Only buffoons think 'man' can be leaped over, and today we find ourselves surrounded by them on all sides. It is the buffoons who have hijacked the idea of the transhuman condition.

## OF THE ENIGMA OF LIBERATION

The identity of the 'we' in Nietzsche assumes various guises in the prefaces he wrote to the new editions of his books published between 1886 and 1887. They are described at various times as the 'affirmers', as the 'self-overcomers of morality', as the 'good Europeans', as the 'free spirits', and as 'tragic pessimists'. On one level, the question of the 'we' in Nietzsche refers to those who will 'read' him, who will read him well (that is, slowly), and so constitute, in an unrealizable sense, his authorship. These are the ones who know how to practise 'the art of intepretation' (*Kunst der Auslegung*), not only by reading the signs of ascending and descending life, but also by knowing how to give those signs 'meaning' (Nietzsche 1994: preface, section 7). But the journey to and beyond Nietzsche will be a perilous one.

The opening sentence of the preface to the first volume of *Human, All Too Human*, written in Nice in the spring of 1886, begins by announcing a series of warnings to Nietzsche's future readers:

> I have been told often enough, and always with an expression of great surprise, that all my writings, from the *Birth of Tragedy* to the most recently published *Prelude to a Philosophy of the Future*, have something that distinguishes and unites them together: they all of them, I have been given to understand, contain snares and nets for unwary birds and in effect a persistent invitation to the overturning of habitual evaluations and valued habits. What? *Everything only* – human, all too human?
> 
> (Nietzsche 1986: preface, section 1)

This passage would be read too quickly if one supposed that Nietzsche here is speaking only of the net and snare of the human, all too human: there is also the net and snare of the overhuman, all too overhuman, which is why he is referring not solely to 'everything only human, all too human'. The 'invitation' to overturn all previous valuations and ideals asks for more than a simple inversion and reversal.

Nietzsche goes on to describe his writings as a schooling in suspicion, in contempt, in courage, and in audacity. It seeks courage to question the land of morality, since morality would prefer us not to question. But, paradoxically, the 'critique' of morality can only be performed '"*out of*" morality', for the simple reason that immorality also places a closure on questioning (Nietzsche 1982: preface, section 4). Immorality deceives itself in thinking that it has gone beyond the question. No wonder Nietzsche tells us that all his thinking may not only be a consolation but also a 'deception'. This, he says, is to speak 'unmorally, extra-morally, "beyond good and evil"'. Nietzsche writes in 'solitude' not by choice but by necessity since his time is not yet; he still wanders. As a critic of the idols of the present age one easily feels oneself alone and isolated. Out of this isolation one artificially invents for oneself a fiction or two. This is the paradoxical practice of an 'artificial art' (*künstliche Kunst*). On one level, therefore, the ideal of the overman is one such fiction, a fiction which Nietzsche devises as his consolation in the face of the world-weary, retired sickness of man and his diminishing returns. On another level, however, the overman is much 'more' than an ideal born out of asceticism and suffering: it is also the excessive invention of an overflowing abundant, newly discovered, newly redeemed, great health. That one cannot simply choose between these two aspects is the profound message of Nietzsche's daybreak contained in the 1886 prefaces. His art of selection is always an 'artifice' and, as such, it can be continually reinvented and rethought. Indeed, of what concern is it that today Herr Nietzsche has become well again?

The 'free spirits' Nietzsche appeals to in his writings are a fictional product of his imagination which he needed to invent for himself so as not to feel alone in his difficult task of teaching man how to go beyond himself by going down to himself. The free spirits do not actually exist; all one can do is to describe their 'coming' and seek to lay down in advance 'under what vicissitudes, upon what paths' it is possible to see them 'coming' (ibid.: preface, section 2). This is to speak of a 'decisive experience' of a 'great liberation'. The liberator discovers that hitherto it has been chained and fettered not only to the past but to its most supreme moments. As a result there necessarily arises a terror and suspicion in the face of what it had loved, producing:

a rebellious, arbitrary, volcanically erupting desire for travel, strange places, estrangements, coldness, soberness, a hatred of love, perhaps a descecrating blow and glance *backwards* to where it formerly loved . . . perhaps a hot blush of shame at what it has just done and at the same time an exultation *that* it has done it, a drunken, inwardly exultant shudder which betrays that a victory has been won – a victory? over what? over whom? an enigmatic question-packed, questionable victory . . . such bad and painful things are part of the history of the great liberation.

(ibid.: preface, section 3)

Even in his desire to overcome himself, to free himself from the bondage not only of the past but of his own self, the liberated prisoner who engages in 'wild experiments' and 'singularities' expresses a kind of sickness. In learning the 'truth' that all values can be turned around, that good is evil, and that God is only an invention of the Devil, the emancipated human being becomes drunk on his curiosity and wicked laughter. Initially, and perhaps for a not inconsiderable duration of time, such a spirit who strives to be free will experience the icy breath of solitude, even running the risk of madness on the road to the achievement of superabundant health. Along the way 'from' man 'to' overman long periods of convalescence are undergone in which the free spirit comes to see himself for the first time (ibid.: 4 and 5). The overturning and inverting of values and all previous ideals is only an initial step on the way, one which must not be taken at face value since it contains a great deception. Ultimately such overturning and inversion have to be put to the 'test':

From this morbid isolation, from the desert of these years of temptation and experiment, it is still a long road to that tremendous overflowing certainty and health which may not dispense even with wickedness, as a means and fish-hook of knowledge, to that *mature* freedom of spirit which . . . permits access to many and contradictory modes of thought.

(ibid.: preface, section 4)

The enigma of liberation involves a process of 'self-mastery' in which one conquers not only one's virtues but also one's own overcomings. This requires a training in perspectivism:

You shall learn to grasp the sense of perspective in every value judgement – the displacement, distortion, and merely apparent teleology of horizons and whatever else pertains to perspectivism . . . You shall learn to graps the *necessary* injustice in every For and Against, injustice as inseparable from life, life itself as *conditioned* by the sense of perspective and injustice.

(ibid.: preface, section 6)

One wants 'more' than the perspective, but even this desire for more is only a perspective, a judgement of a limited horizon of being only from the perspective of the total horizon, a horizon one can never attain (death). In inviting us to make the selection, to be for or against the perspective of eternal return, to be changed or crushed by it, Nietzsche is not inviting us to engage in a blind affirmation of forces, but rather demanding that we affirm the necessary injustice of our willing, which is to be more than human and to be human *again*. The question of their 'active' or 'reactive' nature is not suspended, but simply becomes superfluous, with the result that one 'lives no longer in the fetters of love and hatred, without yes, without no, near or as far as one wishes,' (ibid.: preface, section 4). Health of the productive kind is to be prescribed only in small doses since too much sickness is a good thing. One is to 'remain sick for a long time, and then, slowly, slowly, to become healthy, by which I mean "healthier",' (ibid.: preface, section 5). One has learned to say yes to one's 'yes' and one's 'no'.

Who shall judge? Deleuze proposed a major innovation by replacing the naivety of this question with another, not 'what' is judging, but 'which one' is judging? In *Nietzsche and Philosophy* Deleuze makes central to an active, affirmative, anti-Hegelian mode of philosophy par excellence the doctrine of eternal return, proposing it as an 'ethical and selective thought'. His reading of its vision and riddle is immensely complicated and convoluted, and it pays to return repeatedly to it. A consideration of Deleuze's reading should serve to show 'what' is at stake in the question of the art and artifice of Nietzsche's selection. Deleuze is badly read if it is thought that his construction of the experiment of return simply closes down the question of judgement. While not at all times altogether clear or coherent, showing moments of real blindness, ultimately Deleuze's reading of the doctrine of return is able to show how it is possible, through ultimate affirmation, to move beyond judgement through judgement.

Deleuze reads Nietzsche's philosophy as effecting the realization of 'total critique' in the form of a 'critical reversal'. It does this by directing attention to genealogy as a philosophy of values, in which the problem of critique becomes one of determining the value of values, that is, the evaluation from which values arise and so the problem of their creation. Deleuze would seem to pre-empt the exercise of genealogy as critique, however, at the very outset, since he simply asserts that critique is not the 're-action of re-ssentiment', but the active expression of an active mode of existence (Deleuze 1983: 3). The question of the 'becoming' of critique is not allowed or addressed here. Deleuze devotes a chapter to 'Nietzsche's evolution', but, ironically, the reading he develops in the opening of the book deprives Nietzsche of any 'serious' becoming. This is why the introduction of the thought of eternal return in the unfolding of his reading becomes so crucial. Deleuze places the notion of 'forces' at the heart of his appreciation of Nietzschean critique. In deciding whether values and ideals reflect ascending or descending modes of life attention needs to be focussed not on isolated or reified persons and things but on the forces which constitute them, namely, active or reactive. His argument, however, is not a straightfoward one, since he does not want to posit a simple bifurcation of forces. Under his construction, for example, the eternal return does not simply negate or cancel out the power of the reactive, but rather ensures that the reactive comes back but as active. The issue, however, is how their 'selection' is to be designed and artificed.

An organism can be understood as a play of forces. The important point Deleuze makes is that forces, including reactive ones (such as 'consciousness', 'memory', 'habit', 'adaptation', 'nutrition', 'reproduction', etc.) (ibid.: 41), are precisely that – forces and not merely mechanical means or final ends. As such, they are capable of becoming: 'each time we point out the nobility of action and its superiority to reaction in this way we must not forget that reaction also designates a type of force' (ibid.: 42). In seeking to 'judge' the becoming of forces, Deleuze appeals to Nietzsche's 'art of interpretation' (a 'difficult art', he notes), speaking of the need for a 'concrete physics' over an abstract one, so that it becomes possible to decide whether the forces that 'prevail' are inferior or superior, reactive or active (ibid.: 58). So, how are we to 'decide'? Deleuze notes that one cannot appeal to the state of a system of forces as it is, or the result of the struggle between forces, in order to determine which are active and which are reactive. If one looks at humans now, for example, one will have to conclude, 'contra Darwin', that the thesis on the survival of the 'fittest' is wrong since in this case, the case of mankind, it is precisely the weak and distressed who have survived and flourished (ibid.).[1] Hence 'evolution' establishes nothing. So where is one to look? Deleuze's answer is that one looks not to the facts of history but to the interpretation of qualities of difference. In contrast to the merely 'free *thinker*', whose humanism and positivism bind him to the human, all too human, the free spirit is able to judge forces 'from the standpoint of their origin and quality' (ibid.: 60). But is this to think at all 'genealogically'? Deleuze would seem to go astray at this point since the question of 'quality' gets reduced to a matter of 'origins' (which has little to do with 'becoming'), committing in the process the so-called genetic fallacy. As Nietzsche notes, uncovering the origins of values is not to begin the task of determining their value, but is merely to arouse our suspicion about them and their alleged noble descent (Nietzsche 1968: section 258).

Deleuze demands an ultimate selection and believes that it is the doctrine of eternal return that can provide him with one once it is conceived as a selective experiment guaranteeing only the becoming of the active. But what his reading of return demonstrates is that its willing goes beyond the need which gives rise and calls out for a final selection. The eternal return implements only becoming, neither becoming-active nor becoming-reactive (this kind of 'absolute knowledge' about becoming is denied in the thought-experiment's affirmation). Deleuze notes Nietzsche's fascination with the reactive, even noting that there is something admirable and dangerous about the 'becoming-reactive of forces' (ibid.: 66). Thus, while reactive forces do not take us to the limit but insist on separating us from what we can do, they also bring with them 'new feelings' and teach 'new ways of being affected'. But then, as Deleuze notes, it cannot be the same force which both separates me from what I can do and at the same time endows me with a new power, the power of becoming. It is at this point in the unfolding of his presentation, when the eternal return gets hooked up to becoming as change and transformation, that we can perhaps best locate the import and importance of his construal of the experiment of the eternal return.

Eternal return is deemed a 'selective' thought on Deleuze's reading in that, firstly, it grants the will a practical rule, and secondly, it effects a synthesis of being *as* becoming, repeating: 'whatever you will, will it in such a way that you also will

---

[1] Deleuze simply cites Nietzsche on this point, from *Twilight of the Idols*, and does not recognize the gross anthropomorphism implicit in Nietzsche's 'critical' reading of Darwin. This topic is treated at length in chapter 4.

its eternal return' (ibid.: 68). Thus, for example, a laziness, a stupidity, a baseness, and a cowardice that willed their own eternal return would not come back as the same but as different. They would come back as 'creations'. Consequently, Deleuze claims that it is the thought of return which makes 'willing something whole . . . it makes willing a creation' (ibid.: 69).[2] The willing of eternal return is even more complicated than at first appears since it involves two selections. A second selection is needed simply because one must realize that within the first selection it is possible that reactive forces that can go to the limit can enter into the experiment: 'far from falling outside the eternal return', such forces 'enter into it and seem to return with it' (ibid.: 69). The second selection, Deleuze tells us, involves the most obscure bits of Nietzsche's philosophy, granting eternal return an almost esoteric aspect. Without going into the details of Deleuze's presentation of the second aspect of selection here, we need only note the important point that what is performed in it is ultimately a selection that moves beyond selection, pronouncing the highest 'yes'. In this second selection reactive forces return but are not recognized or treated as such, that is, they have changed and become something different, part of another evolution. No longer is it a question of 'eliminating everything that falls outside this thought'; rather, the task is now to perform an experiment in which things come into being only on the condition that they change their 'nature' (that is, they return not as 'facts' but 'interpretations', not as 'things' but as 'forces') (ibid.: 71). Nietzsche's selection, therefore, consists in the discovery and creation of the forces of 'his' becoming, transmuting reactivity into activity. It is not for Deleuze a question of 'resolution' but only of the movement 'beyond'.

Deleuze is not seeking a 'moment' of selection, then, which will decide once and for all, and in advance, the nature of the return, for it has no 'nature' – it is art and sheer artifice. For Nietzsche, the proof of the test of return lies not in the 'in advance' but in the glance 'backwards', that is, it lies in history constructed as genealogy. To grant the eternal return a 'second' selection, in which the will

---

2 Compare Klossowksi (1985: 115–16). Klossowski's reading maintains that the rewilling of past time which is demanded in the experience of eternal return also requires an admission that *'forgetfulness* alone' is what enabled us 'to undertake old creations as new creations *ad infinitum*'. The 'object' of the rewilling of eternal return is the 'multiple alterity' that is inscribed in the individual. Klossowski concedes that the 'will-to-power' is a 'humanized' term to indicate the nature of the 'vicious circle' that is the eternal return; but he insists that the circle itself is a *'pure intensity without intention'* (ibid.: 117). As such, the teaching does not practise 'expiation', 'purification', or 'immutable purity' since 'Pre-existence and post-existence are always the surplus of the same present existence, according to the economy of the vicious circle' (118).

becomes an object of itself as an object of affirmation, is not to 'solve' the riddle of return but simply to show its conditions of possibility – not, of course, 'once and for all', but for the moment which endures eternity.[3] Deleuze knows this, and he is affirming it in his complicated reading of Nietzsche. In the experiment of eternal return, therefore, what is being affirmed is the necessity of the return of *selection*. It is precisely this insight which informs Deleuze and Guattari's later thinking on 'good' and 'bad': 'Good and bad', they write, 'are only the products of an active temporary selection, which must be renewed' (Deleuze and Guattari 1988: 10). Here they write not as moralists but as metallurgists and ethologists, appreciating that in terms of the functioning of a machinic plane of immanence, in which everything is interconnected and subject to transmutation by heterogeneous forces, good and bad cannot be treated as a dualism or a dichotomy. If 'life' is process and becoming, then nothing can be known 'once and for all' in advance. Hence the desire of the selection of return and necessity of selection: 'You may make a rupture, draw a line of flight, yet there is still a danger that you will reencounter organizations that restratify everything, formations that restore power to a signifier, attributions that reconstitute a subject . . . from Oedipal resurgences to fascist concretions' (ibid.: 9).

The eternal return is designed to offer a responsibility one can freely accede to, providing a burden or a weight one can make joyous. This is to become one's own path and goal, saying yes to one's own secret yes and secret no. In the final section of the preface to *Human, All Too Human*, Nietzsche argues that the imperative of the free spirit, the spirit that has unlearned the command 'thou shalt' and learned the supra-moral autonomous entitlement to 'I may', must become universal by becoming a categorical imperative 'for all and none'. The free spirit generalizes its own singular and unique case and learns to adjudicate on the basis of this experience (the experience of the 'midday'):

What has happened to me, he says to himself, must happen to everyone in whom a *task* wants to become incarnate and 'come into the world'. The secret force and necessity of this task will rule among and in the individual facets of his destiny like an unconscious pregnancy – long before he has caught sight of this task itself or knows its name. Our vocation commands and disposes of us even when we do not yet know it: it is the future which regulates our today.

(ibid.: preface, section 7)

---

3 On the 'once and for all' again see Klossowski (1985: 115). The ruse of return – rewilling the events of one's becoming innumerable times – 'removes the "once and for all" character from all events'.

In affirming the task of his own becoming Nietzsche admits to his own paradoxical and paralogical status as a free spirit and self-overcomer – he speaks only, he tells us, of his overcomings, but then what else is there to speak and write of? His 'greatest danger' has always been '*disgust* at mankind' (Nietzsche 1979a: 'Why I am so Wise', section 8). His thinking is deeply paradoxical in that it seeks an overcoming of the philosophy of the ascetic priest, which teaches humanity always to sacrifice the present for the promise and lie of a better, ill-defined future, by also teaching us to sacrifice the present for the sake of the future: 'I love him', says Zarathustra, 'who justifies the humanity of the future and redeems the humanity of the past, for he wants to perish by the present' (Nietzsche 1969: prologue, section 4). Concealed within the excessive logic of Nietzsche's becoming, therefore, is the necessary return 'of' ascetic ideals (again: who, or which one, will judge?). But if their first willing was tragic, their second will be comic.

Nietzsche desires to live 'beyond' selection, to be only a yea-sayer, to affirm the grand economy of life as it is, without subtraction or addition, without any kind of selection at all. The economy of life, however, is unjust and demands negation as well as affirmation, the creation of new law-tables and their destruction. Nietzsche desires a new supra-moral politics beyond the spirit of *ressentiment*, and yet it is unable to conceal its own disgust towards humanity. Emancipation, however, is implicated in the injustice of perspectivism, and so it is necessary to affirm one's own negations since they constitute an essential part of one's own becoming. There is concealed the 'yes' even in the 'no'. To refrain from judgement is the 'judgement', the yes, of the refrain. This reflection on the necessity and impossibility of judgement shows the extent to which art and artifice are wedded together in Nietzsche. Nietzsche speaks of 'artists of the future' as those who not only belong to the future or come towards it, but also undergo the responsibility for its invention as both a sign of their audacity and as a measure of their gravity. This invention of the future speaks of an art 'of' great politics.

## OF ROMANTICISM AND SICKNESS: NIETZSCHE 'CONTRA' ROUSSEAU

In between the prefaces to the first and second volumes of *Human, All Too Human*, Nietzsche wrote his well-known and esteemed 'attempt at a self-critique' in *The Birth of Tragedy* in Sils-Maria in the August of 1886. Here we find him preoccupied with the nature of romanticism and with distinguishing his own tragic form of pessimism — a pessimism born out of the health of the recovery of invention and its injustice — from the morbidly sick type of pessimism he designates as 'romantic pessimism', that is, pessimism that can only lament the loss and its failed recovery. The attempt to distinguish and separate the two kinds of pessimism, so as not to avoid but to confront contamination, is an overriding theme of the year of Nietzsche's daybreak.

Nietzsche appreciates that he too is a sick animal, for he too, like the priests and moralists he castigates throughout his writings, suffers from life. The question of concern to him is whether he suffers from its impoverishment or from its excess. If the latter, then his suffering may be radically distinct from that of priests and feeble windbags. So he asks:

Is pessimism *necessarily* a sign of decline, decay, degeneration, weary and weak instincts — as it once was in India, and now is, to all appearances, among us 'modern' men and Europeans? Is there a pessimism of *strength*? An intellectual predilection for the hard, gruesome, evil, probematic aspect of existence, prompted by well-being, by overflowing health, by the *fullness* of existence? Is it perhaps possible to suffer from overfullness?

(Nietzsche 1967: 'Self-Critique', section 1)

Here it is a question of appealing not so much to instincts as to their becoming, to their incorporation, and internalization with a process of cultural selection and training. This is where Nietzsche's attempt to affirm the pathos of distance that separates him from Rousseau often appears disingenuous. Recognizing the 'identity in difference' of Rousseau and Nietzsche is not simply a matter of pointing to their common misanthropic moralism, since both despised humans out of love for them. Nietzsche sought to distance himself from Rousseau in truly snobbish, Galtonesque fashion, appealing to a differentiation between Rousseau's plebeian origins and his own noble ones. But does Nietzsche really expect his claim that he is the advocate of life (in all its immorality) and Rousseau the great denier of life to be taken seriously? Perhaps Nietzsche was simply a better artist than Rousseau, more accomplished at artifice because he needed to be because he had so much to conceal. Any attempt to construe their relationship in terms of a simple opposition, such as we find in the early Derrida, where a crude and unconvincing distinction is drawn between Rousseauian seriousness and nostalgia for lost origins and Nietzschean playfulness and mockery of origins, fails to see the 'return' of Rousseau in Nietzsche (Derrida 1973: 292). As we saw in chapter 1, Nietzsche makes the demand that we get very 'serious' about 'lost origins': there is work to be done and a task to be executed. The land of the overman is not simply that of a children's playground. The aim is to get serious about lost origins in order to recover them for a new invention. This is the becoming of genealogy.

In fact, both Rousseau and Nietzsche are compelled to construe the question of their authorship in terms of a destiny which heralds a time 'of' the future. In Rousseau's case this is a providential future, a future of providence, and in Nietzsche's it is an unknown future which regulates the today and which prepares itself as if it were an unconscious pregnancy (the future goes right back 'in time' to conception). In his lifetime Rousseau is widely read but ineffectively understood. When a Frenchman reads one of his books he does not read what is before him, Rousseau protests, but reads only in accordance with the prejudices of morality, that is, the common prejudices of the public imagination which stands in the way, he says, of a true appreciation of his genius (he is not simply a man). One day, he anticipates, there will be a day of 'judgement' in which his teaching will be seen for what it really is, and so will its author (Rousseau 1990). Nietzsche, by contrast, is read neither badly or well in his own lifetime: he is simply ignored. All he can anticipate is a posthumous destiny, but it is still a future in which 'I am not read, I will not be read.' Thus, the one who demands that his readers learn the art of intrepretation also points to the necessary misreading in reading him. So many snares and nets. Like Rousseau, however, Nietzsche construes his destiny in terms of an eventual day of decision in which those who read him will reach a terrible and seductive judgement about their lives and the future of humanity. His writings will have forced them into a making a decision, but this decision will contain necessarily the injustice of every perspectival 'for' or 'against'. His questioning of morality will 'break history into two', into those who live 'before' and those who live 'after' (Nietzsche 1979a: 'Why I am a Destiny', section 8). But still Nietzsche offers himself over to man. The uniqueness of Rousseau and Nietzsche is thus destined to become part of the common 'stock' of mankind.[4] In deliberately removing themselves from their own time, and retreating into solitude, both will assume the guise of the 'inhuman' when they come into contact, in their own time and posthumously, with earthly earnestness (Rousseau 1990: 99).

Even Rousseau could claim with a degree of legitimacy that his sickness concealed the marks and betrayed the masks of a new health. Again, who 'can' or 'may' judge? This becomes an especially acute problem once one recognizes that

---

4 In my study of 1991 I was concerned to show the extent to which for both Rousseau and Nietzsche the malaise of the present age stems from the fact that we moderns are no longer 'material' for society. Thus, both can be seen to articulate a politics of transfiguration in which the possessive individuals of bourgeois society are enticed to overcome themselves.

it is a question of forces and their genealogical becoming. Like Rousseau, Nietzsche experienced the compulsion to write. 'One should only speak when one may not stay silent', he writes. All else is to be treated as 'chatter, "literature", lack of breeding' (Nietzsche 1986, book II: preface, section 1). Nietzsche's aphorisms contain 'precepts of health' which may be recommended to the more 'spiritual natures' of the present generation who will read him in terms of a voluntary discipline ('disciplina voluntatis') (ibid.: preface, section 2). But these are 'precepts of health' that 'come' with the warning of having been contaminated by deep sicknesses. One can only go 'beyond' romanticism by adopting an attitude of mistrust towards oneself, so that one is able to take sides against oneself, become one's greatest enemy as one's deepest friend, and in this way find one's way to 'that courageous pessimism that is the antithesis of all romantic mendacity' (ibid.: preface, section 4). The charm of writing is to write as a sufferer and self-denier while not appearing to be such (ibid.: section 5). Nietzsche identifies the real paradox of his becoming, however, when he writes about his campaign against the 'unscientific tendency' of romantic pessimism which interprets and inflates individual personal existence into 'universal judgement', and into condemnations of the world. He then asks inquiringly:

Shall my experience – this history of an illness and recovery . . . have been my personal experience alone? And only my human, all too-human?

(ibid.: preface, section 6)

Nietzsche seeks to universalize his experience, but in terms that will not not simply inflate merely personal experiences into unjustifiably universal judgements about life and history. He would like to believe that his 'travel books' were not written solely for himself, so that, with growing confidence, he can 'venture to send them off again' (ibid.). But this requires that Nietzsche's self-overcoming is more than merely *his* self-overcoming. The reason this might be possible, he speculates, lies in the fact that what his overcoming speaks of is not only his own personal past – it does not, hence the insignificance of the fact that Herr Nietzsche has become well again – but rather man's genealogical past. Nietzsche is fatally and audaciously claiming that within his being there finds expression the tremendous coming into being and suffering of those form-shaping forces that collide with the present since they are riddled with the past and are pregnant with the future. If he has been infected by the disease of the past (man), he has also been granted the power of the future (overman). And so he addresses himself to those who have to be 'the conscience of the modern soul' and to possess its knowledge.

These are the ones in whom 'all that exists today of sickness, poison, and danger, comes together', and whose 'lot' is to be sicker than 'any other kind of individual because you are not "only individuals"' (ibid.) Something flows on 'underneath' these individuals which explains why they are 'more' than themselves and what they simply appear as.

The preface to the second edition of *Daybreak* was written in Ruta, near Genoa, in the autumn of 1886, and it is here that Nietzsche now speaks of his 'return', of his return to life and his desire to be 'man' again. What could easily have turned out to be a funeral oration – the year of 1886 and all that led to it – can now be celebrated as a self-overcoming to good health and a courageous knowledge of, and for, the forbidden. He has emerged from his questioning of man and morals free of bitterness towards man and his moral past. It is not that he has not been contaminated by coming into contact with it, for he knows he already was poisoned by its sickness. He can simply now recognize it as a formative training or selection in a process of becoming, and not only *his* becoming.

## GAY SCIENCE AND THE RETURN OF ASCETIC IDEALS

To return to the 'name' of 'Nietzsche' is to return to the name that 'comes', the name of the future that is on its way and still wanders. It is of this name that Nietzsche speaks in the preface to the second edition of *The Gay Science* which he wrote again in Ruta, this time in the autumn of 1886. The preface represents the consummation of his daybreak.

He begins by suggesting that the gay science heralds a book which may require more than the one preface, and he doubts whether there is another being alive who has ever lived through such experiences. The book expresses above all the 'gratitude of a convalescent'. 'Gay Science' signifies the 'saturnalia of a spirit' who with patience and time on his side has resisted a terrible, long pressure 'severely, coldly, without submitting, but also without hope', but who is now suddenly 'attacked' by hope, the hope for health and the intoxication of convalescence that has turned out well (Nietzsche 1974: preface, section 1). The book speaks of both a death and a rebirth. After long privation and impotence it can now rejoice in the attainment of a strong spirit that enjoys a 'reawakened faith in tomorrow and the day after tomorrow' since it contains a 'sudden sense and anticipation of the future'. It is in this preface that Nietzsche openly admits for the first time, to himself and to his readers, that his radical retreat into solitude was a *retreat*, since it emanated from a feeling of lofty isolation from the concerns of humanity. Now, however, after undergoing recovery, he realizes that his stubborn pursuit of solitude was nothing more, and nothing less, than a form of self-defence against a contempt for man that had become 'pathologically clairvoyant'. Moreover, he can now appreciate that his nausea at man developed out of a spiritual diet called romanticism. In seeking the beyond of man Nietzsche had, in the retreat of his solitude, forgotten man and his concealed potentialities for future becoming. Now he is ready to leave *behind* Herr Nietzsche since the fact that this gentleman has become well again is of no great consequence (just as his decline into sickness was of no ultimate importance (ibid.: preface, section 2)).

For any philosopher who has a training in psychology, Nietzsche states, the most important question concerns the relationship between health and philosophy. What is it, he asks, that gives rise to all searches for the 'beyond'? In some, he notes, it is deprivation that motivates philosophizing, in which philosophy is reduced to a need, serving as a kind of sedative or self-alienation. In others, however, it is strength and excess of energy flows which lead to philosophizing, and in this case philosophy acts as a beautiful luxury, expressing a 'triumphant gratitude that eventually still has to inscribe itself in cosmic letters on the heaven of concepts' (ibid.: 2). Nietzsche is not here erecting a strict partition between the two since he recognizes that the distinction is largely an arbitrary one. The important thing to be grasped is the extent to which the two species of philosophizing are born from the same soil and the same sun. The question of sickness, however, persists in raising a certain disquiet and alarm:

Every philosophy that ranks peace above war, every ethic with a negative definition of happiness, every metaphysics and physics that knows some finale, some final state of some sort, every predominantly aesthetic or religious craving for some Apart, Beyond, Outside, Above (*Abseits, Jenseits, Ausserhalb, Oberhalb*), permits the question whether it was not sickness that inspired the philosopher.

(ibid.)

However, this question is only a provisional one since it is clear from man's genealogical record that it is indeed a profound sickness that has motivated all constructions and inventions of the beyond and the outside. Here we are not dealing simply with 'truth' but with something much more important which, to speak beyond good and evil, concerns 'health, future, growth, power, life' (ibid.). Philosophy is, in fact, the 'art of transfiguration' which is defined by Nietzsche as the capacity for traversing for many kinds of health, including the health of sickness, and passing through many kinds of philosophies. Great health, therefore, entails, as an essential part of its coming, an *affirmation* of sickness and of the ideals it inspires:

> We are not thinking frogs and registering mechanisms with their innards removed: constantly, we have to give birth to our thoughts out of our pain and, like mothers, endow them with all we have of blood, heart, fire, pleasure, passion, agony, conscience, fate, and catastrophe. Life — that means constantly transforming all that we are into light and flame — also everything that wounds us; we simply can do no other. And as for sickness? Are we not almost tempted to ask whether we could get along without it?
>
> (ibid.: preface, section 3)

The paradox is that this is to judge sickness 'beyond' judgement, to think 'beyond' the beyond. Only this kind of paradoxical involvement in the movement beyond can speak genuinely of the becoming-active of forces. This is not, however, to define a 'moment' of judgement — is this active? is this reactive? — unless the moment be understood genealogically. Unmasking morality — through consolation and deception — entails revaluing values not in terms of a new reverance and canonization. Impiously one is now able to see them as signs of 'the most fateful abortion'. What makes them 'fateful' is the fact that they exert a strange 'fascination'. Why? Because they have 'crossed' the *law of selection* ('das Gesetz der Selektion gekreuzt') (Nietzsche 1979a: 'Why I am a Destiny', section 8).

The experience of going into the depths and then re-emerging with a new-found sense of joy is not designed to make us any 'better' as human beings, only more 'profound' creatures. Through rigorous self-questioning, a questioning that freely draws on all the resources of cruelty and violence of its ascetic past, the trust in life disappears as it becomes a problem. And yet, Nietzsche encourages, we are not to 'jump' to the conclusion that life is without meaning, making us despondent and gloomy. In thinking through the problem of life the task is to imitate chewing cows, not fretful frogs. Instead, one is to 'return' from one's abysses and severest and most secret sicknesses 'newborn' (ibid.: section 4). Our skin has been shed; we have flown away and then returned home. But one discovers that one has not returned as the same but as different, that one's scenery has changed and one has new eyes, more subtle, more sophisticated. One has been trained out of sickness.

The preoccupation with the 'outside', with how one is to get there and to emancipate the flight into the beyond from the desire of secret will to nothingness, informs book 5 of *The Gay Science*, which Nietzsche added in 1886 for its publication in the following year. For Nietzsche the task is to think not of the fact of the future but of its coming, and to attempt to do so in a way that reveals signs of one's liberation from one's romanticism. In other words, the crucial art of selection involves knowing whether it is the spirit of revenge that informs one's willing and invention of the future, or whether it is the spirit that has emancipated itself from the longing of the future, which is nothing more than the cry of the distressed and the impotent. But this is not simply a matter of deciding whether the desire for the future is a human desire or a more than human desire, since the two are entangled. Again the moment of final or ultimate decision is deferred. The doctrine of eternal return is not offered as a resolution of this lack of decision. It only gives us back the overman who has become man again, that is, it gives us back our task:

Finally, our reward is the *greatest* of life's gifts, perhaps the greatest thing it is able to give of any kind – we are given back our *task*.

(Nietzsche 1986: book II, preface, section 5)

Speaking of the 'outside', Nietzsche states that if one wants to know how high the towers in the town are one simply leaves the town. But the case of man would seem to be of a different order since one cannot simply 'leave' behind one's 'flesh and blood' in the search for what lies 'beyond' him (Nietzsche 1974: section 380). But the problem persists since if thoughts about moral prejudices – about humanity – are to be more than mere prejudices about prejudices, they presuppose a position 'outside morality, some point beyond . . . to which one has to rise, climb, or fly'. It is not so much a question of wanting to go out there or up there – it would be more accurate to speak of unfree will than free will in this regard – but rather of knowing whether 'one really *can* get up there' (ibid.). It is the future that is the source of our unfreedom in this regard (recall: it is the future which regulates our today). Nietzsche's reponse to the question of the outside and how one is to get there is simply to appeal to its 'manifold conditions' of possibility. In essence, the question takes us back to the enigma of liberation, namely, that to become a human being of such a 'beyond' who desires to behold the 'supreme measure of value of his time' requires him first of all to overcome (*überwinden*) this time *in himself*. Overcoming one's own time in oneself involves overcoming one's prior aversion to it, one's suffering from it, the kind of suffering that gave birth to romanticism. Again, the eternal return speaks not of the liberation from this time but only of its *enigma*.

Nietzsche is careful to show that the ascetic ideal can be uncovered hiding in the most unlikely places: in science in general, and in the positivist sciences in particular, such as historiography, and, perhaps most surprisingly of all, in the self-proclaimed Antichrists, immoralists, nihilists, and sceptics of every degree. He reserves his greatest mistrust for those preachers of a new faith who desire only believers. He does not, he tells us, deny that faith 'brings salvation' – but it is precisely because it does that he denies that faith *proves* anything. Such faith does not bring 'truth', but only establishes a certain probability – of deception. But all of these 'free, *very* free spirits', spirits of today *only*, are simply the 'last idealists of knowledge', since all they desire to do is to 'jump' (Nietzsche 1994: III, section 24). Since these spirits stand too close to themselves, unknowledgeable about the art of distance or selection, they cannot see that the ascetic ideal is simply their ideal as well, that they are its current 'representatives'. Indeed, Europe is currently experiencing massive 'overproduction' in the field of ideals, opening up a new trade in the marketing of 'little idolatrous ideals' and new 'idealisms'. Nietzsche speculates: how many shiploads of sham idealists, hero-outfits and tinny rattle of great words, how many tons of sugared, alcoholic sympathy, would one have to export in order to make the air of Europe smell cleaner? We are polluted not only by the toxic wastes of industry but much more by the overproduction of our decay, our overproduction of ascetic ideals that simply reveals our inability any longer to overcome ourselves. The only real opposition to the new ascetic idealists is to be found in the 'comedians of this ideal', since they at least arouse in one mistrust (ibid.: III, section 27). So, we learn, Nietzsche's own teaching is not to be taken on trust; on the contrary, and as Nietzsche encourages us, it is to be treated with the greatest suspicion.

Science – especially 'modern science' – offers the best ally for the continuation of the ascetic ideal on account of the fact that it is the most unconscious, voluntary and subterranean. Science suffers from the fact that it lacks independence, that it is always placed in the service of a value-creating power, never creating values. Science suffers from the lack of a great love. As a result it harbours a place for all kinds of discontent, for resentment, and for gnawing worms. Science unconsciously performs its own kind of revenge on man by arriving at results that serve to belittle him (since Copernicus man, Nietzsche notes, has been rolling on a downward path). Nietzsche, by contrast, searches to give articulation to a *gay* science, a science that speaks of both man's tragedy and comedy, a form of expansive knowledge that will heat up the universe and render it conducive for the mixing of all kinds of foreign elements and the explosion of new sparks. If normal science belittles man, hiding its own ascetic ideal, the task of a gay science is to expand his horizon so that it becomes possible to catch a glimpse of the future of the overman and of man again. In working through the real problem of man

Nietzsche does not bind us to the history of morality. Morality is unable to go 'beyond' good and evil, unable to traverse outside itself. It is for this reason that it can be defined as the 'danger of dangers'. Its restricted economy of life makes impossible the actualization of the 'highest potential power (*Mächtigkeit*) and splendour' since it desires that the present exist at the 'expense of the future' (*auf Kosten der Zukunft*) (Nietzsche 1994: preface, section 6). The future is too valuable, however, too compulsive, to be sacrificed to the impoverished economy, the unpayable but always requested, guilty debt of morality. Time waits – indeed it slows down – for the overman.

Nietzsche goes 'beyond' the ascetic ideal by recognizing its tremendous power. From a genealogical perspective it becomes possible to appreciate that – 'you take my *meaning* already' (my italic) – the ascetic priest, the negative man in and for himself – 'actually belongs to the really great forces in life which *conserve and create the positive*' (ibid.: III, section 13). The ascetic ideal has inscribed itself into the 'whole history of man' and in a way that is both 'terrible and *unforgettable*' (my italic) (ibid.: III, section 21). But this 'real catastrophe' on planet earth also offers real promise – for something flows not simply beyond or outside individuals but *underneath* them.

# 3

# DEAD OR ALIVE

## On the death of eternal return

> In effect, death is everywhere, as that ideal, uncrossable boundary separating bodies, their forms, and states, and as the condition, even initiatory, even symbolic, through which a subject must pass in order to change its form or state.
>
> (Deleuze and Guattari 1988: 107)

> Everywhere resound the voices of those who preach death: and the earth is full of those to whom death must be preached.
>
> (Nietzsche 1969: 'Of the Preachers of Death')

> You must want to burn yourself in your own flame: how could you become new, if you had not first become ashes!
>
> (Nietzsche 1969: 'Of the Way of the Creator')

If the eternal return speaks of death and rebirth, of daybreak, what kind of death belongs to the eternal return? A heat-death or a fire-death? The distinction would be between death conceived as a judgement which denies, restricts, and condemns, and death experienced as a transportation, a flight, dissolution and passage, true becoming. This distinction is allowed and invited by Nietzsche himself in the well-known passage on the greatest weight in *The Gay Science*, where he speaks of the impact of the eternal return in terms of either a crushing (*zermalen*) or a transforming (*verwandeln*), depending on the predisposed forces present at the time 'of' the moment (*Augenblick*) when the experiment is undergone and tested. What does it mean to be 'free for death and in death'? Further, how is it possible to distinguish between 'good' death and 'bad' death (Nietzsche 1969: 'Of Free Death')? Does one only die well one when one dies for the sake of the 'beyond'? Is this what happened to Nietzsche when he underwent the experience of eternal return six thousand feet *beyond man and time*? The task: to die at the 'right time' and to make of death a festival. What Nietzsche calls 'the consummating death' (*den vollbringenden Tod*) is a death that contains a promise, a promise 'of' life and of death to life (promise considered as a pledge, *ein Gelöbniss*). What matters is not the death that 'comes' at the end of life but the modes of one's dying in this life.

The theme of 'death' has been little explored in the becoming of Zarathustra. Indeed, for far too long interpretation has concentrated too much on the misguided question of Zarathustra's identity (the question, again and again, 'who is Zarathustra'?). This question is overburdened simply because an essential component of the process of becoming, as Nietzsche understands it, and as governs the becoming of Zarathustra, is that the subject 'of' becoming does not know who or what it is ('Is it *my* teaching? Who am I?', Nietzsche 1969: 'The Stillest Hour'). Repeatedly, Zarathustra's disciples and animals implore Zarathustra to reveal his identity, to disclose who he really is, and to end the uncertain, polysemic character of his becoming. Zarathustra resists their demands, and continues to dance to a different tune: the tune of 'pure becoming'.

In *Difference and Repetition* Deleuze produces a positive conception of death – death conceived as the condition of possibility of difference and as the progenitor of repetition – in the context of a critique of Freud's formulation of the death-drive. Deleuze criticizes Freud for restricting death, conceived as the qualitative and quantitative return of the living to inanimate matter, to an 'extrinsic, scientific and objective' definition. Although he allowed for plural models of existence in the cases of birth and castration, Freud reduced death to an objective determination of matter, with the result that the phenomenon of repetition cannot be thought along any other lines than those of undifferenciation,[1] with the result that repetition becomes real, all too real, existing without displacement or disguise (Deleuze 1968: 147–8; 1994: 111–12).

Deleuze's emphasis on the primacy of the unconscious allows him to conceive of the phenomenon of 'difference and repetition' in terms of a productive and positive unconscious, an unconscious that is not driven by negation and contradiction, but by questioning and problematizing (a novel philosophical interpretation of Freud's well-known declaration that the unconscious knows no negative would be one which posited the unconscious as the genuinely pre-suppositionless organon of 'thinking'). What makes the unconscious productive and positive is that it is driven by the unknown, the immeasurable, the alogical, and so on. It is not restricted either by limitation or opposition. It knows nothing of the

---

[1] The words 'differenciation' and 'differentiation' are used to translate the French *différenciation* and *différentiation*.

world as representation (it is a factory, not a theatre). We should recall the warning which Deleuze and Guattari make in *Anti-Oedipus*, concerning the necessity to avoid the attribution of dark and sombre horrors to the unconscious solely derived from the horrors of consciousness. As they so classically put it, 'The unconscious has its horrors, but they are not anthropomorphic. It is not the sleep of reason which engenders monsters, but vigilant and insomniac rationality' (Deleuze and Guattari 1972: 133; 1983: 112).

Is it possible to formulate death as a question and a problem before it becomes marked as a limitation and a negation? This is precisely the move made by Deleuze in his working through of the question of 'difference and repetition'. Contra Freud's human, all too human interpretation of the death-drive, Deleuze contends:

Death does not appear in the objective model of an indifferent inanimate matter to which the living would 'return'; it is present in the living in the form of a subjective and differenciated experience endowed with its prototype. It is not a material state; on the contrary, having renounced all matter, it corresponds to a pure form – the empty form of time. . . . It is neither the limitation imposed by matter upon mortal life, nor the opposition between matter and immortal life, which furnishes death with its prototype. Death is, rather, the last form of the problematic, the source of problems and questions, the sign of their persistence over and above every response, the 'Where?', and 'When?' which designate this (non)-being where every affirmation is nourished.

(Deleuze 1968:148; 1994: 112)

Deleuze has written that *Beyond the Pleasure Principle* is the place where one can find Freud most directly and penetratingly engaged in 'specifically philosophical reflection' (Deleuze 1989b: 111). By this he means that in setting out to think the 'beyond' peculiar to the pleasure principle Freud is carrying out a 'transcendental' analysis. By the 'beyond', Deleuze argues, Freud does not simply mean to refer to empirical exceptions to the principle, such as the unpleasure the reality principle imposes on us or the circuitous route of its becoming, since these are all merely apparent exceptions that can still be reconciled with the pleasure principle. So, if there are no 'real' exceptions to it, what does the 'beyond' in Freud's title refer to? Deleuze's position is to argue that although nothing contradicts the principle and everything can be reconciled to it, there is an excess that while 'governed' by the principle is not entirely 'dependent' on it. This is to speak of a range of elements and processes that make up its complicated application. If the pleasure principle 'rules', it does so never as the final or highest 'authority' (it has power without legitimacy in this regard). The fact that there is something which 'falls outside' and 'is not homogeneous' with the pleasure principle – something 'beyond' (*Jenseits*) – explains why Freud is involved in a transcendental analysis of the 'phenomenon'. The 'beyond' for Deleuze refers, ultimately, to the higher authority and power of 'repetition', which, he contends, Freud conceives in terms of a transcendental synthesis of time, that is, a repetition which is 'at once a repetition of *before*, *during*, and *after*' (ibid.: 115). From the 'natural standpoint' the past simply follows upon the present and the present upon the future in terms of a linear unfolding. From a transcendental perspective, however, the three modalities of time are constituted 'in time *simultaneously*' (ibid.) (they enfold as much as they unfold). But there is also a further movement, one which makes repetition what it is, which is the fact that one can add the future (the 'after') to the other two dimensions (past and present) because there could be no constitution of time without the opening up to, and the creation of the possibility for, the future (the future that is not only 'in' time but also 'of' time). In his reading of sadism and masochism Deleuze locates the monstrous force of repetition that is at work and play. Here repetition takes on a life of its own, running wild, and becoming independent of all previous pleasure. As a result a fundamental inversion can be seen to have taken place in their practices, since 'Pleasure is now a form of behaviour related to repetition accompanying and following repetition. Pleasure and repetition have thus exchanged roles' (ibid.: 120). For Deleuze there is always a double process of desexualization and resexualization taking place in the economy of pleasure and pain. It is in the 'on between' of the two that the death-drive announces itself. However, because the process is characterized by an 'instantaneous leap', is it always pleasure which endures and prevails. It is here that one might locate what can be termed the 'transcendental illusion' of the pleasure principle. Pleasure – and pain – are real, but what the 'beyond' announces is the coming into play of *new* sensations, *new* affects, and *new* bodies of becoming. To live and die 'beyond' the pleasure principle, therefore, is to enter into the excessive economy of difference 'and' repetition.

However, contra Deleuze, it can be argued that the difficulties which beset Freud's bizarre presentation of the death-drive stem from the fact that his analysis is both 'too' philosophical and not philosophical enough. We need to ask: what is the status of Freud's claim that 'the aim of all life is death', in terms of both its biological validity and its philosophical legitimacy? What kind of teaching of 'life' is offered in *Beyond the Pleasure Principle*? It is by no means obvious that Freud should turn to biology in the way that he does in order to lend scientific support to his metaphysical speculations on the fundamental aim of all life, a speculation that ultimately posits a particular conception of evolution. It seems that he made this turn because only a biological explanation was capable of accounting for the alleged 'primordiality' of the power at work in the compulsion to repeat (that is, repeating past experiences which offer no possibility for pleasure in their relived experience) (see Boothby 1991: 74). There is also a reading of memory offered in Freud's account in which it becomes a faculty that serves the desire to restore an earlier state of things (the inorganic).[2] As such, the death-drive refers to an urge that is inherent in the entire manifestation of organic life. The death-drive is fundamentally ambiguous in that one aspect of its 'beyond' dimension is the curious fact that it leads not to a decrease in psychical tension but to its increase (we get fixated on painful memories; repetition becomes a pain). On the other hand, however, its quest for Nirvana – the reduction of psychical tension to an absolute minimum – also means that, in its ultimate sense, the death-drive does desire equilibrium and stasis, a state beyond the restless and deceiving wanderings and shenanigans of pleasure (this is the point at which the theory comes very close to Schopenhauer, as Freud himself acknowledges in his essay). The paradox here can be resolved by recognizing that Freud's presentation of the death-drive actually involves two (at least) thoughts of the 'beyond'. It is only on the 'psychological' level that Freud is positing a 'beyond' in the sense of a tremendous heightening of psychical tensions; while it is on the level of *biology* that he is construing the 'beyond' in a finalistic sense as that which escapes the senseless striving of pleasure.

Several important questions about Freud's presentation remain to be examined, including his equation of repetition and regression, an identification that colours his thinking on evolution. I shall now seek to explore this and other questions in an inquiry into the death that peculiarly belongs to the eternal return. Important differences between Nietzsche and Freud – in their thinking on life, evolution, and death – will then emerge. Although I am unable to establish the point firmly here, I would contend that the difference between the two is that wheareas Nietzsche conceives death in terms of an open-ended becoming of forces, Freud construes death in terms of a biological lock-in (a *deadlock*), modelling its being along the lines of a Lamarckism in reverse gear. It was one of the

---

2 For a provocative, if theoretically flawed and incoherent, account of memory going back into deep or geological time, see Ballard's novel of 1962, *The Drowned World*: 'The brief span of an individual life is misleading. Each one of us is as old as the entire biological kingdom, and our bloodstreams are tributaries of the great sea of its total memory' (Ballard 1987: 44). As one character in the book says to another: "'That wasn't a dream, Robert, but an ancient organic memory millions of years old. . . . This is the lumbar transfer, total biopsychic recall. We really *remember* these swamps and lagoons' (ibid.: 74).

merits of Deleuze's early reading of Nietzsche to show the extent to which Nietzsche's thinking on life and death was informed by an engagement with thermodynamics, and he successfully located in his writings a critique of modern physics and biology by focussing on their grounding in a reactive metaphysics. According to Deleuze, Nietzsche's thinking of the becoming of forces attacks all forms of the undifferentiated, such as logical identity, mathematical equality, and physical equilibrium (Deleuze 1983: 45). In his reading of eternal return Deleuze seeks to show that the attempt to conceive of becoming without reference to final ends results in an attack on both mechanistic and thermodynamical conceptions of energy. In fact, both mechanism and thermodynamics are based on a depression of difference since in both cases it is possible to identify a passage from a principle of finitude (the constancy of a sum) to a principle of nihilism, such as the cancelling out of differences in quantities, the sum of which is always constant. In mechanism, for example, an idea of eternal return is affirmed, but only by assuming either a balancing or a cancelling out of produced differences between the initial and final states of a reversible system. On this model the final state is *identical* with the initial state, a 'process' is which there is no differentiation in relation to intermediate stages. In thermodynamics differences in quantity cancel each other out in a final state of absolute heat-death and identity vanquishes difference (ibid.: 46; for Nietzsche's engagement with thermodynamics see 1968: sections 1062–7). In effect, Deleuze is endorsing Bergson's trenchant critique of mechanism and finalism, which contends that both regard the future and past as 'calculable functions of the present' with the result that 'all is given' (Bergson 1983: 37). In other words, 'becoming' remains the great monstrous unthought in mechanistic and thermodynamical conceptions and calculations of the energy of the universe. A positive, dynamical and processual conception of death, which would release it from an anthropomorphic desire for death (for stasis, for *being*), speaking instead only of a death that desires (a death that is desire, where desire is construed along the lines of a machine or a machinic assemblage), can only be arrived at by freeing the becoming of death from both mechanism and finalism. To use the language of the contemporary science of complexity, the eternal return is a thought of non-linear becoming in which the stress is on non-equilibrium and positive feedback as the conditions of possibility for a truly 'creative' and complex (involuted) mapping of 'evolution' (as we shall see in later chapters, the notion of 'evolution' simply proves inadequate to the task). This is to posit the world as a *'monster of energy'* without beginning and without end, a Dionysian world of 'eternal' self-creation and 'eternal' self-destruction, moving from the simple to the complex and then back again to the simple out of abundance: cold/hot/

hot/cold, 'beyond' satiety, disgust, and weariness, a world of becoming that never attains 'being', never reaching a *final* death. For death (becoming) lives on itself; it is its own food and excrement.

## II

Deleuze's reconfiguration of the death-drive can be illuminated by considering the distinction he makes, drawing on Blanchot, between 'personal' and 'impersonal' death. 'Personal' death refers to the death of the 'I' which is encountered as the ultimate limit, the 'present' which causes everything to pass but beyond which 'I' cannot pass. This is what Blanchot calls 'inevitable and inaccessible death'.[3] The difference between the 'I' or ego is a difference which exists, says Deleuze, only in order to die, which can only be represented in terms of a return to inanimate matter, 'as if calculated by a kind of entropy'. This is the negative image of death formed from the restricted point of view of the 'ego'. Even when this death seems to constitute our ownmost possibility, it is a death which comes from without (as Blanchot says, in it I do not die). The other death, the one Deleuze is so keenly interested in, refers 'to the state of free differences when they are no longer subject to the form imposed upon them by an I or an ego, when they assume a shape which excludes my own coherence no less than that of any identity whatsoever' (Deleuze 1968: 149; 1994: 113). There is, therefore, always a 'one dies' which is more profound than 'I die', the death – exemplified in, but not restricted to, the death of the gods – which takes place endlessly and in a variety of ways. Deleuze contends that Freud modelled the death-drive on the first kind of death, and could not, therefore, access the more profound death, which is the death of repetition, the death 'of' eternal return. Of course, informing Freud's (re-)presentation of

---

3 Blanchot is put to use in the same way to problematize Freud's death-drive in Deleuze and Guattari 1983: 329–31, where it is maintained that to speak of a death-drive that stands in qualitative distinction from the life-drive is absurd. It is not death that is desired, but rather death which desires. The question becomes: what kind of desire is it within its machinic operations and functionings? It is necessary in speaking of the desire of life and that of death to speak of two parts, 'two kinds of desiring-machine parts', that of the working organs and that of the body without organs. Viewed as a part of the desiring-machine, death cannot be treated, as it is in Freud, in the abstract and independently of its functioning in the machine and its system of energetic conversions. Deleuze and Guattari ultimately appeal to Nietzsche's analysis of the ascetic priest and ascetic ideal to account for Freud's erection of a transcendent death instinct.

the death-drive is the opposition between the conflictual forces of Eros and Thanatos.[4] But it is precisely this negative opposition which Deleuze's positive thinking of death undermines. The death-drive cannot be distinguished from Eros, either in terms of a difference in kind between two forces, or by a difference in rhythm between two movements. To posit the difference in either of these ways would be to take difference as already given. Instead, Deleuze proposes that Thanatos is conceived as indistinguishable from the 'desexualization of Eros' (Deleuze 1968: 149; 1994: 113) ('desexualization' in the sense of forming a neutral and displaceable energy). There is no 'analytic difference' between Eros and Thanatos. This is to introduce differenciation where Freud argues there can be none, namely, in death. Deleuze's attempt to introduce difference into death is anticipated by Nietzsche. In an astonishing *Nachlass* passage he demands that we cease to think of 'the return to the inanimate as a regression'. Rather, we are to 'perfect ourselves' in the 'reinterpretation' and revaluation of death, and thereby 'reconcile ourselves with what is actual, with the dead world'. False evaluations of the dead world stem from the fact that we judge it from the 'vantage point' of the sentient world. But it is 'a *festival*', he writes, 'to go from this world across into the "dead world"'. The task is to see through the comedy of sentient being 'and thereby *enjoy* it!' (Nietzsche 1987: volume 9: 11[70]). In a fundamental inversion we are to treat death not as the opposite of life but as its true womb.

Indeed, Freud's whole model by which he seeks to understand the biological evolution of death – death's invention – is an entropic one. If death is not visible in earlier, primitive organizations of life, this is not because it was not there, he argues, but simply because the internal processes that cultivate death have not yet revealed themselves and overtaken the processes of life. Against Weismann's contention that death is a late acquisition of evolutionary life, and one that may not even be present in protista, Freud argues that this assertion applies only to the 'manifest phenomena' of death, and in no way imperils his assumption concerning the fundamental internal proccesses that reveal a tendency towards it. The result of Freud's inversion is to make the human death-drive into the telos of the entire evolution of life. In other words, death becomes in Freud's schema the endogenous motor of life: 'the

---

4 See Freud, 'Beyond the Pleasure Principle' in 1991, volume 11: 269–339, especially 322–3, where Freud confesses that his thinking on life and death has unwittingly steered him into the harbour of Schopenhauer's philosophy. In addition Freud notes the similiarity of his thinking on the life and death instincts to August Weismann's distinction between soma and germ-plasm. Weismann collaborated with Wilhelm Roux on the theory of 'mosaic development' that influenced Nietzsche. On Roux's influence on Nietzsche see chapter 4.

aim of all life is death'. He maintains this position in the face of the evidence of natural selection, which he construes in terms of decisive external influences obliging the living substance to diverge ever more widely from the original course of life and make ever more complicated detours *before* attaining the ultimate aim of death. In spite of apparent evidence to the contrary, therefore, such as the evidence of increasing complexity in evolution, Freud is able to insist that the goal of life is not life but death. This insistence is a direct result of his privileging of the 'conservative' nature of the living substance. Change and development are thus placed not in the service of variegated life but in that of entropic death.

How does the thought of eternal return connect to a model of productive and engendered death? The relation can only be thought by working through the notion of repetition. Repetition demonstrates that it is impossible to die one time, impossible to die *once* and *for all*. And yet the eternal return of death does not mean that one undergoes the same death again and again. The death belonging to eternal return is a plural one assuming multiple guises. Death is disguise itself, the mere appearance and apparition of another becoming. The repetition implicated in the eternal return is not the repeating of an original model since there is no original moment which can be subjected to a law of repetition. Eternal return already takes place within the element of difference and simulacra. This is why Deleuze is so insistent that the 'Same' in Nietzsche's elliptical formulation cannot be taken to denote a content (since none exists prior to the creation of repetition), but rather must be taken to refer to the act of returning (*revenir*) itself. What returns is repetition and the difference it engenders (eternal return as a 'groundless law', or as the law which shatters and explodes law, decoding and deregulating it). If it was the One which Nietzsche intended to return in his thought-experiment, then surely it could begin only by never being able to leave itself. As a 'force [or power] of affirmation' ('puissance d'affirmer'), eternal return affirms 'everything' of the multiple (the 'moment' which is 'eternity') (Deleuze 1968: 152; 1994: 115). The connection between eternal return and (negative) death is that it actualizes the death of the 'One' (what dies 'once and for all', never to return, is the 'One'). The repetition of eternal return affirms only excessive systems, machines of chance and strategies of risk. This is the 'divine game' of life in which there are no pre-existing rules, in which the game bears only upon its own rules, in which the child-player can only win, the 'whole' of chance being affirmed 'each' time and for 'all' times. If notions of the 'same' and the 'similiar' are to be allowed, it will be in the form of simulations, not in the form of error but as inevitable illusions. 'Identity' and 'resemblance' would be products of systems relating the different to the different by means of difference.

The difference of eternal return – the difference of *its* repetition – comes out clearly when contrasted with the test of repeatability and universalizability presupposed in Kant's formulation of the categorical imperative. Here repetition is made subject to 'law' in which it is known and decided in advance what is 'good' and what is 'evil'. The demonic is to be defeated by the 'man of duty' through devotion to the consistency and coherence of the test. As a result repetition is turned into a moralism. In thinking repetition 'beyond good and evil' in the thought-experiment of eternal return Nietzsche juxtaposes repetition to the moral law 'to the point where it becomes the suspension of ethics' (Deleuze 1994: 6), that is, a genuine willing and creating that is beyond the law of good and evil (see Nietzsche 1974: section 335) (compare Blanchot 1993: 279; Ansell Pearson 1991/1996: 194–9). There takes place in Nietzsche, therefore, an ironic and humorous overturning and overcoming (*Überwindung*) of Kant. The formalism of the eternal return defeats the categorical imperative on its own ground, pushing the test to the extremities of excess, since instead of relating repetition to a (pre-)supposed moral law, it makes repetition itself the only form of a 'law' beyond morality. Repetition becomes for Deleuze the thought of the future, opposed to both the generalities of habit and the particularities of memory. Or, as Blanchot enigmatically expresses it, the eternal return forces desire to return without beginning or end, and, as such, it 'does not belong to the temporality of time. It must be thought outside time, outside Being, and as the Outside itself; this is why it can be named "eternal" or aevum' (1993: 280).[5]

To use the form of paradox we could say that the eternal return 'is' the same of the different, 'is' the one of the multiple, 'is' the resemblant of that which returns, etc. The distinction here, between the unconscious becoming of eternal return (a force which seizes and overtakes) and consciousness of a willing and desiring of repetition, 'resembles' the analysis presented in section 354 of *The Gay Science*. In this section Nietzsche speaks of the 'superfluous' and superficial nature of consciousness, which for him is the domain of identity, representation,

---

[5] For another, truly innovative reading of the thought-experiment of eternal return as 'outside' time see Caygill 1991: 216–40, who provides what is arguably the finest essay on the eternal return in the English language. For Caygill the *question* of eternal return deranges the power of judgement – it asks, do you want this once and again and innumerable times more? – revealing both its compulsion and its conditions of *impossibility*. Within the experience of return is contained the 'wicked parody' in which the heaviest burden turns into the greatest joy (ibid.: 236).

resemblance, measurement, etc. Consciousness develops through the pressure for communication and sociability. By contrast, that which is incomparably unique and infinitely 'individual' (different) cannot be accessed through the human, all too human 'faculty' of consciousness. The inhumanity of 'difference', the sheer non-human monstrosity and cruelty of it, requires that we undergo a fundamentally other kind of experience – of the shattering and explosive kind presaged in the down-going and perishing of eternal return. Perish man! Perish consciousness! Perish common sense, perish good sense! Perish identity! Perish representation! Perish Zarathustra! Perish one more time again and again! Perish thought! Experiment!

### III

Of course, things are never this easy. The matter of death is rendered more complex in *A Thousand Plateaus*. In this text of multiple texts the figure of death is traversed by lines of flight: death in itself is meaningless, but death for-itself becomes the point of access to the fluid and the mobile. The discussion of death takes place in the context of an exploration of language. The distinction made between 'major' and 'minor' refers to two different treatments of language: the 'major' extracts constants and norms from language, while the 'minor' places language in constant variation and mutation. What Deleuze and Guattari call the 'order-word' is the 'variable enunciation' which brings about the condition of possibility of language and which defines the deployment of its elements according to either major or minor. As a result, the usage of language is doubled. In the order-word we can locate both a death sentence – a major deployment – and a signal of flight – a minor becoming. Order-words, such as 'you will not do this' or 'you will do that', bring the threat of death to those who receive the order. This is death as judgement and punishment. At the same time, however, the order-word contains a warning cry, a message to escape. It would be mistaken to reduce the cry or message to a state of reaction; rather, the escape or flight is included in the death judgement as an integral part of its complex assemblage. The roar of a lion – an example which could not be more appropriate in the context of Zarathustra, conceived as the dark precursor of eternal return – enunciates at one and the same time negation (death) and transportation (flight). The words of the prophet speak of both a longing for death and a longing for flight. Death heralds transformation. As Deleuze and Guattari point out, even though death concerns bodies, that which lives, grows, and dies, the immediacy and instantaneousness of death lend it the character of an incorporeal transformation. 'Death' is the figure of the uncrossable and unsurpassable. It is the ultimate challenge, the limit to the practice of sovereignty which lies at the extremity of the body. Death would like to limit metamorphoses, to give figures clear and stable contours. *Empty space, time void.* Death completes and gives shape. However, the revolutionary force of the line of flight lies in the fact that it is capable of making death a variable of itself. The overcoming, but not the elimination, of death. An incorporeal transformation is still attributed to death, but now, rendered in the language of the minor, it is a passage to the limit. Deleuze and Guattari write:

> We witness a transformation of substances and a dissolution of forms, a passage to the limit or flight from contours in favour of fluid forces, flows, air, light, and matter, such that a body or a word does not end at a precise point. We witness the incorporeal power of that intense matter, the material power of that language. A matter more immediate, more fluid, and more ardent than bodies or words. . . . Gestures and things, voices and sounds, are caught up in the same 'opera', swept away by the same shifting effects of stammering, vibrato, tremolo, and overspilling. A synthesizer places all of the parameters in continuous variation.
> 
> (Deleuze and Guattari 1980: 138–9; 1988: 109)

At the moment when a conjunction between death and flight occurs, defined as the moment when 'fundamentally heterogeneous elements end up turning into each other in some way' (ibid.), the point of the abstract machine, the diagram of the assemblage, has been reached. As Deleuze and Guattari modishly put it, the 'synthesizer' takes the place of 'judgement', music replaces law, the plane of consistency assumes the role of a defunct morality, and there occurs a creative synthesis of, on the one hand, biological, physio-chemical, and energetic intensities, and, on the other, mathematical, semiotic, and aesthetic intensities. The question should not be formulated in terms of how to elude the order-word, but rather how to erupt the death sentence it envelops, and, moreover, how to prevent escape or flight from veering into the unproductive black hole. To bring into play the musicality of death, to interpret life in terms of continuous variation, is to bring forth the 'virtual continuum of life' (ibid.: 139; 110). Beneath the order-words (for example, 'God is dead! And we have killed him!') there lie pass-words ('The overman shall now be the meaning of the earth'). When words pass, when they presage passage, the compositions of order and organization are transformed into the compositions of passage and consistency: 'In the order-word, life must answer the answer of death, not by fleeing, but by making flight act and create' (ibid.). Or, as Zarathustra sings it:

> One does not kill by anger but by laughter. Come, let us kill the Spirit of Gravity!
>
> I have learned to walk: since then I have run. I have learned to fly: since then I do not have to be pushed in order to move.
>
> Now I am nimble, now I fly, now I see myself under myself, now a god dances within me.
>
> (Nietzsche 1969: 'Of Reading and Writing')

> I know how to speak the parable of the highest things only in the dance – and now my greatest parable has remained in my limbs unspoken! . . .
>
> I am invulnerable only in my heels. You live there and are always the same, most patient one! Always you break on through out of all graves!
>
> (ibid.: 'The Funeral Song')

As Bataille points out, in one sense death is the common inevitable (the great equalizer and normalizer). In another sense, however, it is 'profound, inaccessible' (the great differenciator). Must one not be a god in order to experience, to live, a sovereign death? In speaking in *Inner Experience* of the necessity of anguish in the face of death as man's mark of distinction, of his inhabiting a tragic world in contrast to the untragic world of the animal, Bataille is perhaps granting too much significance to the one, ultimate, final heat-death, disregarding the seminal importance of the many little deaths which the productive unconscious entices us to undergo, again and again. The joyful quality of this kind of repeated death – death as repetition – is poetically captured by Bataille in another piece appropriately entitled 'The Practice of Joy Before Death'. As always in the case of Bataille, the difficulty resides in determining whether his dream of annihilation represents the human pushed to its limit, and crushed under the weight of it, as a kind of infinite tragedy of the human, of the impossibility of overcoming it, or whether in the practice of joy there is prefigured a comprehension of something genuinely inhuman. We might speak of Bataille's ode to the practice of joy before death in terms of a translation of the non-human into the human. In his darkest dreams, Bataille imagines 'the earth projected in space, like a woman screaming, her head in flames' (Bataille 1985: 239). To conceive of the limitless possibilities of human movement and excitation is to imagine the 'gift of an infinite suffering, of blood and open bodies, in the image of an ejaculation cutting down the one it jolts and abandoning him to an exhaustion charged with nausea'. 'Only a shameless, indecent saintliness', Bataille writes, 'can lead to a sufficiently happy *loss of self*'. 'Joy before death' means that life can be celebrated from root to summit, since it is in and for itself the apotheosis of the perishable – beyond conservation, beyond reservation, and beyond preservation. This is death lived as pure life. Bataille: 'it appears that no less a loss than death is needed for the brilliance of life to traverse and transfigure dull existence, for it is only its free uprooting that *becomes in me* the strength of life and time. In this way I cease to be anything other than the mirror of death, just as the universe is only the mirror of light.' Bataille is imagining nothing less than the transformation of man into overman, now waiting the arrival of 'the first lightning' (Nietzsche 1969: 'Of The Tree on the Mountainside'):

Before the terrestrial world whose summer and winter order the agony of all living things, before the universe composed of innumerable turning stars, limitlessly losing and consuming themselves, I can only perceive a succession of cruel splendours whose very movement requires that I die: this death is only the *exploding* consumption of all that was, the joy of existence of all that comes into the world; even my own life demands that everything that exists, everywhere, ceaselessly give itself and be annihilated.

I imagine myself covered with blood, broken but transfigured and in agreement with the world, both as prey and as jaw of TIME, which ceaselessly kills and is ceaselessly killed.

There are explosives everywhere that perhaps will soon blind me. I laugh when I think that my eyes persist in demanding objects that do not destroy them.

(ibid.)

The problem of death as transformation (flight) or as a leap into a black hole revolves around the task of determining the extent to which the desire to perish is motivated by a desire for destruction borne of the spirit of revenge – the spirit which animates the desire of despisers of the body and the preachers of death – or by an emancipated desire for the heights which is propelled by a love of freedom. As Zarathustra says to the 'young man' he meets in the mountains surrounding the town known as 'The Pied Cow':

You are not yet free, for you still *search* for freedom. . . . You long for the open heights, your soul thirsts for the stars. But your bad instincts too thirst for freedom.

Your fierce dogs long for freedom; they bark for joy in their cellar when your spirit aspires to break open all prisons.

To me you are still a prisoner who imagines freedom: ah, such prisoners of the soul become clever, but also deceitful and base.

The free man of the spirit must also purify himself. Much of the prison and rottenness still remain within him: his eye still has to become pure.

(ibid.)

In another reading Deleuze has thought death in relation to the aporetic structure of truth and power, seeking a way of thinking beyond, or across, 'the line'. 'How can we cross the line' which will not re-establish the 'truth of power' over the 'power of truth' (Deleuze 1988: 94–5)? Furthermore, much further in fact, how is it possible to 'attain a life that is the power of the outside' which is not the outside of a 'terrifying void', in which life is lived as though it were not the simple distribution within the void of '"slow, partial and progressive" deaths?' (ibid.: 95). In other words, how is it possible to escape the 'reality' of Freud's beyond, his ultimate death-drive that would mercilessly destroy everything in order to guarantee the realization of life's one true goal, final heat-death? But Nietzsche shows, and Deleuze shows that he shows, that the question of death, of its voluntary or servile nature, of its good or bad condition, cannot be settled once and for all: it has to be made subject to the higher 'law' of eternal return.

## IV

The problem of determining the difference between lines of flight and lines of death informs Deleuze and Guattari's reworking of Freud in *A Thousand Plateaus*. In speaking of a line of death, they are not, they insist, invoking a mysterious 'death-drive' (*pulsion de mort*). As they say: 'There are no internal drives in desire, only assemblages (*agencements*). Desire is always assembled' (Deleuze and Guattari 1980: 280; 1988: 229). It is important that they do not succumb to the temptation of positing within life a desire for death (death as stasis, as final end, as entropic becoming), since such a desire is nothing more than life turning against life, and is a phenomenon which is human, all too human. The positing of a death-drive is nothing less than a reification of death, placing it within a restricted human economy of life. Take, for example, as they do, the example of suicide. The option of suicide is taken by the one who is world-weary and exhausted: one would rather engage in uncreative destruction than embark upon radical transformation. One recalls in this context Zarathustra's speech to the 'beyondworlders' (*Hinterweltlern*), in which he speaks of the 'weariness which wishes to reach the ultimate in a single leap', a leap he describes presciently as a 'death-leap' (*Todessprünge*). This is a 'poor, ignorant weariness, which no longer wants even to want'. It is the suffering of the weary and impotent which lies behind the creation of all 'beyond worlds'. Deleuze and Guattari follow Virilio in arguing that the fascist State, such as the National Socialist State, is best understood, not in terms of a totalitarian State, but in terms of a 'suicidal State'. Nazi statements invoke the cause of 'sacrifice' not for the sake of the generation of new life, but for the preservation of reactive, dead life: 'They always contain the "stupid and repugnant" cry, *Long live death*!, even at the economic level, where the arms expansion replaces growth in consumption and where investment veers from the means of production toward the means of pure destruction' (ibid.: 282; 231). In appropriating the war machine for its own ends, the State apparatus can reach a state where the war machine is placed solely in the service of war, substituting destruction for mutation.[6] In an astute insight they note that mutation does not signal a transformation of war; on the contrary, war signifies the fall, or failure, of mutation. At this point 'the war machine no longer draws mutant lines of flight, but a pure, cold line of abolition' (ibid.: 281; 230). The blind, senseless 'passion of abolition' is the passion which turns lines of flight into lines of death. Of course, this is not to devalue the suicide that takes away life out of fidelity to its failed promise. Such a suicide does not serve to denigrate life but, on the contrary, it keeps alive its burning desire. Here the act of suicide is not a lazy one but vital and generous since it still bestows the poisonous gift of life on the living and the dead. This is to write, with Nietzsche, of the 'proud death': 'Death of one's free choice . . . with a clear head and joyfulness, consummated in the midst of children and witnesses, so that an actual leave-taking is possible while the one who is leaving *is still there*. . . . From love of *life* one ought to die . . . freely, not accidentally' (Nietzsche 1979b: 88). When nihilism has become truly contagious then voluntary death needs to be practised with a scientific conscientiousness, and a 'new responsibility' may be granted to the physician, allowing the living the 'right time' to die. Such a praxis of death liberates life from the fatal objection. The 'will to love' must be coupled with the willingness to die, since from eternity 'loving and perishing' have gone together (Nietzsche 1969: 'Of Immaculate Perception'). Thus speaks a new innocence and a new beauty: 'For it is already coming, the glowing sun – *its* love of the earth is coming! All sun-love is innocence and creative desire!' All that is deep rises to greet the coming of the sun (ibid.).

The death 'of' eternal return, therefore, must be taken out of the bounds of the death-drive, at least as formulated in Freud. The drive in itself is interpreted by Freud in terms of conservation and retention: 'It seems, then, that an instinct is an urge inherent in organic life to restore an earlier state of things', Freud writes in *Beyond the Pleasure Principle*. The 'organic elasticity' revealed by the curious drive amounts to nothing less than the discovery of inertia as inherent in all organic life. Far from being the progenitors and agents of change we thought they were, the

---

6 The 'war machine' in Deleuze and Guattari's work does not refer to a machine that makes war an object of life; only the forces of State-capture do that (1980: 535ff.; 1988: 429ff.). It would be absurd to attribute to them a desire to naturalize war as a permanent metaphysical feature of historical existence. Their concern is to establish its machinic conditions of existence.

drives now reveal themselves to be the expression of the conservative nature of all living substance (Freud 1991: volume 11, 308–9). In this positing of the goal of life as death, death is understood in terms of a negative, unproductive conception of repetition: repetition not as the condition of possibility of perpetual difference, but as the 'restoration' and maintenance of an 'earlier state of things', in short, as the eternal return of identity. This is not life conceived in terms of a law of 'self-overcoming' (Nietzsche 1994: III, section 27), but in terms of a law of self-penitence (Freud 1991: volume 11, 310). Life is condemned from the start. As soon as it begins it is dead matter, a fatal return which wants its final end right at the beginning. This is the self, this is life, conceived as becoming-entropic, as heat-death, as self-same identity. In Freud's depiction of the death-drive one might say that the future 'comes' without 'becoming'. For Freud it is equally impossible to imagine the coming into being of the new, the unique, and the different and to entertain the possibility of self-generating life. The only law of organic life he will allow is the eternal return of death *as* death:

Let us suppose, then, that all organic instincts are conservative, are acquired historically and tend towards the restoration of an earlier state of things. It follows that the phenomena of organic development must be attributed to external disturbances and diverting influences. The elementary living entity would from its very beginning have had no wish to change; if conditions remained the same, it would do no more than constantly repeat the same course of life. In the last resort, what has left its mark on the development of organisms must be the history of the earth we live in and of its relation to the sun. Every modification which is imposed upon the course of the organism's life is accepted by the conservative organic instincts and stored up for further repetition. Those instincts are therefore bound to give a deceptive appearance of being forces tending towards change and progress, whilst in fact they are merely seeking to reach an ancient goal by paths old and new alike. Moreover it is possible to specify this final goal of all organic striving. It would be in contradiction to the conservative nature of the instincts if the goal of life were a state of things which had never yet been attained. On the contrary, it must be an old state of things, an initial state from which the living entity has at one time or other departed and to which it is striving to return by the circuitous paths along which its development leads.

(ibid.)

Ultimately, one must recognize that informing Freud's entropic model of death (which does not become: it always *is*) is a negative appraisal of destruction and disintegration. While the aim of the life instinct is to bind energy together and so establish stable unities, that of the death-drive is to unbind and disintegrate. Instead of locating positive possibilities for emancipation from the tyranny of the ego in unbound energy, Freud chose to privilege the organism (as he did the imaginary unitary ego) – the production of which he simply takes as a 'given'

– and to interpret the passages and tunnels of death mechanistically and entropically. In declaring the aim of all life to be that of death, Freud places death within a restricted economy of the organism. This economy is then read back into biology as if it constituted a general economy of 'life'. In Freud the conflict between psychic representation and unrepresented somatic forces does not lead to the productive and machinic unconscious but to an anthropomorphization of death. The 'practice of joy before death' – the 'festival' of death Nietzsche speaks of – is inaccessible to Freud. If there can be no subject 'of' death – if death is dead – it is because death is its own becoming: 'Dionysus cut to pieces is a promise of life – it will be eternally reborn and return again and again out of destruction' (Nietzsche 1968: section 1052).[7]

## V

Deleuze acknowledges that Freud's great innovation in *Beyond the Pleasure Principle* consists in linking up the death-drive not simply with destructive tendencies, but with phenomena of repetition. If the 'pleasure principle' is only a 'psychological' principle, the death-drive by contrast serves as an 'originary, positive principle' for repetition. To this extent, it can be conceived as a 'transcendental' principle (Deleuze 1968: 27; 1994: 16). Informing Freud's linking up of the death-drive and repetition, Deleuze contends, is his realization that a negative schema, such as amnesia, is insufficient for explaining repetition. We do not repeat because we repress; we repress because we repeat. At this point in his discussion Deleuze proposes a highly novel revision of Freud's formulation of the death-drive. In effect, he destroys its credibility as a material model (the desire of living matter to return to an inorganic state), and in its place, he construes its reality and efficacy in terms of a play of repetition. Deleuze contends that in praxis the death-drive can be seen to affirm repetition only in the form of disguise. The disguises, which can be located in the work of dreams and symptoms, such as condensation, displacement, and dramatization, do not actualize a 'brute repetition' (a repetition of the Same). Does not 'Dora' elaborate her role and repeat her love for her father only through the enactment of other roles and the

---

7 Marcuse offers a powerful critique of Freud's death-drive and its 'biological rationale' in terms of its stifling of 'utopian' energies of overcoming: 'The powers that be have a deep affinity to death; death is a token of unfreedom, of defeat' (Marcuse 1987: 236).

creation of disguises, the donning of masks and costumes – masks and costumes which are not secondary to the original sin, but which constitute the internal genetic element of repetition itself? If one is to utilize the idea of a drive for death (or rather, of a death that desires, that wants to live) and in terms of a thought of production, not simply representation, then it can only be in terms of its relationship to masks and costumes, to the dramatization of repetition phenomena. The constitution of repetition takes place, in effect, through disguise. Repetition does not lie under or behind the mask, but is formed from one mask to another. Does not everything profound, such as the phenomenon of repetition, love the mask? The mask is profound out of superficiality: it hides nothing but another mask. It desires nothing but another mask.[8] This means that there 'is no first term which is repeated, and even our childhood love for the mother repeats other adult loves with regard to other women'. In other words, 'there is no bare repetition which may be abstracted or inferred from the disguise itself' (ibid.: 28; 17). In order to make the move from the 'really real' to the fantastical (the element of the death-drive where everything is always masked and disguised), Deleuze argues that it was necessary for Freud to abandon the hypothesis of real childhood events. It is in these terms that it is possible to account for 'difference':

> Difference is included in repetition by way of disguise . . . This is why the variations do not come from without, do not express a secondary compromise between a repressing instance and a repressed instance, and must not be understood on the basis of the still negative forms of opposition, reversal or overturning. The variations express, rather, the differential mechanisms which belong to the essence and origin of that which is repeated.
>
> (Deleuze 1968: 28; 1994: 17)

Repetition *defies* representation: its true subject, which will always be unfaithful to it, is the mask. The repeated as such must always be signified, never represented. And yet, it is masked by what signifies it, and it itself masks what it signifies. As for Freud, so for Deleuze: becoming conscious amounts to little. Healing and sickness are not generated by simple anamnesis, but rather operate

---

8 See Nietzsche (1966: section 278):

'Wanderer, who are you? I see you walking on your way without scorn, without love, with unfathomable eyes . . . who are you? what have you done? Rest here: this spot is hospitable to all – recuperate! And whoever you may be: what do you desire now? what do you need for recreation? Name it: whatever I have I offer to you!'

'Recreation? Recreation? You are inquisitive! What are you saying! But give me, please –'

'What? What? say it!'

'Another mask! A second mask!'

through a much more theatrical and dramatic enactment – as in the theatre and drama of Zarathustra's *Untergang* (he is sick, but he is becoming health) – namely, 'transference'. As Freud himself points out in his essay on 'Remembering, Repeating, and Working Through', 'the patient does not *remember* anything of what s/he has forgotten and repressed, but *acts* it out'. Transference is nothing other than repetition, Deleuze claims (Freud had acknowledged this himself). Transference takes place in a manner similar to scientific experimentation. The patient is expected to reproduce their disturbance in privileged, artificial conditions. However, in transference, repetition does not serve to authenticate people, places, and things, but rather it selects masks and erects symbols. Repetition then assumes the guise of a transformative power, a 'demonic' power which both makes us ill and cures us, both enchains and liberates us (Deleuze 1968: 30; 1994: 19). In Deleuze's reworking and rewriting of the death-drive, it is no longer a desire on the part of life to endure a bare repetition by returning to a previous, initial state of inorganic life, but is now that which gives repetition its 'disguising power' and its immanent meaning, mingling the actuality of terror with the movement of active selection and freedom. In repetition, in eternal return, one consumes oneself in one's own flames – consummation (*Vollendung*) as constant productive death and going beyond. Admittedly, Deleuze's emphasis on the work of production performed by the immense power of repetition remains highly formalist. But what it succeeds in showing is that the 'death-drive' enjoys no teleological governance over life since it too is subject to the production of difference through repetition which constitutes the costumes and drama of a life that is lived in terms of a creative and destructive evolution.[9]

## VI

That 'other world', that inhuman, dehumanized world, which is a heavenly Nothing, is well concealed from humans; and the belly of being does not speak to man, except as man.

Truly, all being is difficult to demonstrate, it is difficult to bring it to speech. Yet, tell me, my brothers, is not the most wonderful of all things most clearly demonstrated?

(Nietzsche 1969: 'Of the Beyondworlders')

---

[9] In his own critical reading of the *Fort-Da* refrain and the death-drive, Guattari has argued that it is a question of making a choice between a 'mechanical conception of deathly repetition and a machinic conception of processual opening'. See Guattari 1992: 106–7; 1995: 74–5.

Not only does the work of Deleuze, and that of Deleuze and Guattari, illuminate the becoming of Nietzsche's philosophy, its lines of death and flight, but, and most appositely in the context of this chapter, the becoming peculiar to Zarathustra and to the playful repetition which is affirmed in the thought-experiment of eternal return. Here, in this final section of the chapter, I can only begin to show how a utilization of Deleuzian-inspired thought can make novel sense of the complex, acentred narrative structure of Zarathustra's going-down and going-across.

Towards the end of *Difference and Repetition*, in the conclusion when all is to begin again, Deleuze notes that *Zarathustra* is radically incomplete and unfinished as a text. He also notes that in the *Nachlass* of the plans of the text, Nietzsche set himself the task of composing a further part which would revolve around the meaning and significance of Zarathustra's death. However, Deleuze leaves the significance of this irresolution concerning Zarathustra's life and death suspended in mid-air, and fails to realize that his own thinking through of the question and problem of difference and repetition provides us with the key that will unlock the mystery and the riddle of Zarathustra's aborted final death. Might it not be that Nietzsche did not have Zarathustra die a final dramatic death because he knew that such a death both was rendered superfluous by and ran counter to the import of Zarathustra's 'pure becoming'? Zarathustra does die in the text, not once but many times; he dies many little deaths (*petites morts*), again and again, in the duration of his perishing and transforming. A final heat-death would undermine the counter-entropic principle of eternal return, which demonstrates that it is impossible to die 'once' and 'for all'. An examination of the *Zarathustra-Nachlass* serves to validate these claims. There are plans and outlines of acts and parts in which Zarathustra not only suffers a fatal and final death, but is also murdered. For example, in a plan from the period November 1881 to February 1883, Zarathustra forgets the misery of life through teaching 'recurrence', but then his pity increases when he realizes that the theory cannot be 'endured'. The plan then reads: 'Climax: the sacred murder. He devises the theory of the overman' (Nietzsche 1987, volume 10: 152–3). In another plan, this time from June/July 1883, Nietzsche has Zarathustra die at the moment when the 'vision' of the overman departs from him and he becomes aware of the suffering he has caused (he dies of the pity he feels towards man, precisely that which, in *Zarathustra*, Nietzsche says 'killed' God) (ibid.: 495–6). In a plan from late 1884, by which time the first three parts of *Zarathustra* have been finished, Nietzsche has Zarathustra teach the eternal return, which is at first presented in *menschliche* terms, depressing the nobler and enervating the 'lower natures', and then outlines a scene in which the teaching has to be suppressed and Zarathustra killed (ibid., volume 12: 281).

As this *Nachlass* material so clearly demonstrates, the relationship between the teachings of eternal return and the overman is highly complex and underdetermined. While in the 'completed', published text it is the teaching of the overman which is announced first, with that of the eternal return not appearing, in disguised form as well, until the end of part 2 (in the discourse on 'Redemption'), in the *Nachlass* it would seem that Nietzsche formulated the teaching of return first and was led to positing a notion of the overman as a result of his inability to conceive of its affirmation by man: the thought of eternal return is not human at all, hence its 'undecidable' and uncanny quality. Only the overman is able to endure the thought of eternal return, to dance and play with it, and then deploy it 'as a means of discipline and training' (ibid., volume 10: 378). It is only the prospect of the overman which can make the thought of return conceivable (an immaculate conception). Once possible, however, the overman then becomes the progenitor of the thought of eternal return as an affirmative, *über-menschliche* thought.[10] One of the most enigmatic confessions from this period runs as follows:

Goal to reach the overman for a moment. For that I would suffer *everything*. That triad!

(ibid.: 167)

This is paradoxical on a number of counts: to begin with, the 'suffering' referred to is a suffering grounded in infinite joy (O *Ewigkeit!*). Secondly, to 'reach' the overman for a moment would be to reach him forever (O *Ewigkeit!*). And, finally, to suffer everything, in the sense that one would gladly perish oneself in order to attain that which is 'over', would, in effect, amount to an affirmation of *eternity* since what has been attained, or 'reached', is nothing other than eternal return,

---

10 This involuted and convoluted play between the two doctrines, or thought-experiments, has been overlooked and downplayed by the great majority of readers of *Zarathustra*, including the most diligent and astute, such as Maurice Blanchot. See, for example, Blanchot 1993: 148–9, where Blanchot contrasts the categorical clarity with which Zarathustra announces the overman with the anxious and hesitant announcement of the eternal return, suggesting that the profound truth of the latter supersedes the superficial truth of the former. I remain one of the few readers of Nietzsche to insist on the creative entwinement of the two doctrines and call for the affirmation of the promise and the danger of the doctrine of the *Übermensch*. Such an insight becomes attainable when one ceases to think of the production of the overman in terms of a linear process of 'evolution' but recognizes that it can be attained 'at every moment'. The 'trick' is to 'see' (*blicken*) the 'moment' (*Augenblick*) of the overman from the 'perspective' of a genealogical becoming.

the very thought of 'difference and repetition' (as the eternal return of the 'moment' (see Nietzsche 1968: section 1032)). The 'evolution' of Zarathustra in the book can be understood in terms of this excessive economy of repetition, in which Zarathustra evolves or becomes in terms of a passage through masks and disguises. It proves impossible for Zarathustra to reveal at any point, least of all at the end, who he truly is, for he 'is' *not*, he only becomes. Zarathustra is already dead when he descends to the market-place from his mountain retreat. He appears to men as a cross between a fool and a corpse. What is not perceived by those gathered around Zarathustra is that his dying is only a bridge and not a goal. 'Sacrifice' — the act of perishing through active auto-destruction — is to be affirmed when the perishing it inaugurates is for the sake, not of the stars beyond, but of the earth, not for the sake of the preservation of the present, but of the creation of the future and the redemption of the past. Invoking himself in terms of an uncanny fate, a dark precursor, Zarathustra declares:

I love all those who are like heavy drops falling singly from the dark cloud that hangs over mankind: they prophesy the coming of the lightning, and as prophets they perish.

(Nietzsche 1969: prologue)

In terms of this aspect of Zarathustra's identity as a prophet, Deleuze's reading is apposite and correct. As the herald of the new, the unique, and the incomparable, and as the concomitant destroyer of the identical, the same, and the similar, Zarathustra must perish, must die. But what perishes is not Zarathustra in-himself but rather Zarathustra as 'hero', as 'redeemer'. Zarathustra as liberator and creator lives on to fight another day:

Zarathustra-hero became equal, but what he became equal to was the unequal, at the cost of losing the sham identity of the hero. For 'one' repeats eternally, but 'one' now refers to the world of impersonal individualities and pre-individual singularities. The eternal return is not the effect of the Identical upon a world become similar, it is not an external order imposed upon the chaos of the world; on the contrary, the eternal return is the internal identity of the world and of chaos, the Chaosmos.

(Deleuze 1968: 382; 1994: 299)

The ultimate death of Zarathustra, as a kind of fatal perishing (the perishing of the dice-throw of existence), if possible and conceivable, would be equivalent to a sovereign dissolution and sacrifice. But even such an 'ultimate' death can be no more than a passage to an 'over-death', a creative transformation of the chaos which gives birth to a dancing star. Towards the end of the prologue — and here I concur with Deleuze when he argues in *Nietzsche and Philosophy* that the prologue of *Zarathustra* contains 'the premature secret of eternal return' (Deleuze 1983: 70) – Zarathustra, who up to this point has been plagued by death (by his own corpse, by the dead buffoon, etc.), resolves not to be what he is not: namely, herdsman to the herd and universal gravedigger. He needs 'living companions' who follow him because they wish to follow themselves and who go where he desires to go (Nietzsche 1969: prologue). He has 'spoken to a dead man for the last time', and now resolves to 'make company with creators, with harvesters, with rejoicers'. This is the line of death turning into a line of flight: 'I will show them the rainbow and the stairway to the overman' (ibid.).

The experiment unfolds. Here, through a reading of the prologue, I have sought to show how it is possible to read the repetitive figure, mask, and symbol of Zarathustra in terms of a thinking of pure becoming, of 'difference and repetition'. A reading of the rest of the book would, I believe, consolidate this interpretation. In the crucial and deeply enigmatic discourse in part 2 on 'The Prophet', for example, Zarathustra once again repeats his encounter with death, what he now calls 'the rasping silence of death, the worst of my companions'. But far from being overwhelmed and depressed by death's persistence, Zarathustra has now learned how to combat the screams of coffins with 'a thousand peals of laughter' (Nietzsche 1969: 'The Prophet'). Zarathustra has detected the hidden, negative death-drive within the 'despisers of the body: 'Even in your folly and contempt, you despisers of the body, you serve your Self. I tell you: your Self itself wants to die and turn away from life' (ibid.: 'Of the Despisers of the Body'). It is not a question of death being contra life, but of a certain kind of death fighting another kind, another species, of death and the dead: 'Everyone treats death as an important event: but as yet death is not a festival . . . one should learn to die, and there should be no festivals at which such a dying man does not consecrate the oaths of the living!' (Nietzsche 1969: 'Of Free Death').

I propose that the becoming of Zarathustra, the becoming of Nietzsche's philosophy, be read as a monstrous fire-machine. The machine of chance – the machine of the dice-throw which is eternal return – is utterly different from the steam engine, the engine of final and ultimate heat-death, the engine of entropy, which inspired thermodynamic conceptions of time and becoming (but for nineteenth-century entropic thought there ain't no becoming, only death, only the death 'of' being and the being 'of' death). In *Nietzsche and Philosophy* Deleuze compares the 'power' of return to fire in that it signals an affirmation of multiplicity 'all at once'. Fire is the element which plays with being, the becoming of being and the being of becoming (Deleuze 1983: 30). The fire-machine is a machine which affirms chance by cooking and boiling it, in which immense forces are released by small, multiple manipulations. If the task of transfiguration is one involving the transformation of suffering into joy, negation into affirmation, the same into the different, the heaviest of burdens into the lightest of weights, then the ultimate test and challenge must surely consist in the transformation of death: from the undifferentiated black nothingess of the death-drive to the differentiated fire-death of eternal return.

The task, then, my friends? To traverse the line of flight beyond good and evil, but not beyond 'good' and 'bad' death. Again, this is a training in life and death that requires cultivation, the cultivation of an animal capable of living even beyond the 'beyond'. From Zarathustra's teaching on 'Free Death' (*Vom freien Tode*):

> Free for death and free in death, a solemn No-sayer when there is no longer time for Yes: thus he understands life and death.
> That your death many not be a blasphemy against man and the earth, my friends: that is what I request from the honey of your soul.
> In your death, your spirit and virtue should glow like a sunset glow around the earth: otherwise your death flies into a bad death.
> Thus I want to die myself, that you friends may love the earth more for my sake; and I want to become earth again, that I may have peace in her who bore me.
> Truly, Zarathustra had a goal, he threw his ball: now may you friends be the heirs of my goal, to you I throw the golden ball.
> But best of all I like to see you, my friends, throwing on the golden ball! So I shall move on earth a little longer: forgive me for it!
> Thus spoke Zarathustra.

## VII

The death of eternal return, conceived in accordance with a mode of production and reproduction, ceases to be an objection to life, becoming its only possible ultimate and unequivocal affirmation (*Bejahung*). The eternal return does not establish a totality or unity of life, but is, above all, a teaching of the fragment, of fragmentary death and fragmentary life.[11] In undergoing its convoluted experience one does not become whole, an organic unity, or an organism that

---

11 The emphasis on the fragment here is potentially misleading. I do not mean to suggest that the eternal return lacks completeness or wholeness; on the contrary, conceiving the eternal return as a positive and affirmative teaching of the fragment is designed to bring out the

knows in advance what it shall become and wants to become, but rather a machine of partial objects and open boxes. The time of eternal return introduces the death that is always half, always incomplete, the time of severed deaths. For Deleuze it is this neither entirely alive nor entirely dead condition that makes it possible to describe humans as 'monstrous beings' (Deleuze 1973: 143). They are 'monstrous' precisely because their condition is punctuated and pricked by the half-death; their time is that of an infinite and immeasurable horizon, and these tiny creatures walk through life as if giants on account of the measureless depth granted to them by time, plunged into years and stretched along aeons that exist in vast remoteness from each other. When Nietzsche declares that he is all the names in history he is not arrogating to himself some great, immodest cosmic identity, but rather affirming the immeasurability of his 'identity' and stretching history out into the distances of aeonic becoming. It is far from being a mad thought, though it may be overhuman, quite overhuman.

'Death is an invented state', repeats Artaud, advising us to be suspicious of the preaching of warlocks, gurus, and conjurers of nothingness. But if death is an 'invented state' then it can be reinvented anew and repeated again and again. This conception of death as invention corresponds to Deleuze and Guattari's construal of the experiment of eternal return as involving the deterritorialized circuit of all the cycles of desire. According to their energetics of desire there is no death instinct simply because both the 'model' and 'experience' of death reside in the unconscious. Locating death in the context of a machinic (mal-)functioning means that death can no longer be treated as an abstract principle, but has to be evaluated in terms of the system of 'energetic conversions' and the desiring-machines of which it is part. There is no death-drive, no being-for-death, not even a speculative investment of death, because the 'experience of death' belongs among the most common events of the unconscious, which 'occurs in life and for life, in every passage or becoming, in every intensity as passage or becoming. It is in the very nature of every intensity to invest within itself the zero intensity starting from which it is produced' (Deleuze and Guattari 1983: 330). There cannot be either a mechanist or a finalist (entropic) model of death since death is '*what never ceases and*

---

processual/machinic character of the test and experiment. In the plateau entitled '1730: Becoming Intense, Becoming-Animal, Becoming-Imperceptible . . . ' in *A Thousand Plateaus*, Deleuze and Guattari contend that it is not fragmentary writing that is the real issue in Nietzsche, but rather the production of speeds and movements between particles. They thus proclaim Zarathustra's teaching of eternal return in terms of 'the first great concrete freeing of nonpulsed time'.

*never finishes happening in every becoming*' (ibid.). Death is folded within and enveloped by intensity. Death happens, but only in terms of a 'becoming'. Its experience is thus not at all a personal one, amounting to an existential deepening, but a function of the cycles of the desiring-machines. Construed as the operation of a static dualism, as in Freud's human, all too human schema, the death-drive (death working itself to death contra Eros) does not function as a simple limitation but as the very liquidation of the libido. The product of analysis is not the free and joyous 'person' who is the carrier of life flows, and who has the courage to carry them into the desert of life and decode them, but the person who is weighed down by sadness and anxiety, whose *Dasein* gives off only the sour smell of entropic decay (on non-heroic courage see Deleuze and Guattari 1983: 341).

The human body dies, Artaud says, only because we have forgotten how to transform it and change it. And all the while Nietzsche dies among his 'daughters of the desert', seeking to remind us of the 'over-death':

> Wonderful, truly!
> Here I now sit,
> beside the desert, and
> yet so far from the desert,
> and not at all devastated:
> for I am swallowed down
> by this little oasis
> – it simply opened, yawning,
> its sweetest mouth
> the sweetest-smelling of all little mouths . . .
>
> Here I now sit
> in this smallest oasis
> like a date,
> brown, sweet, oozing golden,
> thirsting for a girl's rounded mouth,
> but thirsting for more girlish,
> ice-cold, snow-white, cutting
> teeth: for these do
> the hearts of all hot dates lust. Selah . . .
>
> The desert grows: woe to him who harbours deserts!
> Stone grates on stone, the desert swallows down.
> The monstrous death gazes glowing brown
> and *chews* –, its life is its chewing . . .
> *Forget not, O human, burnt out by lust:*
> *you – are stone, desert, and death.*
>
> (Nietzsche, 'The Desert Grows', *Dithyrambs of Dionysos*, 1889)

# 4

# NIETZSCHE CONTRA DARWIN

I write for a species that does not yet exist.

(Nietzsche 1968: section 958)

History ultimately proves something quite different than what man wanted: it turned out to be the surest means of destroying those principles. Darwin. . . . One gets to know better the real forces in the movement of history, not our 'beautiful' ideas!

(Nietzsche 1987, volume 9: 10 [D88])

Humankind likes to put questions of descent (*Herkunft*) and beginnings out of its mind: must one not be almost inhuman to detect in oneself a contrary inclination?

(Nietzsche 1986: section 1)

Nietzsche's writings, both published and unpublished, are riddled with critical reflections on Darwin and the theory of natural selection. While Nietzsche's explication of the *Übermensch* as involving a non-Darwinian style of evolution is often noted (if little understood), his engagement with Darwin has not received the kind of attention it merits.[1] Where it has been treated, it has been so cursorily, without any serious effort being made by commentators to render comprehensible Nietzsche's 'philosophical biology', including its problematic aspects. This is not a 'minor' issue in Nietzsche-reception, since at the very heart of Nietzsche's outline of his fundamental concerns in his major text, *On the Genealogy of Morality*, we find a critical engagement with the Darwinian paradigm of evolution. The *Genealogy* is a

---

1 The connection between Nietzsche and Darwin is touched upon by Heidegger in his 1930s lectures on Nietzsche, but the treatment of Darwin is perfunctory and cavalier. See Heidegger 1961, volume 1: 72; 1979: 60. Heidegger's reading of Nietzsche's 'biologism' and Heidegger's own engagement with modern biology will be examined in the final section of this chapter.

text steeped in nineteenth-century biological thought and ideas, and is unthinkable without this heritage. The task of determining Nietzsche's relation to Darwin and Darwinism is an immensely important one, but also complicated. No attempt will be made here to pit Nietzsche against Darwin in any simple or straightforward sense. This is for a number of reasons. Firstly, it is necessary to appreciate that there is an essential 'evolutionary' basis to Nietzsche's most radical philosophizing (as when, for example, he argues in the opening of *Human, All too Human* that there are no absolute values or eternal truths, and argues in favour of the adoption of a 'historical' mode of philosophizing).[2] Secondly, it is important to appreciate that even when Nietzsche presents himself as 'contra' Darwin, he is, in fact, frequently writing 'pro' Darwin and refuting only an erroneous image of Darwin which he has derived from popularizations of his thought. Now that these important qualifications have been made, however, it remains to be examined whether in some vitally important sense Nietzsche is a philosopher whose essential thinking poses a serious challenge to Darwin's ideas on evolution, and can thus be construed in some crucial sense as a thinker who is indeed 'contra Darwin'.[3] I shall endeavour to show that Nietzsche's position 'contra' Darwin is flawed and does not amount to a decisive critique or attack. Rather, what is decisive is the critical perspective which Darwin's thinking on natural selection brings to bear on Nietzsche's *Lebensphilosophie*, since it is able to show the extent to which it rests on an untenable anthropormorphization of nature, life, and evolution.

Many of Nietzsche's most penetrating insights into the genealogy of moralities and molarities gain their potency by having their basis in the insights of scientific materialism. The burgeoning disciplines of physiology, thermodynamics, and atheistic biology in the nineteenth century left a decisive mark on his critique of modernity and his attempt to evolve a philosophy of the future. This does not prevent him, however, from criticizing natural science for displaying residues of moral theology, as in the apocalyptic 'heat-death' vision of the second law of

---

2 In fact the influence of an evolutionary paradigm on Nietzsche's thinking on life is evident as early as 1867 in his speculations on Kant and the question of teleology. In this early outline of a planned dissertation Nietzsche comes close to arguing that Kant's thinking on nature is irredeemably pre-Darwinian on account of its inability to conceive of nature producing through contingent mechanistic means life-forms that are capable of complex self-organization. In this essay it is perhaps significant that Nietzsche embraces an Empedoclean standpoint since Empedocles is often portrayed as an ancient precursor of Darwin. See Nietzsche 1933–42, volume 3: 371–94. For Empedocles see Wheelwright 1966: 122–54.

3 For insight into the reception of Darwin in Germany in the period of Nietzsche's writing see Kelly 1981.

thermodynamics. Science halts before the 'petty facts' and is unable to generate new visions and riddles of life that could be placed in the service of the cultivation of 'higher' types and forms of life. I intend in this chapter to concentrate on Nietzsche's engagement with modern biology, especially Darwin's theory of natural selection, since it reveals novel insights into the difficulties of Nietzsche's thinking. There is plenty of evidence to suggest that Nietzsche was familiar with the work of the English Darwinians (and prominent German Darwinians too, such as Ernst Haeckel), but no evidence to suggest that he had any direct acquaintance with the work of Darwin itself.[4] Besides Herbert Spencer and Thomas Henry Huxley, for example, Nietzsche was familiar with the work of a figure like Walter Bagehot, whose *Physics and Politics* of the late 1860s was sub-titled 'Thoughts on the Application of the Principle of "Natural Selection" and "Inheritance" to Political Society' (a reference to this work can be found in the final section of *Schopenhauer as Educator*). It can be quite easily shown that at the points at which Nietzsche thinks he is differing from Darwin, he is, in fact, endorsing the subtler Darwin he never cultivated an appreciation of. These points also show the extent to which Nietzsche is, in fact, closer to Darwin in his thinking on evolution and adaptation than to the explicit Lamarckian position frequently attributed to him.[5] In using Huxley contra Spencer in the second essay of the *Genealogy of Morality*, for example, Nietzsche is, by implication, endorsing the attack made by, among others, William James on Spencer's Lamarckism.[6] Lamarckism offers a too perfect

---

4 It would be erroneous to attempt any strict determination of Darwinian and Lamarckian components in the biological thought informing Nietzsche's ideas. It is early in the 1880s with the work of Weismann (never cited in Nietzsche's work) that Darwinism emerges as a theory wholly distinct from its Lamarckian heritage. Haeckel, for example, freely incorporated Lamarckian elements into his Darwinism. In the *Origin of Species* Darwin is ignorant of the genetic causes of hereditary variation, and so freely incorporates into his theory of descent with modification Lamarck's theses on the use and disuse of organs and on the inheritance of acquired characteristics.

5 See, for example, Kaufmann 1974: 294–5, who speaks of Nietzsche as remaining faithful to Lamarck's doctrine of the inheritance of acquired characteristics throughout his intellectual life.

6 Nietzsche's remarks about Spencer are always contemptuous. In Nietzsche 1974: section 373, for example, he refers to him as 'that pedantic Englishman' who raves tediously about the eventual reconciliation of egoism and altruism, and argues that a human race that adopted a Spencerian perspective would be worthy of 'annihilation'. The *Nachlass* makes it clear that the text Nietzsche was making notes from and commenting on was Spencer's *Data of Ethics* (translated into German in 1879). See Nietzsche 1987, volume 10: 550; volume 11: 525. For further references to Spencer see Nietzsche 1979a: 'Why I am a Destiny', section 4, and 1979b: 'Expeditions of an Untimely Man', sections 37 and 38. See also Nietzsche 1966: section 253 where Darwin, J. S. Mill, and Spencer are lumped together as 'mittlemässiger Engländer'.

model of adaptation and does not place the emphasis in evolution, as Darwin and as Nietzsche do, on the role of functional indeterminacy in complex evolution. In Darwin it is clear that the process by which adaptive traits are produced is initially independent of their potential usefulness in adaptation. This is what contemporary theorists have called 'exaptation', denoting an adaptation which either originated as a non-adaptive characteristic or one which evolved with a different function from that which it enjoys in the present.[7]

Nietzsche reads natural selection as lending support to the reactive forces of life and to their triumph in modernity.[8] Nietzsche does not refute natural selection, but emphasizes the extent to which it is the 'mechanism' by which reactive forces are able to attain a position of dominance. Natural selection is conceived by Nietzsche as a largely negative feedback mechanism that encourages the physiologically weak and ill-constituted to gather together in herds in order to maximize their opportunities for self-preservation.[9] Natural selection reveals an entropic tendency; as one commentator on Darwin has succinctly expressed the

---

7 For an account of exaptation see Plotkin 1995: 54ff.

8 One of the few commentators to expose this point is Deleuze, who refers to 'adaptation, evolution, progress, happiness for all, and the good of the community' as examples of new reactive values peculiar to modernity that take the place of the old discredited reactive values associated with God and a Christian-moral culture. See Deleuze 1983: 151. Earlier in this essay (61) Deleuze characterizes reactive force as (a) a utilitarian force of adaptation and partial limitation; (b) a force that separates active force from what it can do (such as the example of the separation of the lightning and its flash that Nietzsche gives in the parable of the lamb and bird of prey in the *Genealogy of Morality*, I, section 13); (c) a force that denies and turns against itself (the process that Nietzsche refers to as the 'internalization of man', which is almost constitutive of his very being).

9 The influence of thermodynamics on the theory of natural selection is more readily apparent if one looks not at Darwin's conception of it, but that put forward by Alfred Russel Wallace. Just a few years before the publication of Darwin's *Origins* in 1859, Wallace 'discovered' the principle of natural selection after a psychedelic experience caused by a malaria attack, resulting in delirium, while in Indonesian rain forests. Wallace explained his 'discovery' by comparing the action of the principle as 'exactly like that of the centrifugal governor of the steam engine, which checks and corrects any irregularities almost before they become evident'. Wallace makes the analogy with the centrifugal governor of the steam engine in the context of a discussion of the role of mimicry in evolution and how evolution works in favour of counteracting the potentially disastrous effects of unbalanced deficiencies. Thus, a deficiency in one set of organs (say, weak feet) is always compensated by an increase in the development of other organs (powerful wings, for example). See Wallace 1958, reprinted 1971: 268–80. In his *Mind and Nature* Gregory Bateson went so far as to claim that if it had been Wallace, rather than Darwin, who steered the theory of natural selection, then today we would have a very different theory of evolution and

essential import of the tautologous 'survival of the fittest' thesis: 'natural selection is the *differential* loss of differently constituted individuals'.[10]

It is clear, however, that natural selection reveals both aspects of feedback. Natural selection – which would be more accurately characterized as 'natural destruction' since nature does not in this schema so much positively select the fittest as 'exterminate' the ill-adapted in a purely mechanistic fashion – compels organisms and species to strive for stability and preservation (the important task in evolution is not to be selected against), but the selective pressures of a changing and variable environment mean that they must learn to operate their capacities for adaptation innovatively at the 'edge of chaos'. The 'Red Queen hypothesis' provides another example of feedback in evolution in which even stable environments can be upset, that is, rendered unpredictable and non-linear.[11] It is by no means certain that life-forms evolve by maintaining a tightly adjusted relationship with their 'environment'. Natural selection, in which the emphasis is placed on preservation, is one means of measuring the adaptive success of life-forms, but it is, in Nietzsche's eyes, a highly conservative, if not 'bourgeois', measure of evolution. It is on this level of argument that Nietzsche is engaging with Darwin's theory of natural selection and proposing 'self-overcoming' as an alternative 'law of life'. In his 'mature' thought Nietzsche seeks to articulate an alternative conception of life. He was immersed in the debates which took place after the publication of Darwin's *Origin of Species* about the precise mechanisms of evolution (exogenous or endogenous). Indeed, it is in the context of this fundamental debate

---

cybernetics may have appeared one hundred years earlier. For further insight into Wallace see S. J. Gould, 'Natural Selection and the Human Brain: Darwin vs. Wallace', in Gould 1983: 43–51, P. J. Vorzimmer 1970: 187–213, and Cronin 1991. For further insight into negative and positive feedback, and for a discussion of the Watt governor in terms of its application to biology, see the chapter on 'Explosions and Spirals' in Dawkins 1991: 195–220. See also Sigmund 1995: 47, 59, 128ff. In one of the most important contributions to biology in recent years, Manfred Eigen has argued that 'selection' is not the blind sieve people have considered it to be since Darwin, but rather is to be conceived as a highly active process that is 'driven' by an internal feedback mechanism. His reformulation of selection in such terms is capable of making a valuable contribution to a Darwinian conception of *creative* evolution. Eigen maintains that selection does not possess an inherent drive towards some predestined goal; rather, it is on account of its inherent *non-linear* mechanism, which gives the *appearance* of goal-directedness, that selection functions as a discriminating searching device looking for the best route to optimal performance (but note, since optimality is never final in life, that selection is a continuing process). See Eigen 1992: 121–7, 'Resume: Darwin is dead – long live Darwin!'.

10 See Howard 1992: 22.
11 For an account of the Red Queen hypothesis see Sigmund 1995: 148ff.

about the nature and motor of evolution, which still divides the community of biologists today, that Nietzsche specifically provides the most succinct formulation of his notion of 'will-to-power' (in essay 2 of the *Genealogy of Morality*). Ultimately, Nietzsche will *read* natural selection as positing a certain *evaluation* or measurement of life, arguing that it rests on particular 'values', notably, the value and utility of preservation.[12] Thus, a fundamental aspect of the revaluation of values conducted in a genealogy of morality will be a revaluation of 'Darwinian' values. This revaluation, however, as I shall endeavour to illuminate, is not without major problems since it raises the complex issue of unwarranted anthropomorphizations of nature and corresponding reifications of natural and technical life.

In the *Genealogy*, in which he calls for a fruitful exchange between philosophy, physiology, and medicine, Nietzsche's overriding aim is to expand the horizon of value, so that the fundamental question, 'what is the value of this or that table of values and morals?', can be examined with the benefit of a wide array of perspectives. Nietzsche advocates such a pluralism in order to prevent any simple-minded reductionism concerning the fundamental questions of 'life'. He sees natural selection as lending itself to such reductionist approaches, and he is keen to point out that something which possessed obvious and enormous value in relation to the survival of a 'race' (*Rasse*), such as the improvement of its power of adaptation (*Anpassungskräfte*) to a particular climate, or to the preservation of the greatest number, would not at all enjoy the same value if it were, say, a question of the production (*herausbilden*) of a 'stronger' type. It is, he contends, only the naivety of English biologists which permits the two questions of value to be conflated (Nietzsche 1994: I, section 17). This particular confrontation shows, I would argue, the extent to which Nietzsche is responding to Darwinism not so much as a biological theory but more as a social theory, as *social* Darwinism.

---

12 It is not at all clear that Darwin was supplying a mechanism in order to explain evolution with the principle of natural selection. For example, in the third edition of *The Origin of Species* he makes it clear that natural selection is not to be construed as inducing variability; rather it implies only the preservation of variations that arise and that prove beneficial 'to the being under its conditions of life'. In the same passage he stresses the solely metaphorical quality of the expression 'natural selection' so as to ward off any personification of nature. For further analysis of this issue see Young 1985: 95ff. It was Wallace who tried to get Darwin to drop the misleading phrase 'natural selection' and replace it with 'the survival of the fittest'. In a letter to Darwin he maintains that 'natural selection' is 'indirect' and 'incorrect' as a metaphorical expression. If one must personify nature, he argues, it is better to speak of 'natural extermination' since nature does not so much *select* variations as *exterminate* unfavourable ones. See Paul 1988: 411–24.

Nietzsche construes the experimental creation of the *Übermensch* not in 'Darwinian' terms as a superior type evolving through natural selection; rather, he configures it in terms of a notion of emergent cultural complexity and deterritorialization, laying particular stress on the hybridic emergence of diversity and difference within the order of things. The *Übermensch* operates on a number of planes in Nietzsche's thought: as the thought of singularity and incomparability; as the supra-economic thought of a cyborg future; as a vision of the 'higher' type of a complex evolution, and so on. Its meaning is both radically other and relative to what we know of the human and what we think still might become of it: 'a relatively overhuman type, is overhuman precisely in its relation to the good – the good and the just would call this overman the devil' (Nietzsche 1979a: 'Why I am a Destiny', section 5). The higher type, and the stronger, more evolvable, 'species', signified in the overman represents the 'secretion of a luxury surplus of mankind' made possible by mankind's 'machinery of interests and services' becoming integrated in more and more intricate terms. On the plane of human cultural evolution there will occur, as there is occurring now, Nietzsche argues, a kind of stationary adaptation. Once the common economic management of the earth has been attained, 'mankind will be able to find its best meaning as a machine in the service of this economy'. Economic development will result in such an intelligent symbiosis of man and machine that the need for command and domination will become superfluous: 'a tremendous clockwork, composed of ever smaller, ever more subtly "adapted" gears; as an ever-growing superfluity of all dominating and commanding elements; as a whole of tremendous force, whose individual factors represent *minimal forces, minimal values*' (Nietzsche 1968: section 866; 1987, volume 12: 462–3). On another plane, evolution will take place in an opposite direction, away from a specialized utility and the production of a 'synthetic, summarizing human'. The existence of the 'transformation of mankind into a machine' is a precondition of the emergence and cultivation of this new overhuman type. If one wanted to look at this picture of the future morally, it would have to be conceded, Nietzsche admits, that this 'overall machinery' and 'solidarity of all gears' of the human-social machine represents a high point in the maximum exploitation of man. Nevertheless, he insists, this higher evolution 'presupposes those on whose account this exploitation has meaning'. Nietzsche offers this vision of the overhuman as a rival to the 'economic optimism' which governs at the present time, holding that the increasing expenditure of everyone will involve the increasing welfare of everyone (ibid.; see also section 898). Here we find Nietzsche combating what he regards as the 'levelling tendencies' of modern social evolution with an entirely different conception of the engineering of man and his future becoming, one which rests on a particular praxis of selection that is radically at odds with the 'natural' type posited by Darwin. Nietzsche's artificial selection of 'man' aims to combat the animalization of man into the dwarf animal of equal rights and claims' (Nietzsche 1966: section 203). In his writings Nietzsche will often equate English empiricism and liberalism with the preservation of the perfect herd animal (see Nietzsche 1979b: 92–3). 'Humane Englishmen' such as Darwin, Spencer, and John Stuart Mill simply lack music; the movements of their thinking are devoid of rhythm and dance. Indeed, what these thinkers lack is 'the real *profundity* of spiritual perception; in brief, philosophy' (1966: section 252). The only vision of the highest human achievement which English clumsiness and peasant seriousness can offer is that of a 'Salvation Army' type (ibid.).

In the crucial section on 'historical method' in the *Genealogy of Morality* Nietzsche puts forward a novel valuation of evolution and selection. The theory of will-to-power does not place 'adaptation' (*Anpassung*) in the foreground (as inner adaptation to external circumstances and provocations). For Nietzsche, this is an entirely 'reactive' notion of life. An 'active' notion of life can only be given articulation if the emphasis is placed, not on adaptation, but on the priority of the 'spontaneous', 'expansive' (*übergreifenden*), and self-organizing 'form-shaping forces (*gestaltenden Kräfte*) that give new directions and interpretations' (Nietzsche 1994: II, section 12). 'Adaptation' is a secondary effect which takes place only after the formative powers have exerted their influence. Nietzsche does not mention Darwin in the section of the *Genealogy* where he formulates his own conception of evolution through the priority of form-building forces, but refers instead to Herbert Spencer. The *Nachlass* note of this crucial section, however, from the end of 1886/early 1887 (simply stated as 1883–8 in the Kaufmann translation of *The Will to Power*), makes clear that a scientifically informed if inaccurate critique of English Darwinism lies at the heart of Nietzsche's postulation of a notion of 'will-to-power' to account for the primacy of spontaneous and form-giving 'activity' (*Aktivität*) in the becoming of complex life (Darwin, not Spencer is the figure Nietzsche mentions in the original formulation of this passage). In contrast to an emphasis on the influence of 'external circumstances' (*ausseren Umstände*), he stresses that the essential phenomenon in the life process is precisely the 'tremendous shaping, form-creating force' (*ungeheure gestaltende herformschaffende Gewalt*) that works from within and then utilizes and exploits 'external circumstances'.[13]

---

13 Nietzsche 1968: section 647; 1987, volume 12: 304–5.

  A similar critique of Darwinism can be found in Bergson's *Creative Evolution* of 1907 (which curiously nowhere refers to Nietzsche). See, for example, Bergson 1983: 101–3, where Bergson

It has been little noted that the notion of will-to-power is, in large part, inspired by work Nietzsche read in the early 1880s in experimental embryology (notably Wilhelm Roux) and orthogenesis (notably Carl von Nageli). One of the original passages in the *Nachlass* where Nietzsche develops the ideas that will inform the crucial section 12 of the second essay of the *Genealogy of Morality* is entitled 'Gegen den Darwinismus'. It begins by insisting upon a principle of method that Nietzsche will make fundamental to the understanding of 'evolution' or becoming which he propounds in that work, namely, that the 'use' of an organ in no way serves to explain its 'evolution' (*Entstehung*) (Nietzsche 1987, volume 12: 304). This principle finds an exact correspondence in von Nageli's theory of evolution (*Abstammungslehre*).[14] Von Nageli construes evolution taking place in terms of the synthesis of external causes and internal causes that operate under the influence of molecular forces (*Molecularkräfte*). Von Nageli construes evolution by adaptation as taking place in terms of the primacy of internal factors that result in increasing complexity (ever more elaborate 'configurations' of forces) corresponding to external conditions. Natural selection prunes the phylogenetic tree but does not cause new branches to grow. The phylogenetic process is a double one, with the combination of forces producing a new configuration while the new configuration produces new combinations of forces. This process of a continually 'increasing complexity of configuration by the action of internal forces' constitutes the 'automatic perfecting process . . . and entropy of organic matter' (von Nageli 1898: 8). For von Nageli it is this double process and resultant play between the interior and the exterior which account for the complex reality of variation: 'The same external causes may, according to the nature of the organism and other

---

endeavours to steer a course beyond the opposition of mechanism (neo-Darwinism) and finalism (neo-Lamarckism), by developing a conception of evolution which places the emphasis on an 'internal push' that carries life 'by more and more complex forms, to higher and higher destinies'. The issue of vitalism should not serve to downplay the continuing significance of Bergson's text. On this point see Kampis 1991. Bergson's thinking on evolution and entropy has been defended against the many charges of mysticism levelled against it by Georgescu-Roegen (1971: 192).

14 Von Nageli published his theory of evolution, *Mechanisch-physiologische Theorie der Abstammungslehre* (Leipzig, Oldenburg, 1884), in two volumes, *1: Die Schranken der naturwissenschaftlichen Erkenntniss*, and *2: Kräfte und Gestaltungen im molekulären Gebiet*. This correspondence between Nietzsche and von Nageli has been expertly annotated by Andrea Orsucci (1993: 380ff.). See also Orsucci 1996: 53–7. I am grateful to the author for sending me an advance copy of his most recent study. The English translation of this work (see von Nageli 1898) simply amounts to a translation of Nageli's summary of his research. The original work runs to well over 500 pages.

circumstances, have very unlike variations as a result. But the internal rearrangement produces in a definite case very definite variations' (ibid.: 20).

For Nietzsche the will-to-power is active in a complex evolution in terms of an unconscious process of interpretation and connection that results in 'greater complexity, sharp differentiation, the contiguity of developed organs and functions'.[15] Nietzsche's argument is that mere variations of power could not feel themselves to be such; rather, 'there must be present something that wants to grow and interprets the value of whatever else wants to grow' (Nietzsche 1968: section 643). Indeed, Nietzsche goes as far in his privileging of a shaping force as to claim that this force 'desires an ever new supply of "material" (more "force")', and speaks, in this regard, of the 'masterpiece' of the construction of an organism from an egg (ibid.: section 660). Moreover, greater complexity does not simply mean greater power in terms of greater mass: the emphasis is on the quality, not the quantity, of power. As recent 'complexity' theorists have emphasized, the marker of evolution in a complex adaptive system is not the number of components but the number of different types of components.[16] Nietzsche's whole attack on mechanism has its source in this qualitative understanding of force and form (mechanistic theory, he argues, can only describe, not explain the processes of evolution) (ibid.). The notion of 'utility' in evolution is clearly problematic. Nietzsche himself formulates a notion of the 'individual' that recognizes its complex evolution, speaking, for example, of the individual's evolution in terms of a struggle between parts — for food, for space, etc. — which proceeds through atrophy and '"becoming an organ" of other parts' (ibid.: section 647). Moreover, he insists that the 'new forms' generated and moulded from within are not formed with any end in view.[17] In the spontaneous becoming of organs the struggle of the

---

15 Nietzsche understands organic memory precisely in these terms of an unconscious formation: 'One must revise one's ideas about *memory*', he writes. 'Here lies the chief temptation to assume a "soul", which, outside time, reproduces, recognizes, etc. But that which is experienced lives on "in the memory"; I cannot help it if it "comes back", the will is inactive in this case, as in the coming of any thought. . . . Before judgement occurs, the process of assimilation must have already taken place; thus here, too, there is an intellectual activity that does not enter consciousness. . . . Probably an inner event corresponds to each organic function; hence assimilation, rejection, growth, etc.' (Nietzsche 1968: sections 502, 532).
16 On this point see Saunders and Ho 1976: 375–84 and 1981: 515–30. These authors argue that it is not 'organization' but 'complexity' which signifies growth in evolution. An increase in organization is treated as a secondary effect that comes about simply because the more a system evolves in complexity the more organization is required to faciliate survival.
17 Compare Wicken 1987: 62: 'Adaptation is an "end" of evolution in the sense of *consequence* rather than goal.'

different parts results in a new form which is eventually related to a partial usefulness, which then develops itself more and more completely in accordance with its use. It is not so much, therefore, a question of refuting Darwin's conception of utility, where 'useful' is synonymous with proven advantageousness in the struggle with others,[18] but of constructing an order of rank, in which the 'real development' is located in the feeling of increase in power, 'the feeling of becoming stronger', apart from any usefulness in the struggle of life as the 'survival of the fittest' (a formulation long recognized by biologists as tautologous) (ibid.: 649).[19] Nietzsche thus does not accept that the 'drive for preservation' is the cardinal drive in the evolution of organic life:

> One cannot ascribe the most basic and primeval activities of protoplasm to a will to self-preservation, for it takes into itself absurdly more than would be required to preserve it; and, above all, it does not thereby 'preserve itself', it falls apart. The drive that rules here has to explain precisely this absence of desire for self-preservation.
>
> (ibid.: section 651)

Darwinism overestimates utility in evolution on account of its privileging of the influence of external circumstances. In positing 'self-preservation' as the principal law of life Nietzsche argues that modern natural sciences are entangled in a 'Spinozistic dogma' that erroneously universalizes as a general principle of evolution particular conditions of existence (such as the idea that every living thing desires to maintain itself in its own being) (see Spinoza 1955: 136–7). He

---

18 For Darwin's justification of a utilitarian approach see Darwin 1985: 227ff. Darwin's thinking on utility is a great deal more subtle than Nietzsche allows. He concedes Nietzsche's point, in fact, when he argues that 'many modifications, wholly due to the laws of growth, and at first in no way advantageous to a species, have been subsequently taken advantage of by the still further modified descendants of this species' (1985: 232). It is not the case for Darwin, therefore, that every modification and formation are acquired through natural selection. Rather, selection operates as 'preservative power' by making 'profitable variations' of modifications in the struggle for life.

19 Of course, Nietzsche wilfully misreads Darwin for his own purposes and in order to bring out the radical difference of his own position. It is clear that 'fitness' for Darwin only makes sense in relation to a given environment. It does not refer to an absolute scale of perfection, and so lacks the teleological intent that Nietzsche ascribes to the theory of natural selection read as a *social* theory or theory of culture. However, Nietzsche is correct to insist that 'survival of the fittest' denotes a passive, if not reactive, principle of life. The only criterion of usefulness or fitness is the process of natural selection itself, namely, the outcome of selection. For clarification of the phrase 'survival of the fittest' see Dawkins 1982: 179–94.

warns us, in speaking of the 'incomprehensibly onesided doctrine of the "struggle for existence"', that Malthus is not nature.[20] On the contrary, the species of English Darwinism breathes the 'musty air of English overpopulation, like the smell of the distress and overcrowding of small people'.[21] He thus insists contra Darwinism that it is not conditions of distress (*Nothlage*) and scarcity that are

---

20  As early as 1875 Nietzsche is contesting the extent to which the 'struggle for existence' can be posited as the most important principle within an economy of life. See the note labelled 'Zum Darwinismus' in Nietzsche 1987, volume 8, 12 [22]: 257–9. For Darwin's reference to Malthus see Darwin 1985: 117, where he states that his conception of evolution is 'the doctrine of Malthus applied with manifold force to the whole animal and vegetable kingdoms'. Evolution by natural selection is conceived by him as nature's check on an infinite exponential increase and spread of the striving of organic beings to increase their numbers: 'The face of Nature', he writes in a graphic passage, 'may be compared to a yielding surface, with ten thousand sharp wedges packed close together and driven inwards by incessant blows, sometimes one wedge being struck, and then another with greater force' (119). When Darwin returned home to England in 1836 at the end of his five-year-long voyage of discovery on the *Beagle*, he returned, in the words of his biographers, to a 're-energized Malthusian world', in which the new poor law had put into effect the Whig philosophy of 'middle-class Malthusian values'. See Desmond and Moore 1992: 196. Malthus presents a lucid account of his views on population growth in terms of solid 'laws of nature' in the opening chapter of his classic *Essay on the Principle of Population* (1798/1993).

21  Somewhat cryptically, and perhaps unfairly, Nietzsche locates the source of Darwin's conception of evolution not only in Malthus but also in Hegel: 'without Hegel there could have been no Darwin', Nietzsche 1974: 357. The Hegel–Darwin nexus was first outlined and explored by Nietzsche in his scathing attack on David Strauss, his first 'untimely meditation' of 1873 (section 7). It should be clear: what links Hegel and Darwin is that both are worshippers of the 'real' as the rational and hence 'deifiers of success'. What he abhors in Strauss is the disingenuous attempt to derive from evolutionary theory a possible 'genuine Darwinian ethics'. Nietzsche's point is a strong one, namely, that any attempt to derive ethical values from the laws of natural science represents the 'extreme anthropomorphism of a reason that has overstepped the bounds of the permitted'. An echo of Nietzsche's position contra Strauss can be heard in Stephen Jay Gould's 1990 Edinburgh Medal Address (Gould 1995). See also Nietzsche 1987, volume 11: 34 [73]: 'What separates us as much from Kant, as from Plato and Leibnitz, is that we believe that becoming (*das Werden*) even in the realm of the spirit (*Geistigen*), we are historical (*historisch*) through and through. This is the great reversal: Lamarck and Hegel – Darwin is only an aftereffect.' Of course, we know that the most important influence on Darwin came from the geologist Charles Lyell. The only significant scientific treatise Darwin took with him on the *Beagle* voyage was the first volume of Lyell's *Principles of Geology* (the second volume he picked up later during his travels).

 Interestingly, Nietzsche's own conception of history (*Geschichte*) operates not under the influence of Hegelianism but rather under that of *geology* and its notion of 'strata' (*die Schichten*). It is because he reads history geologically in terms of processes of stratification that Nietzsche

dominant in nature but rather conditions of overflow *Überfluss*) and squandering (*Verschwendung*), even to the point of absurdity (*Unsinnige*). The struggle for existence has to be regarded as a 'temporary restriction of the will to life' (*der Wille des Lebens*). This is to recognize the 'will to power' as the formative principle of the 'will to life' (Nietzsche 1974: section 349).

The extent, therefore, to which Nietzsche formulated his conception of life as will-to-power in terms of an alternative to the depiction of life offered by 'English Darwinism' has been overlooked. For Nietzsche the life process evolves in terms of the shaping, form-creating forces working from within, utilizing and exploiting external circumstances as the arena to test out its own extravagant experimentations. The 'useful' establishes itself as an indirect result of this complex process. Thus, for example, Nietzsche argues that a deficiency or degeneration can prove to be of the highest utility insofar as it acts as a stimulant to other organs (Nietzsche 1968: section 647).[22] He even goes so far as to estimate the evolution of strength, the 'maximal feeling of power', in terms of its intensity, not its extensity (that is, the feeling of becoming stronger does not have to depend on one's comparative advantage over others, as in the Darwinian struggle for existence). In his theory of

---

opposes all forms of historical evolutionism or historicism. Geology affords insight into the *virtual plane of becoming* that established 'history' conceals and covers over. On this point in Nietzsche see the astonishing section 223 of *Assorted Opinions and Maxims* entitled 'Whither to one must Travel', where he speaks of the past as continuing to 'flow within us in a hundred waves'. In order to 'discover' the past genuinely, it is not necessary that one travel thousands of miles, constantly moving from place to place and traversing vast distances. The process is rather one of activating and actualizing the buried virtuality of past time in a new becoming ('thus I willed it!' being precisely the moment which captures the temporal flow of geological-historical time). The passage from *Assorted Opinions and Maxims* closes with the intimation of a possible future/futural humanity (*zukünftige Menschenthum*) in which 'self-knowledge' and 'self-determination' have become *universal* knowledge and *universal* determination.

22 The aforementioned *Nachlass* note from 1875 (8, 12 [22]) stresses, contra the essential import of the principle of the struggle for existence (*Kampf um's Dasein*), the significance of degenerative natures in the context of a discussion of how the 'infection of the new' gets accepted and assimilated. This note from 1885 became section 224 of *Human, All To Human*, entitled 'Ennoblement through Degeneration' (Veredelung durch Entartung), which, in part, states: 'Degenerate natures are of the highest significance wherever progress is to be effected. Every progress of the whole has to be preceded by a partial weakening. The strongest natures *preserve* the type, the weaker help it to *evolve* . . . the celebrated struggle for existence does not seem to me to be the only theory by which the progress or strengthening of an individual (*Menschen*) or a race (*Rasse*) can be explained.' Nietzsche's construal of the feedback mechanism brought into play by degeneration and deficiencies brings him close to Wallace's argument at the conclusion of his aforementioned essay.

life Nietzsche sharply criticizes the view that the aim and goal of life is self-preservation (Hobbes, Spinoza, Adam Smith, Darwin), and places all the emphasis on the enjoyment a living thing gets out of simply discharging its force (with preservation a consequence of this overcoming) (ibid.: section 650). The 'instinct of preservation' is a superfluous teleological principle in the comprehension of life.

Nietzsche's thinking on this question of struggle between parts evolves under the influence of Wilhelm Roux (1850–1924) and his work of 1881, *Der Kampf der Theile im Organismus. Ein Beitrag zur Vervollständigung der mechanischen Zweckmässigkeitslehre*, which contended that natural selection was unable to account for *Organbildung* since it relied on a purely exogenous influence.[23] Nietzsche cites key insights from this text in the notes of 1883 (Nietzsche 1987, volume 10: 272–5 and 302–4). It is only several years later in the *Nachlass* material of 1886/7 that he begins to explore its significance in the context of his formulation of 'form-shaping forces' and his critique of Darwin (see ibid., volume 12: 304ff.). It is from Roux that Nietzsche borrows the notion of 'form-shaping/building forces' (or 'formative powers'). However, the notion is not restricted in Nietzsche to the evolution of 'organs' but plays a fundamental role in his positing of the will-to-power as a principle of 'historical method' that is applicable to variegated forms of evolution, whether they occur in biological, physiological, cultural, or technological domains:

there is no more important proposition for all kinds of historical research than that which we arrive at only with great effort . . . namely, that the origin of the emergence of a thing and its ultimate usefulness, its practical application and incorporation into a system of ends (*Zwecken*), are *toto coelo* separate; that anything in existence, having somehow come about, is continually interpreted anew, requisitioned anew, transformed and redirected to a new purpose by a power superior to it . . . everything that occurs in the organic world consists of *overpowering* (*Überwaltigen*), *dominating* (*Herrwerden*), and in their turn, overpowering and dominating consist of re-interpretation, adjustment, in the process of which their former 'meaning' and 'purpose' (*Zweck*) must necessarily be obscured or completely obliterated.

(Nietzsche 1994: II, section 12)[24]

---

23 For full details of Nietzsche's utilization of the work of Roux see the editorial comments provided in Nietzsche 1987, volume 14: 684–6, and Müller-Lauter 1978: 189–223. There can be little doubt that Nietzsche's contention that 'exploitation' (*Ausbeutung*) belongs to the 'essence of what lives' as a basic organic function (as a consequence of the will-to-power) is derived in large part from his reading of Roux. See Nietzsche 1966: section 259.

24 For a contemporary statement of functional indeterminacy see Dennett 1995a: 245–75: 'there is no ultimate User's Manual in which the *real* functions, and *real* meanings, of biological artifacts are officially represented' (270).

Nietzsche further insists that as a major principle of historico-genealogical method the 'development' (*Entwicklung*) of a thing or of an organ is in a way to be treated in terms of its 'progressus' towards a goal, and most definitely not as a 'logical progressus'. Rather, 'evolution' must be approached as operating in terms of a 'succession' (*Aufeinanderfolge*) of more or less profound and independent processes of overpowering in which powerful transformation and resistance play the role of an immanent, open-ended dynamics. If the 'form is fluid, the meaning even more so' (ibid.). Nietzsche then makes the analogy with the individual organism, clearly drawing on the embryological work of Roux, arguing that every time the whole grows significantly, so the meaning of the individual organs also shifts, with the result that the partial destruction of organs is to be regarded as a sign of their increasing vitality and perfection. He thus reaches the 'strange' conclusion that decay and degeneration, as well as loss of meaning and purposiveness (*Zweckmässigkeit*) (in other words, 'death'), are all to be regarded as the conditions of an actual progressus.

The notion of 'form-shaping forces' operating in terms of a non-linear and non-teleological becoming is crucial to understanding the morphological basis of his *Kulturkritik* — democracy and its modern misarchism, the hegemony of herd morality, the triumph of reactivity, etc. As Nietzsche tells readers of the 'genealogy', stress is to to be placed upon the major points of a historical method in order to combat the prevailing instinct and fashion which would rather accept the view that a randomness (*Zufälligkeit*) and mechanistic senselessness governs all events than that a 'theory of a *power-will (Macht-Willens)*' is played out in all that happens and evolves. It is thus woefully inadequate to claim, as one commentator on Nietzsche's critique of Darwin has, that Nietzsche was an opponent not of 'scientific Darwinism' but only of the attempt to derive moral formulations or conclusions from Darwinism (Stegmaier 1987: 264–88). Nietzsche is arguing that the mechanism of Darwinism has influenced physiology and biology to the extent that the basic concept, that of 'activity' (*Aktivität*), of the objective sciences, is 'spirited away'. When this 'passive' model of evolution is moved into the foreground, through a notion of 'adaptation', the 'essence of life', namely, its will-to-power conceived as the becoming of the reinterpeting, redirecting 'formative powers', is lost sight of. Nietzsche *politicizes* this conflict within the 'natural sciences' by claiming that mechanistic physiology and biology serve to lend support to the cause of the modern democratic idiosyncrasy, the political philosophy of the last man, which is opposed to everything that dominates and wants to dominate as a higher power. At the same time Nietzsche *biologizes* the question of the political by upholding a theory of will-to-power which seeks to demonstrate that a system of law conceived as sovereign and universal is 'anti' the fundamental 'activity' of life. A society that employs law not as a means 'for use in the fight between units of power' but as a means '*against* fighting in general' not only is hostile to life but would equally represent 'an attempt to assassinate the future of man', concealing a 'secret path to nothingness' (Nietzsche 1994: II, section 12).

It is only by understanding the theoretical basis of Nietzsche's celebration of immanent diversity and variety, which he sees as 'evolving' spontaneously and endogenously through the surplus of overpowering and architectural excess, that we can make sense of his attempted critique of Darwin (and, by extension, social Darwinism). He views the 'struggle for life', vulgarized in socio-biological thought of the nineteenth and twentieth centuries to the level of the 'survival of the fittest', as the exception rather than the rule. The 'general aspect of life', he contends, is not lack (hunger) and distress, but rather wealth, luxury, and prodigality (*Verschwendung*) (Nietzsche 1979b: 'Expeditions of an Untimely Man', section 14). If we admitted that the popular Darwinian-Malthusian view of life predominates in nature, then it would be necessary to acknowledge that history proves the theory wrong, for, in the case of man, it is not the 'strong', active type that has flourished but the weak, reactive type. Nietzsche argues that we can only account for such a perverse history of the animal 'man' in terms of the evolution of the 'mind' (*Geist*) (the weak have become strong through cunning, patience, diligence, self-control, mimicry, etc.: in short, through morality). It is only on the level of history and culture that the triumph of the Darwinian-Malthusian view of life as a general economy of nature can be accounted for, and it is precisely such a 'history', that of man and of morals, that Nietzsche sketches in his genealogy of morality.

Nietzsche attacks biologists for importing into the logic of life moral evaluations (the altruism of the herd, for example). Both the 'species' and the 'ego' are illusions. If we are to posit a notion of the 'ego' it should be in terms of a complex unit in a chain of members, and not as an isolated, self-sufficient monadic entity. The notion of the species is merely an abstraction from the multiplicity of chains. The theory of descent, on Nietzsche's view, must construe individuation as degeneration (the falling apart of one into two, the becoming of multiplicity, difference, heterogeneity) (Nietzsche 1968: section 679). In a note of 1881 he maintains, 'In any case there are no species (*Gattung*), but only different kinds of individuals (*Einzelwesen*)! . . . Nature does not desire to "preserve the species"!' (Nietzsche 1987, volume 9: 11 [178]). The future of evolution for Nietzsche belongs not to species but to individuals who embody ever greater levels of complexity, by which Nietzsche means 'a greater sum of co-ordinated elements'. He appreciates that greater complexity means that such a higher type renders itself more vulnerable to disintegration ('The genius is the most sublime machine (*die sublimste Maschine*) there is – consequently the most fragile', 1968: section 684; 1987, volume 13: 315). Nietzsche's affirmation of the higher type goes against the grain of evolution, which favours the gradual selection of that which endures. The higher type, by contrast, squanders itself; it does not last, and is but a lucky stroke; it cannot be bred or passed on through heredity. It is precisely for this reason – the fact that natural selection so rigorously favours the weak and the mediocre – that Nietzsche argues for the protection of the strong (the lucky strokes, the fragile complex types) from the herd-desires of the weak (1968: section 685; 1987, volume 13: 303–5). Nature is blind and dumb; the intelligence of the lucky stroke is a freak, a quirk, of evolution. If man is the product of natural selection, the overman – considered as the *future* of evolution – will be the invention of a wholly different kind, and it is in the context of Nietzsche's engagement with Darwin that we can perhaps best understand his positing of the eternal return as promoting an alternative principle of selection to be placed in the service 'of strength (and barbarism!!)'[25]: 'My philosophy brings the triumphant idea by which all other modes of thought will ultimately perish. It is the great cultivating idea (*züchtende Gedanke*): the races that cannot bear it stand condemned; those who find it the greatest benefit are selected for mastery (*Herrschaft*)' (Nietzsche 1968: 1053; 1987, volume 11: 250).

Nietzsche recognizes that his 'contra Darwin' position is deeply problematic since it overturns the basis on which a Darwinian perspective evaluates evolution. The attainment of the 'highest types' – by which is meant 'the richest and most complex forms' (Nietzsche 1968: section 684) – takes place only rarely, and once attained has to be nurtured with extreme care and attention. The problem of culture, as that which gives culture its *raison d'être*, is nothing other than that of how to cultivate the conditions which give rise to the flourishing of the highest types. Nietzsche does not think, however, that one can manufacture the genius. Rather, a culture can only lay down conditions that are favourable to the unpredictable and non-calculable lightning-like appearance of unique, singular beings. Types are hereditary, but then a type is not a 'lucky stroke', 'nothing extreme' (ibid.). The task is to make 'the scales more delicate and hope for the assistance of favourable accidents' (ibid.: section 907; see also sections 933, 957, 960).

Nietzsche is compelled to engage with Darwin simply because he appreciates that natural selection stands opposed to the fundamental concerns of his own

---

25 A point made several decades ago by Haas (1929).

conception of life and of selection (artificial selection by means of the experiment of eternal return) (Nietzsche 1968: section 1053; 1987, volume 11: 250). Nietzsche's appraisal of Darwinism, however, is awkward and ambiguous. While the thrust of his thinking is to dereify the naturalistic claims of the theory, there are places in his work where he appears to be arguing that on the level of 'natural' selection Darwinism is correct. Survival of the fittest, *even at the level of the 'will-to-power'*, he suggests at one point, translates itself into a cultural history and evolution that favours the organization and dominion of the weak over the 'lucky strokes' and 'select types'. Nietzsche's conclusion is that if one translates 'reality' into a 'morality', then this morality will assert the primacy of the will to nothingness over the will to life, and prize the value of the mediocre over that of the rare and the exceptional. It is as if Nietzsche is making the claim that history could only have developed in the way it did, in the direction of the triumph of the slave revolt in morality, since 'history', like 'nature', favours the organization and moral intelligence of molar formations (such as flocks and herds). This is akin to his argument in the *Genealogy of Morality* that the animal 'man' was destined to develop a bad conscience as soon as he became trapped within the walls of society and peace (indeed, is it possible to speak of 'man' before this tremendous event?). Encouraged by the tendency of natural selection to lead in the direction of the formation of homogeneous totalities and equilibrial unities, the molecular forces become captured by molar aggregations, resulting in the dominion of herds over packs (such as the blond beasts of legend) and the general victory of reactive forces on the level of both nature and culture. It is out of his confrontation with 'Darwinism' (what he took to be the Darwinian theory of evolution) that Nietzsche is forced to become a philosopher of culture as breeding and an advocate of artificial selection. Nietzsche locates within natural selection the prevalence of negative feedback. The struggle for existence does not reveal a continual growth in perfection through the perishing of the weaker creatures and the survival of the most robust and gifted, since in this struggle chance and accident serve the weak as well as, if not better than, the strong. The reality of natural selection has promoted among weaker forms of life the cultivation of cunning, patience, dissimulation, and mimicry in the attainment of the goal of self-preservation:[26] 'one nowhere finds any example of *unconscious selection*. The most

---

26 On the role of mimicry in evolution see Nietzsche 1982: section 26. In section 14 of 'Expeditions of an Untimely Man' in Nietzsche 1979b, Nietzsche argues that Darwin could not entertain the possibility that evolution might favour the survival of the weak because he left out of his account the mind or spirit (*Geist*). The weak dominate the strong though large numbers

disparate individuals unite with one another, the extremes are submerged in the mass. Everything competes to preserve its type' (1968: section 684; 1987, volume 13. 315ff.).[27] Nietzsche contends that every type has its limits beyond which there can be no evolution. He refuses to construe the victory of slave values and reactive forces as 'antibiological'; rather, this triumph has to be explained in terms of the interest life has in preserving the type 'man' through the 'method of the dominance of the weak' (Nietzsche 1968: section 864; 1987, volume 13: 369–70). The problem is ultimately one of 'economics', in which 'duration' as such (the longevity of species of forms of life) has no intrinsic value from the perspective of a transvaluation of values that places itself in the realm of Nietzschean 'justice', where justice is conceived as the 'highest representative of life itself (Nietzsche 1987, volume 11: 141) and as a 'panoramic power' that functions beyond the narrow perspectives of good and evil (Nietzsche 1987, volume 11: 188).

The molar aspect of Darwin's conception of natural selection is evident in the chapter on 'The Struggle of Existence' in *The Origin of Species*, where Darwin speaks of the necessity of a 'large stock of individuals of the same species, relatively to the numbers of its enemies' if the goal of preservation is to be

---

(majorities) and through cleverness. It is this insight into the role played by mimicry in evolution which informs his contention that the 'entire phenomenon of morality', including the Socratic virtues, has an animal origin, that is, the virtues are adaptive traits which have served to facilitate human survival. In 1982: section 26 he writes: 'animals learn to master themselves and alter their form, so that many, for example, adapt their colouring to the colouring of their surroundings . . . pretend to be dead or assume the forms and colours of another animal or of sand, lichen, fungus. . . . Thus the individual hides himself in the general concept "man", or in society, or adapts himself to princes, classes, parties, opinions of his time and place: and all the subtle ways we have of appearing fortunate, grateful, powerful, enamoured have their easily discoverable parallels in the animal world.' Deleuze and Guattari have argued that mimicry is a bad concept since it relies upon a logic of mimesis which fails to appreciate that evolution does not take place through imitation but through what they call 'transversal communications'. Hence they claim that the crocodile no more reproduces a tree trunk than a chameleon can be said to reproduce the colours of its surroundings. See the introduction on 'The Rhizome' to Deleuze and Guattari 1988.

27 There are a number of passages, like this one, which lend support to the view that Nietzsche had no direct familiarity with the work of Darwin, including *The Origin of Species*. Darwin explicitly discusses examples of 'unconscious selection' in the opening chapter of the book entitled 'Variation under Domestication' (see 93–5 especially). Another example is Nietzsche's erroneous view that 'there are no transitional forms', a view he expresses in Nietzsche 1987, volume 13: 315ff (1968: section 684), and a topic about which Darwin has many interesting things to say in *The Origin* (see 1985: 206ff. in particular).

attained.[28] The only writers to have picked up on the importance of the problem of selection — that natural selection works in the favour of large numbers — for Nietzsche's philosophy are Deleuze and Guattari, in the final chapter of *Anti-Oedipus*. The key insight, which is a crucial one for their own molecularization of thought and reality, is that large numbers, or aggregates (molar identities such as species, organisms, and complete whole persons), do not exist prior to a selective pressure that elicits singular lines from them; on the contrary, large numbers arise out of the pressure of selection which either regularizes singularities or eliminates them altogether. The 'herd instinct' and 'morality' are the outgrowth of the pressure of selection. Culture, Deleuze and Guattari argue, works in the same way, inventing through 'inscription' the large numbers in whose interests it is exerted. Only once molar formations have effected a unification and totalization of molecular forces through a statistical accumulation that operates in accordance with the laws of large numbers do the partial machinic objects of the molecular order appear as a *lack* (the slave revolt in morality succeeds, therefore, when it manages to seduce the masters into thinking that they lack morality and need the recognition of identity freely offered by the slaves).[29] For Deleuze and Guattari it is only when desire becomes welded to lack that it acquires collective and personal ends and intentions (Deleuze and Guattari 1972: 410; 1983: 342–3). At the point of molar takeover, we might say, desire no longer desires.[30] It has become a will *for* power in terms of a unitary subject that persists in its identity and that has internalized desire in terms of a representation, not a production.

Nietzsche clearly felt compelled to respond to Darwin and was baffled by the lack of any real challenge to his theory on the level of a radical cultural critique: 'The error of the school of Darwin becomes a problem to me: how can one be so blind as to see so badly at *this* point?' (Nietzsche 1968: section 685; 1987, volume

---

28 Darwin 1985: 122.

29 See Nietzsche 1994: I, section 13 on the slave revolt in morality and its invention of the fiction of the subject in terms of the separation of 'doer' and 'deed': 'This type of man *needs* to believe in an unbiased "subject" with freedom of choice, because he has an instinct of self-preservation and self-affirmation in which every lie is sanctified. The reason the subject . . . has been, until now, the best doctrine on earth, is perhaps because it facilitated the sublime self-deception whereby the majority of the dying, the weak and the oppressed of every kind could construe weakness as freedom, and their particular mode of existence as an *accomplishment*.'

30 The notions of 'large' and 'small' should not, however, lead one to think that the molecular/molar distinction functions solely in terms of issues of size and scale. Much more important is the matter of organization and composition. For a much fuller insight see Deleuze and Guattari 1988: 217.

13: 305). If the evolution of the species is guaranteed by the survival of the mediocre and the unexceptional, then, ironically, the species that Nietzsche writes for not only does not yet exist but is not, strictly speaking, even a 'species'. This openness and complete experimentation is part of Nietzsche's promise to write for the '*barbarians* of the twentieth century' (ibid.: section 868).[31] The degeneration and decay of the human can, however, make possible the conditions of a true *progressus* once a transhuman perspective on life is attained. In Nietzsche's economy and machine of life the amount of 'progress' is to be measured by how much has had to be sacrificed to it. Thus, 'the sacrifice of humanity *en masse* (*die Menschheit als Masse*) to the flourishing of one single *stronger* species of man (*Species Mensch*)' would, he challenges, be progress (Nietzsche 1994: II, section 12). It has been my intention to demonstrate in this chapter the extent to which, in a formulation of this kind, Nietzsche is speaking neither simply of a 'species' nor simply of 'man'.

Critical questions remain in this consideration of Nietzsche 'contra' Darwin. Let me address what I see as the most salient ones. It is by no means clear that Nietzsche's critique of Darwin is either coherent or convincing. In seeking an alternative conception of 'selection' and 'value' is Nietzsche not guilty of anthropomorphizing nature and life? This is an important issue which Nietzsche himself admirably treats in section 109 of *The Gay Science*, where he warns against anthropomorphizing nature. Let us beware, he argues, of treating the world as a 'living being' and the universe as an 'organism'; equally let us beware of treating the universe as a 'machine' (this is to do it too much honour, he suggests). 'Let us beware', he continues, of proposing that nature follows 'laws', such as a drive for self-preservation, or that the world is either purposeful or accidental. If you get rid of one of these notions, he suggests, you immediately cancel the force of the other. 'Death', he writes, is not opposed to life, is merely a type of what is dead, and a rare one at that. The world simply 'is' and none of our 'aesthetic anthropomorphisms' apply to it. He concludes by proposing a new task for thought, that of de-deifying nature so as 'to begin to "*naturalize*" (*vernaturlichen*) humanity in terms of a purely, newly discovered, newly redeemed nature' (Nietzsche 1974: 109).

Seen in the light of this trenchant passage, Nietzsche's outline of a theory of will-to-power as a rival to Darwinian mechanism looks decidedly awkward and

---

31 Nietzsche points out that a 'species' as such can only increase its powers of preservation through a process of molarization and the preponderance of average and lower types over the strong members and children of fortune. See Nietzsche 1968: section 685; 1987, volume 13: 303.

hugely problematic. If it is illegitmate to suggest that life and the universe manifest a desire or struggle for self-preservation, on what basis, and with what legitimacy, can Nietzsche claim that the fundamental essence of life is 'will-to-power'? Is this also not an anthropomorphism? The real illegitimacy in Nietzsche's 'philosophical biology' lies in his attempt in *Beyond Good and Evil* to employ the theory of will-to-power – here expressed as the view that 'exploitation' (*Ausbeutung*) belongs to the *essence* of what lives as 'basic organic function' – to legitimize an aristocratic radicalism (Nietzsche 1966: sections 257, 259).[32] This is as philosophically dubious and pernicious as the attempt of *social* Darwinism to derive social and political values from Darwin's original theory of natural selection.[33] It is curious that Nietzsche himself does not appear to recognize the predicament he is in. In *Twilight of the Idols*, for example, he is astute in recognizing crucial 'social' elements and historical determinations within Darwinian 'biological' theory. How is it possible, therefore, for Nietzsche to claim that his theory of 'will-to-power' is exclusively and solely a principle of so-called 'natural life'? With what legitimacy can he then read off from the text of nature a social and political philosophy, as he clearly does? In neglecting to attend to these critical questions Nietzsche has forgotten the earlier trenchant critique he had developed of David Strauss, in which he argued that any natural scientist or philosopher who sought to assert anything regarding the ethical and intellectual value of so-called laws of nature was guilty of an 'extreme anthropomorphism' that oversteps the 'bounds of the permitted' (Nietzsche 1983: 31).

Finally, it needs to be noted that the crucial section on historical method in the *Genealogy of Morality*, which in the *Nachlass* material of 1886–7 is labelled as 'contra Darwinism', is wholly ineffectual as a critique of Darwin's theory of natural selection. Nietzsche's position on functional indeterminacy, for example, is, in fact, a reformulation of a central insight of Darwin's theory.[34] Natural selection is, in fact, best construed not in terms of a 'senseless mechanism', but in terms of a complex 'mechanistic purposiveness' (a variation on the title of Roux's study on

---

32 'Every enhancement (*Erhöhung*) of the type "man" has so far been the work of an aristocratic society – and it will be so again and again.'

33 It should perhaps be noted that Spencer's own social and moral theory is not so much based on a social Darwinism, as is often supposed, but rather on a social *Lamarckism*. On this see Bowler 1992: 193.

34 This has been cogently pointed out by Dennett in his recent study, which I read after this chapter had gone through several drafts. See Dennett 1995b: 461ff., where he has some interesting things to say on the 'is/ought' problem in relation to Nietzsche and to socio-biology.

the struggle between the parts of an organism that so influenced Nietzsche). This aspect of the theory of natural selection has been captured well by one commentator in defining its operations – which involve a complex temporal dynamic – in terms of '*trans*generational changes in the properties, propensities, or capacities of organisms' (Burian 1992: 7). Natural selection operates mechanistically, or algorithmically, on functions, which means that the evolutionary history of an organ (an eye or a wing, for example), can only be explained by conversion of function and not by an analysis of its current usage or present 'purpose'. This means that on Darwin's model there cannot be such a thing as 'perfect adaptation'. Natural selection does not consciously or deliberately select traits and organs for their high adaptive value, but does so purely mechanistically. On this model notions of 'active' and 'reactive' would be understood not as expressions of an internal will-to-power intrinsic to life but rather as historically variable and mutable 'values' contingent upon the environmental circumstances which particular life-forms inhabit. This is not to deny the importance in evolution of endogenous powers of spontaneous self-organization; rather, in Darwinism the emphasis is on natural selection as the complex temporal factor, or 'agent', involved in real evolutionary change. This is an agent that does not require the notion of a 'subject' controlling or steering evolution; instead it refers to evolution as a complex machine made up of multiple component parts. Darwin was well aware of the danger of 'personifying nature', and sought to clarify his position by insisting that selection does not induce variability but simply implies the 'preservation' of variations that occur and that prove, in the wider context and timespan of evolution, 'beneficial' to the conditions of life beings operate in. This leads present-day champions of Darwin to argue that while indeed it is the case that not all features of organisms can be explained as adaptations, natural selection can be posited as the exclusive agent of any well-articulated notion of evolutionary change (Dennett 1995b: 277). Nietzsche departs from this natural selectionist perspective by attributing the evolution of organs in terms of a functional indeterminacy to the spontaneous and expansive force of 'will-to-power'. But what is to prevent us from regarding *this* conception, in contrast to the mechanism of natural selection, as enmeshed in a highly anthropomorphic model of purposive, active evolution or becoming? It would appear that Nietzsche, in upholding his 'contra Darwin' position, is fatally propelled back into that hangman's metaphysics – of intentionality, of willing, of teleological purposiveness – that he was so keen to deconstruct and overcome. It would seem, in a final irony, as if Darwinian natural selection is far closer to being a doctrine of the '*innocence* of becoming' than Nietzsche's own celebrated and complicated theory of life as 'will-to-power'. This is not to be so naive as to believe that Darwin's theory of evolution, as a theory about 'descent with modification', is completely shorn of metaphysical elements. The contrast does, however, I believe, serve to show the extent to which Nietzsche's own efforts to overcome metaphysics and to read nature free of deification — to de-deify it — need to be approached critically in terms of their problematic biophilosophical aspects.

In terms of the force (philosophical, political, biological, and historical) of the theory of 'will-to-power', this critical questioning would seem to indicate that the difficulties arise from Nietzsche's ambiguous deployment of it in terms of its transcendental and empirical (genealogical) aspects. As a principle of 'historical method' the will-to-power serves to explain how values and morals have arisen out of particular circumstances and conditions. It thus rules out the possibility of any abstract and ahistorical (agenealogical) law of selection. As a transcendental principle of 'life', it shows that functionally indeterminate change, through the dynamics of overpowering and self-overcoming, is a constitutive component of life's complex becoming. This means that even 'reactive' values can be shown to reveal an active dimension when they are grasped historically (Nietzsche 1968: 55). The problems arise when Nietzsche seeks to impose upon his reading of history and culture a normative conception of life — to assert that life is will-to-power can only be the beginning of a philosophy of life, not its entire, consummate definition — and to appraise signs of life in terms of their active or reactive conditioning, and then from such an appraisal advocate a new politics of breeding devoted to bringing about an end to history hitherto considered as the reign of chance and accident (Nietzsche 1968: section 1009; 1974: section 370). Nietzsche's genealogy of morals is most successful when it shows the extent to which a 'selection' of man can only be properly and fully developed when the past is taken into account in terms of its genealogical becoming. The transhuman only becomes meaningful and intelligible when it involves an affirmation of the totality and fatality of human becoming. Considered in these terms genealogy can then be understood as moving beyond the call for any simple-minded, arbitrarily conceived, and uncultivated test of selection. The previous two chapters have shown the extent to which the thought-experiment of eternal return can be construed as one that attempts to think beyond the 'beyond', that is, beyond judgement and beyond a selection that simply condemns and denies. It is at the point at which Nietzsche seeks to turn the experiment of return into a new 'contra' Darwinian model of selection, and to cultivate with it the selection of the strong and the weak 'once and for all' at a moment in history, that his thinking fails in its task.

## II

In the final part of this chapter I want to show how it might be possible to read Nietzsche's will-to-power – and a 'contra Darwinism' position – in non-anthropomorphic terms so as to be able to begin to map non-human becomings of life. To do this it is necessary to engage with Heidegger's reading of Nietzsche, in particular his examination of the vexed issue of Nietzsche's 'biologism'. Heidegger wishes to show the naivety of reducing Nietzsche's innermost thinking to something like the 'physiological' and the 'biological'. Such reductions might yield interesting insights into his thinking, but they fail to realize the extent to which Nietzsche is first and foremost a 'metaphysical' thinker; indeed, for Heidegger he is 'the last metaphysician'. This means for Heidegger that Nietzsche's project of thinking the will-to-power only makes sense and becomes meaningful when read in the context of the history of Occidental metaphysics. This is a history that has to be rendered 'historical' since it is not simply given. According to Heidegger, Nietzsche's philosophy brings to 'completion' the subjectivism and anthropomorphism of modern (Cartesian) metaphysics.

In his lectures on Nietzsche of the 1930s and 1940s Heidegger maintains that to remain on the level of biologism in one's reading of Nietzsche is to situate oneself solely in the 'foreground' of his thinking (Heidegger 1961, volume 1: 526–7; 1987: 47). To read Nietzsche in terms of a biologism, he says, is not to 'read' him at all. Why is Heidegger so hostile to a biologistically read Nietzsche? Is this not to ignore, and to underplay the significance of, the extent of Nietzsche's immersion in the literature and debates of modern biology? Heidegger believes that he has good reasons for resisting the temptation of a biologistic reading of Nietzsche's philosophy of will-to-power. The term 'biologism' can refer to two things. One is an unfounded extension and transfer of concepts from the field 'proper to living beings' to that of other beings; the other, and much more important, is the failure to recognize the metaphysical character of the propositions of the science of biology. 'Biologism is not so much the mere boundless degeneration of biological thinking', Heidegger writes, 'as it is total ignorance of the fact that biological thinking itself can only be grounded and decided in the metaphysical realm and can never justify itself scientifically' (Heidegger 1961, volume 1: 525; 1987: 45). Biology is metaphysical in the sense that it fails to inquire into its own conditions of possibility and grounds of construction. It simply does not reflect on itself and its historical determination by the tradition of metaphysics. Nietzsche's thought is metaphysical in that it seeks a determination of the beingness of beings in the ontology of will-to-power, but it never opens itself up to the question of being *qua* being, that is, it does not pose the question of being free of anthropomorphic reasoning but instead installs a subjectivism through the positing of the self-assertion and self-expansion of the will-to-power that speaks of a desire for constant self-overcoming on the part of 'life'. Heidegger notes that Nietzsche's emphasis on self-transcending enhancement contests the primacy accorded to self-preservation within Darwin's theory (1961, volume 1: 488; 1987: 15). However, he wishes to maintain that on a fundamental level there exists no essential difference between them since both Darwinism and Nietzscheanism are trapped within anthropomorphism. The predicament of anthropomorphism is more prevalent and explicit in Nietzsche's work on account of the fact that it makes the question of *value* central to its thinking on life. As Heidegger notes, for Nietzsche only 'what enhances life, and beings as a whole, has value – more precisely, *is* a value' (1961, volume 1: 488; 1987: 16). The paradox of Nietzsche's position is that the appeal to 'life' is not at all an appeal to its furtherance in terms of a natural selection, at least not on the level of 'man'. There appears in Nietzsche's depiction of it to be nothing 'natural' about life's enhancement and overcoming in the case of man (on the contrary, nature for Nietzsche, as we have seen, favours the weak and the ill-constituted), hence the need for the artificialization of his evolution through methods of discipline and breeding. It is in the context of his formulation of a model of 'artificial selection' that one can appreciate the force of Nietzsche's proclamation concerning the need to bring about an 'end' to the 'accident' and 'nonsense' of history (Nietzsche 1966: 203). As Heidegger notes, the 'consummate absoluteness' of the will-to-power in 'man' requires that 'the kind of humanity proper to such subjectivity will itself, and that it can will itself only by wilfully and consciously giving shape to itself as the breed of nihilistically inverted man' (1961, volume 2: 308; 1987: 230). Nietzsche's demand for the philosophical legislation of a new politics of breeding and cultivation, which owns up to the artificial character of its own artful techniques of selection, reveals its own revenge against time, against the time of evolution, exposing a fear and loathing of contingency and the reign of chance hitherto. Nietzsche's 'pain' stems from the sight of the extraordinary human being straying from its path and degenerating. Moreover, 'anyone who has the rare eye for the over-all danger that "man" himself *degenerates*; anyone who, like us, has recognized the monstrous fortuity (*ungeheuerliche Zufälligkeit*) that has so far had its way and play regarding the future of man . . . anyone who fathoms the calamity that lies concealed in the absurd artlessness (*Arglosigkeit*, or innocence and naivety) and blind confidence of "modern ideas" and even more in the whole Christian-European morality – suffers from an anxiety that is past all comparisons'

(Nietzsche 1966: section 203). Nietzsche responds, or reacts, to the dominion of Christian-European morality, however, by anthropomorphizing (moralizing) its rise and so takes (human) evolution to its selective extremes. Nietzsche's vision of the overhuman is thus haunted by the 'most painful memories' (*Erinnerung*) of the overhuman possibilities of the human past that were 'broken' and went to waste in the process of becoming.

Nietzsche by no means stands alone in thinking the time to be ripe for an explicit and deliberate breeding of man. Even arch-Darwinians such as Alfred Russel Wallace, the co-founder of the theory of natural selection, eventually recognized that the real problem facing Darwin's theory was that of the (artificial) nature of 'man'. 'We can anticipate the time', he wrote, 'when the earth will produce only cultivated plants and domestic animals', and when 'man's selection shall have supplanted natural selection' (Wallace 1891: 182). For Wallace man's evolution has been determined not by the laws of natural selection but by the artificial and technical character of his own making. Through the fabrication of tools, weapons, and clothing, man has succeeded in taking away from nature the power of 'slowly but permanently changing the external form and structure in accordance with changes in the external world, which she exercises over all other animals' (ibid.: 175). Humans so transform their nature through the art of weaponry, the division of labour, the anticipation of the future, the cultivation of moral, social, and sympathetic feelings, that the material which natural selection would act upon if it remained a power of 'selection' in their case is fully artificialized (ibid.: 179). Wallace is a curious example of the Darwinian species since the only way he could ultimately make sense of evolution – of the fact that, as he saw it, it has created beyond itself in the form of mankind – was by invoking a theory of 'mind' based on a notion of a driving force that operates in evolution and serves to promote complexity and progress, which he named 'will-power' (see ibid.: 213). However, this curious teleological Darwinism is neither peculiar to Wallace nor restricted to the nineteenth century. Julian Huxley, for example, in his postwar account of the theory of evolution, maintained that mankind can regard itself as the sole agent of further evolutionary change on the planet, and as one of the 'few possible instruments in the universe at large'. As the 'purely biological process' of evolution comes to an end and gives way to that of 'human progress', mankind finds itself fulfilling the role not of a shepherd of Being but rather of a 'business manager for the cosmic process of evolution' (Huxley 1953: 132).

According to Heidegger, the manner in which Nietzsche thinks the problem of man is separated from biologism by an 'abyss' (Heidegger 1961, volume 1: 567;

1987: 80). He is adamant that in the explicit or tacit characterization of his metaphysics as biologism 'nothing is being thought, and all Darwinistic thought processes must be extruded' (ibid.). Moreover, while conceding that Nietzsche does indeed view man and his world in terms of the perspective of the body and his animality, in no way, he contends, does Nietzsche decide that man simply 'originates' from the animal – or 'more precisely from the "ape"' - since he maintains that such a doctrine of origin is able to say little about man. Heidegger's emphasis here is obviously on the *Dasein* character of human existence, on the ways in which 'man confronts the *Da*, the openness and concealment of beings, in which he stands' (Heidegger 1961, volume 1: 55; 1987: 45). Heidegger wants to show that what makes man such an 'interesting' animal for Nietzsche is the fact that he is not 'firmly defined' (1961: 573; 1987: 86). Of course, it needs to be noted that Nietzsche approaches the question of man's 'difference' not in terms of *Dasein* but from the perspective of a genealogy of morals.

Heidegger's attempt to save Nietzsche from biologism does succeed in yielding important insights into the 'metaphysical' character of Nietzsche's 'political' thinking on the future of man. However, it exhausts neither the meaning of the doctrine of will-to-power nor the resources the notion offers for the articulation of a more complex biology. Before these possibilities are explored, it is necessary to say something about the anthropomorphic character of Darwin's own theory of evolution.

In its failure to read Darwin properly Heidegger's reading of Nietzsche misses something important, namely, the fact that Darwin's formulation of the general laws of natural selection assumes an anthropomorphic form, and exceeds it, as a result of the fact that it too is ultimately based on a technological model of evolution. It too finds artifice working in nature and in natural selection. The anthropomorphic character of Darwin's articulation of natural selection is evident in his description of it in terms of 'nature's power of selection'. The natural mechanism enjoys 'visual powers' that are 'always intently watching'. Natural selection is described as a 'scrutinizer' which rejects what is 'bad' and which 'preserves' and 'adds' what is 'good'. It works 'silently' and 'insensibly' 'whenever and whatever opportunity offers' in order to 'improve' each being in relation to its organic and inorganic conditions of life (Darwin 1985: 132–3). It is well known that Darwin began the *Origin of Species* with a discussion of animal breeders ('breeding' being a paramount technological notion) and sought to establish the laws of natural selection by making analogies with animal breeding and cultivation. Darwin chose the term 'natural selection' and stuck with it, adding 'survival of the fittest' to it at the insistence of Wallace, because he found it a term used repeatedly in works on breeding, in which it refers to an agency that operates outside the sphere of human control. He conceded that the term 'natural preservation' might be preferable since it eliminates some of the voluntarist overtones from the interpretation (see Young 1985: 95). The principal difference that he posits between the 'selection' of nature and that of artifice is one of 'time'. Although it does not work with a view to the future – it is not teleologically driven, in other words (or at least this is the claim of Darwinians) – natural selection is a power that is 'incessantly ready for action' and one that is 'immeasurably superior to man's feeble efforts'. It is so because it works insensibly, imperceptibly, and slowly over vast stretches of geological time without deliberate design. But it still functions technically (or, as Kant would say, 'intelligently' – purposively – if not 'designedly'). It is this point which is often lost sight of in accounts of Darwin (for an exception see Cornell 1984: 303–44). The products of nature are superior to those of man not because they are not produced technically, but rather because they take place during whole geological periods. By contrast, the time of human productions in breeding is short, and it is this factor which accounts for their inferior quality and 'design'. Nature's 'productions', Darwin writes, are far '"truer"', and they 'bear the stamp of far higher workmanship' (Darwin 1985: 133). Where humans simply select for their own immediate good, nature by contrast acts 'on the whole machinery of life' (ibid.: 132). However, as one commentator has pointed out, Darwin's appeal to time does not amount to a conclusive empirical argument. On the contrary, it rests strangely on an anthropomorphizing of the event of evolution in nature since it presupposes that the effects of nature correspond to what is producible by external environmental causes: 'time cannot even appear causally adequate for Darwin's mechanism without a reinterpretation of the natural phenomena that have been produced' (Cornell 1984: 333). In this respects, Darwin's account of the temporal mechanism of natural selection is decidedly utilitarian, even though it allows for complexity (functional indeterminacy) in the evolution of utility (see Darwin 1985: 227ff.).

It is not clear in Darwin's construal of natural selection whether he has read technology into nature, or whether he has revealed artifice to be the common factor in the technical evolution of both nature and human breeding. What is clear is that his view of natural selection is entirely conditioned by considerations of utility. It is this aspect above all others which makes his theory anthropomorphic (natural selection is very much a theory of the true, the good, and the beautiful). This suggests, I would contend, that there is needed a notion of artifice – of technics – applicable to both nature and art (or industry) that can allow for the excess of invention, an invention of technics that exceeds the claims of a 'naive' anthropomorphic model of evolution. The emphasis within modernity on the artificial character of the engineering of life is based on the discovery that not only mankind but the entirety of evolution is undetermined and open-ended. The deterritorialization of life is not a 'property' peculiar to mankind. Such an insight can serve to disable and disconcert the hubristic view which would posit both nature and mankind as acting in terms of some notion of an 'anthropomorphic engineering deity', in which developmental creation or evolution is based on notions of mastery and control (Cornell 1984: 312). The question is whether technics itself is to be treated as intrinsically and irredeemably anthropomorphic. What we need to think is a technics of excess, in which the inventiveness of evolution would be seen to exceed a utilitarian calculation, so making possible the becoming of more complex, non-linear, and 'machinic' models of evolution. While recognizing that any firm and fixed opposition between nature and technology, between art and artifice, is deeply problematic, one must be careful not to collapse the distinction too quickly or hastily. One can posit the evolution of life in terms of an originary technicity, but this should not be at the expense of serious historical labouring. The danger of neglecting the formation and deformation of these notions, of constructing a 'history' of them in some sense, is that of mystification and reification. This is a matter, however, that I want to leave open for exploration in the next two chapters.

A revealing and 'indecisive' moment in Heidegger's reading of Nietzsche takes place when he argues that although Nietzsche relates everything to 'life', he still does not think life 'biologically'. His reading then undergoes a twist in which the designations of 'human' and 'non-human', of 'biological' and 'extra-biological', cry out for a major revaluation and reconfiguration:

*Nietzsche thinks the 'biological', the essence of what is alive, in the direction of commanding and poetizing, of the perspectival and horizonal: in the direction of freedom.* He does *not* think the biological, that is, the essence of what is alive, biologically at all. So little is Nietzsche's thinking in danger of biologism that on the contrary he rather tends to interpret what is biological in the true and strict sense – the plant and animal – *non-biologically*, that is, *humanly*, pre-eminently in terms of the determinations of perspective, horizon, commanding, and poetizing. . . . Yet this verdict concerning Nietzsche's biologism would need a more comprehensive clarification and foundation.

(1961: 615; 1987: 122)

In this passage what is 'biological' and 'non-biological' and what is 'human' or 'non-human' are cast into question, and not only in regard to Nietzsche's speculations on life. For the most part, however, Heidegger finds Nietzsche stuck within the iron cage of anthropomorphism. However, for him this is not to hold a charge against Nietzsche but to open oneself up to his provocation. Heidegger's challenge is to insist that the emphasis within modernity on viewing life in terms of experiments in 'breeding', evident in Darwin and taken to extremes in Nietzsche, is the reflection not simply of an unconditioned biologism, but of the fact that modernity is fundamentally metaphysical, resting on a voluntarism, subjectivism, and anthropomorphism. The 'philosophy of life' found in Nietzsche thus reveals the 'truth' of modernity. It is for this reason that Heidegger insists (a) that while one cannot deny that Nietzsche extensively deploys in his writings biological language, the attribution to him of biologism 'presents the *main obstacle* to our penetrating to his fundamental thought' (1961, volume 1: 519 ; 1987: 41); and (b) that the charge of 'anthropomorphism' in no way constitutes a criticism of Nietzsche's thinking, or even that of modernity; on the contrary, it is deemed to provide us with genuine insight into the character of modernity and its discontents:

Anthropomorphism pertains to the essence of the history of the end of metaphysics. It determines indirectly the decision of the transition (*Überganges*), inasmuch as the transition brings about an 'over-coming' (*Überwindung*) of the *animal rationale* together with the *subiectum*. . . . This ruthless and extreme anthropomorphizing of the world tears away the last illusions of the modern fundamental metaphysical position; it takes the positing of man as *subiectum* seriously.

(1961, volume 1: 654; 1987: 155)

A move beyond the impasse of Heidegger's reading of Nietzsche — the impasse of anthropomorphism and animalism which then leads to a devotional mourning of the question of Being in Heidegger's later work, to waiting for a god — is possible by questioning the anthropocentric prejudices of Heidegger's own determination of biology as biologism. It is classic anthropocentrism on Heidegger's part to assume that the animal is firmly defined and closed in its rapport with the 'environment', that it is, as he maintains, 'poor in the world' (see Krell 1992: 121). It is also bad biology. The problem, I want to argue, is that Heidegger, along with the modern German tradition of thought that he is working within (notably Kant and Hegel), is trapped within an 'organismic' conception of life (and death), and so is unable to articulate the kind of 'machinic' conception of evolution that is necessary to free the logic of life from anthropocentric naivety and blindness.

The most extended treatment of the organism in Heidegger is to be found in his lecture course on biology in 1929–30. Heidegger's consideration of biology is motivated by what he perceives to be the need, already expressed in *Being and*

*Time*, for a distinction to be made between the animal's world and the world of the human. His investigation into the matter yields positions that are remarkably close to Hegel's emphasis on the structural unity of the organism in which movement or motility (what Heidegger calls 'captivation', *Benommenheit*) constitutes its essential 'nature' (for Hegel see the neglected section on 'Observing Reason' to do with species and genus in the *Phenomenology of Spirit*). In other words, it is not that the organism gets caught up in motility since this motility determines the being of the organism as such (the organism does not find itself 'in' movement). Heidegger then goes on to carve out a distinction between the human world and that of the animal by suggesting that the motility of the animal is not a 'historical' motility. Here the crucial matter concerns death: consonant with the analysis in *Being and Time* Heidegger maintains that whereas the death of the human is always a 'dying', the death of the animal is simply always that of a 'coming to an end' (Heidegger 1995: 267). His central claim in this chapter of the book, therefore, is that 'the animal is poor in world'.

Such a position, I would contend, is based on a phenomenological bias in favour of the molar and the organismic over the molecular and the machinic, which is decidedly anthropocentric. This bias can be seen to be already fully at work in Hegel's reflections on the organism, where the molecular (what is called 'singularity' or 'singleness', *Vereinzelung*) is represented in terms of a *descent* into particularity. Hegel thus speaks of the 'chaos of animals and plants, of rocks and metals' in which only undetermined universal evolves. Instead of finding an immeasurable wealth in this opening up of an immense field of organic and non-organic life, 'we' discover only 'the bounds of Nature and its own activity', the lack of intrinsic being and the rule of contingency. Such 'life', Hegel maintains, cannot even be described since it reveals only a 'rudimentary indeterminateness' (Hegel 1970a: 189; 1980: section 245). It is hardly surprising, therefore, that Hegel, like Heidegger after him, will restrict biology – organic nature – to the domain of the pre-historic which produces the process of becoming merely in terms of a contingent evolution (*zufällige Bewegung*). The molecular simply lacks history (*Geschichte*) conceived in terms of a self-determining formative becoming in which substance becomes subject (ibid.: section 295).

For Heidegger the animal is deficient in that it lacks *recognition* of itself. He is thus able to write that the bee is simply given over to the sun and the period of its flight without being able to grasp them as such, 'without being able to reflect upon them as something thus grasped' (Heidegger 1995: 247). Heidegger moves from anthropocentric prejudice to bad biology when he claims that the animal is withheld from the domain of 'possibility' since it is taken away and captivated by things. The animal is thus both 'taken away' from possibility and and 'unrelated to anything else' (ibid.). As we shall see, Nietzsche's speculations on the becoming of the animal contain a radical and far-reaching overturning of such anthropocentric naivety.

Heidegger's unfolding of the question of the organism is notable for its meticulous character. He is also attentive to the immense difficulties in delineating the machine and the organism. As he notes, once the question of the organism is posed this raises a whole series of problems to do with how we are to distinguish between material things, equipment, devices, machines, tools, organs, organisms, animalisms, etc. (ibid.: 213). He also critically considers the 'autopoietic' character of organismic life – that is, questions concerning self-production, self-regulation, and self-renewal – as a way of making the distinction between machine and organism. The move that Heidegger resists is that of being forced to choose between mechanism and vitalism. The former has no genuine notion of movement or becoming (here Heidegger is very close to Bergson), while the latter reduces the question of becoming to one of internal and mysterious causal factors, and as a result it simply eliminates the problem (ibid.: 223). Ultimately, Heidegger will seek to make a move 'beyond' biology by insisting on a more 'originary' structure of animality, such as the 'unity of animal captivation as a structural totality'. It is 'this fundamental conception of captivation' which should form 'the prior basis upon which any concrete biological question can first come to rest' (ibid.: 260).

What is most interesting about Heidegger's 'privileging' of captivation/motility is the way in which it challenges the Darwinian emphasis on evolution by adaptation. The problem in Darwinism is that it construes the animal as if it were something present at hand which then subsequently adapted itself to the world as if it too were also something present at hand. As a result it loses sight of the 'relational structure' between the animal and its environment. It fails to appreciate, therefore, that the 'environment' is an intrinsic feature of the becoming of the 'movement' of the organism (ibid.: 263–4). In this rethinking of the 'becoming' of life Heidegger's thinking comes close to Deleuze's emphasis on ethology, although Deleuze's analysis takes place on a much more molecular and machinic level, which renders the notion of the organism hugely problematic both philosophically and politically. A Deleuzian-inspired reading of the will-to-power would point to its attempt to conceive reality in dynamical and processual terms in which the emphasis is placed on acentred systems of forces, and in which 'evolution' is seen to take place in non-linear terms without fidelity to the distinctions of species and genus. What interests Deleuze most about complex evolution – a process he will call 'involution' – is the manner in which the becoming of the animal can be seen to be open-ended and subject to an interrelated process of deterritorialization and reterritorialization that cuts across organismic boundaries. Every territory encompasses or cuts across the territories of other species. The deterritorialization and reterritorialization that characterize the becoming of life gives expression to what Deleuze calls, following the work of the modern vitalist Jacob von Uexküll (whom Heidegger also describes as the most perceptive of contemporary biologists in the 1929–30 lecture course, 1995: 215), 'a melodic, polyphonic and contrapuntal conception of nature' (Deleuze and Guattari 1994: 185).[35] Examples of this musical character of complex evolution (which was of concern to Bergson in his attempts to map a creative model of evolution) include birdsong, the spider's

---

35 Von Uexküll (1864–1944) founded the Institute of Umwelt Research in Hamburg University in 1926. His approach to the 'invisible worlds' of animals is inspired by Kant, seeking to explore in highly novel ways the 'phenomenal world' of the animal (its 'self-world'), while 'nature' itself is invoked as the great noumenon which lies 'eternally beyond the reach of knowledge' (von Uexküll 1992: 390). One of the most radical aspects of his thinking is to seek to break down the distinction between machine and organism by insisting that the machines, devices, and technologies of animal and human life, such as spectacles, telescopes, microphones, lathes, and so on, are to be viewed as 'perceptual tools' and 'effector tools' that are a constitutive feature of the 'worlds' of living things. However, he does not accept the theory of those mechanists who claim that animals function as 'mere machines', since this is to neglect the dynamic and formative aspects of animal becomings, that is, the fact that there is 'acting' and 'perceiving' taking place. In other words, a machine cannot be understood without the input of the engineer who 'operates' the machine. The relation between machine and organism is examined at some length in the next chapter in relation to the 'machinism' advanced by Deleuze and Guattari. In *A Thousand Plateaus* Deleuze and Guattari stress the importance of those 'active, perceptive, and energetic characteristics' which serve to inform the 'associated milieus' of various animal worlds. The associated world of the tick, for example, is defined by 'its gravitational energy of falling, its olfactory characteristic of perceiving sweat, and its active characteristic of latching on: the tick climbs a branch and drops onto a passing mammal it has recognized by smell, then latches onto its skin. Active and perceptive characteristics are themselves something of a double pincer, a double articulation' (Deleuze and Guattari 1988: 51). As they point out, as associated milieu is closely related to 'organic form'. However, such a form is not a simple structure but, rather, a *structuration* so that an animal milieu such as the spider's web has to be seen as no less 'morphogenetic' than the so-called autonomous 'form of the organism' (ibid.). Deleuze and Guattari thus credit von Uexküll with the first attempt to elaborate a theory of 'transcodings' in which the components of a biological system act as 'melodies in counterpoint', each serving as a motif for another. This is to construct 'Nature as music' (ibid.: 314). Heidegger, by contrast, restricts von Uexküll's insights solely to the domain of the 'ecology' of the animal, maintaining that the animal is separated from man 'by an abyss' on account of the fact that it does not 'apprehend something *as* something' (1995: 264).

web, the shell of the mollusc which upon the death of the mollusc becomes the habitat of the hermit crab, and the tick (this latter example is taken, in fact, from von Uexküll; compare Heidegger 1995: 263–4 and Deleuze 1988a: 124–5, Deleuze and Guattari 1988: 257–8). For Deleuze this is to replace a teleological conception of nature with a melodic one in which the distinction between art and nature (natural technique) is revealed as an arbitrary one. It is the relationship of 'counterpoint', such as that of the shell of the dead mollusc and the hermit crab, which joins planes together and forms compounds of sensations and blocs, which then can be seen to be the principal influence on 'becomings' (Deleuze and Guattari 1994: 185).

In contrast to the anthropocentric privileging of the 'historical' that we find in Heidegger, which results in a denigration of the world of the animal, Deleuze conceives of becoming in 'geographical' terms, which allows him to conceive of the movements of evolution not in terms of organs, organisms, and species, and their functions, but in terms of the affective relationships between heterogeneous bodies. This is to define things not in terms of determinate organs and fixed functions, not in terms of either substance or subject, but in terms of lines of longitude and latitude. As Deleuze points out, a 'body' can be anything – an animal, a body of sounds, a mind or an idea, a social body or collective, and so on (Deleuze 1989: 127). Deleuze is attracted to the so-called 'mystical vitalism' of a biologist like von Uexküll because of the attempt to describe animal worlds in terms of overlapping territories in which becomings take place in terms of affects and capacities for affecting and being affected. Since an animal cannot know in advance what affects it is capable of, and neither can it know in advance which liaisons will be good or bad for it (Is this poison or food I am eating? Poison can be food!, etc.), this means that 'evolution' must assume the form of an 'experimentation' (ibid.: 125). This experimental evolution speaks, in fact, of an 'involution', that is, the dissolution of forms and the indeterminacy of functions, as well as the freeing of times and speeds (Deleuze and Guattari 1988: 267).

Deleuze and Guattari are adamant that 'none of these formulations carries the slightest risk of anthropomorphism' (Deleuze and Guattari 1988: 318). It is only in the counterpoint that the sonorous, rhythmic, or melodic character of life 'becomes'. Uexküll was similarly criticized in his day for putting forward a new romantic philosophy of nature that rested on a possible anthropomorphization of animal worlds (for him, however, it was solely a matter of empirical research). Deleuze and Guattari go much further than Uexküll in rendering the levelling of such a charge against their work inapplicable and based on a deep misconception of its import. Their conception of 'unformed matter', of an intense 'anorganic' or 'non-organic' life, and of non-human becomings, goes beyond traditional hylomorphic models of the creative relationship between form and matter, seeking to effect what they describe as a 'postromantic turning point' in thought by placing the emphasis on matter as *immanently* creative (ibid.: 343) (this is to think matter deterritorialized and molecularized). One is no longer dealing with metaphysical dichotomies, antinomies, or oppositions, such as form and matter, or subject and object. On the plane of immanence (nature, life, technics), there is no longer any subject or object. The organism has been unbound (compare Nietzsche: 'The organism must be studied in all its immorality', 1968: section 674). Indeed, the 'essential thing' is no longer questions of subject and object, and of form and matter, but of forces, densities, and intensities. In short, this is to arrive at 'the immense mechanosphere' beyond the opposition of nature and artifice (technics, assemblages) in which the 'cosmicization of forces' is harnessed (ibid.).

It is this plane of immanence, the domain of affects and capacities, that informs some of Nietzsche's most novel thinking on the life of the animal, in which the animal 'becomes' art and art 'becomes' animal. Here it becomes possible to unsettle Nietzsche's attempted humanization of the forces of evolution and locate in his thinking a tapping into the transversal character of life's functionally indeterminate and complex becoming. On this model of becoming the will-to-power is to be conceived neither as subject nor substance but as marking out the affective and pathic dimension of life in which transversality can be shown to take place. This is why it is is necessary, contra Heidegger, to take Nietzsche's biology seriously. It is not through a deconstruction of metaphysics that anthropo-centrism and -morphism is to be overcome, but only through an improper biology that is faithful to the complex, non-linear, and machinic/pathic character of 'evolution'.

For Nietzsche the Apollinian and the Dionysian – dream and intoxication – appear in man as if they were forces of nature, compelling him to undergo visions and orgiastic states. The former releases in us the artistic powers of vision, association, and poetry, while the latter releases in us those of gesture, passion, song, and dance. The passion of intoxication speaks of the attainment of an increase in power, where power is conceived as potential for further becoming. This is the strength or potential for 'new organs, new accomplishments, colours, and forms' (Nietzsche 1968: section 800; 1987, volume 13: 294–5). This is life lived as the 'grand style', and involves the 'becoming beautiful' of an enhanced will through the increased co-ordination and harmonization of strong desires. In other words, what this 'becoming' of the will-to-power speaks of is a becoming of the animal:

The sensations of space and time are altered: tremendous distances are surveyed and, as it were, for the first time apprehended; the extension of vision over greater masses and expanses; the refinement of organs for the apprehension of much that is extremely small and fleeting . . . 'intelligent' *sensuality* –; strength as suppleness and pleasure in movement, as dance, as levity and *presto*.

(ibid.)

Nietzsche insists that good artists are those who are full of surplus energy like 'powerful animals'. Indeed, he goes so far as to describe 'the aesthetic state' as one in which the transfiguration and fullness of existence amounts to a positive, affirmative response on the part of the animal which experiences excitation of all the spheres in which pleasurable states are attained and is able to 'blend' the delicate nuances of animal well-being and desire. The primary artistic force is precisely this animal potency, a kind of readiness for excitation and harmonization of heterogeneous forces. Art enhances and excites the muscles and the senses, increasing strength and inflaming desire through the operations, Nietzsche says, of a 'special memory' that works to penetrate the states of intoxication undergone (ibid.: section 809). The aesthetic state is thus attainable for Nietzsche only by natures capable of the 'bestowing and overflowing fullness of bodily vigour' (ibid.: section 801). This is why the sober, the world-weary, and the exhausted – such as modern *Menschen* – are unable to receive anything from art since they lack abundance. And those who cannot give, Nietzsche adds, also cannot receive. How the animal is elevated and man degraded in this consideration of art! The animal thus figures in Nietzsche's thinking as, extraordinarily and profoundly, the 'highest sign of power', namely, a life lived beyond violence and in terms of pure potential becoming (ibid.: section 803). The highest power is attained when life is lived beyond opposites without tension and domination, since obedience has simply become superfluous.

Art thus speaks of states of animal vigour, which, on the one hand, expresses an excess of physicality into a world of images and desires, and, on the other hand, provokes an excitation of the animal functions through the images and desires of intensified life (ibid.: section 802). Considered in this context of vigour and physicality, art can be conceived as no more and no less than the enhancement of life and a stimulant to it. Art does not simply resemble life or bear testimony to it; it incites and excites it, and expresses its real becoming. Art for Nietzsche is quite literally 'an organic function' (ibid.: section 808), a function of the transversal *becoming* of life. Here it matters little, Nietzsche insists, whether one is human or animal. In animals the experience of the transposition of values produces 'new weapons, pigments, colours, and forms, above all, new movements, new rhythms, new love calls and seductions. It is no different in the case of man' (ibid.). Art is the great bestowing virtue and is not the peculiar property of the animal 'man'. For Nietzsche it is modern man whose world is impoverished since he lacks the real need of art, desiring only the will to nothingness. The animal remains rich in the world, which is why we need to denigrate it out of a concealed spite and envy. What we are in danger of most is the perishing of 'truth' – namely, the truth of man, the truth of an exhausted and world-weary will that knows no longer how to affirm the beautiful illusions and form-shaping forces of artistic becoming.

In his essay on 'The End of Philosophy' of 1964 Heidegger speculated on the completion and consummation of philosophical modernity in the 'scientific attitude of socially active humanity' that finds expression in cybernetics, the science of control and communication in the animal and the machine, that privileges a 'technologistic' modelling of evolution (Heidegger 1972: 58). But again he too readily assimilates the thinking of this new science, and of physics and biology, into the alleged anthropomorphic project of Western metaphysics. It is to questions of the machine and of technology – and the related questions of evolution and of entropy – that I now want to turn attention in the next two chapters. My aim is to explore the 'transhuman' possibilities of a new 'machinic' paradigm that has emerged both within the new biology, such as autopoiesis and complexity theory, and within a neglected and marginalized strand of so-called continental philosophy, namely, the innovative work of Deleuze and Guattari.

# 5

# VIROID LIFE

## On machines, technics, and evolution

> The possibility of metaphor is disappearing in every sphere. This is an aspect of a general tendency . . . affecting all disciplines as they lose their specificity and partake of a process of contagion – a viral loss of determinacy which is the prime event of all the new events that assail us.
>
> (Baudrillard 1993: 7)

> *This* is evolution: the use of new technics. There is no such thing as 'biological evolution'. . . . The most terrible mistake of the nineteenth century: the abandonment of creation theory was based on a biological rather than a technical-artificial foundation. We are the children of the consequences of this mistake. Instead of technical practices, we inherited the master-race as our God-function. As good children of the master-race elders, 'we' believe (*green* as we are) that we can protect ourselves against fascism with 'nature' (instead of realizing that only technics can abolish fascism).
>
> (Theweleit 1992: 260)

Current continental philosophy contends that the human is necessarily bound up with an orginary technicity: technology is a constitutive prosthetic of the human animal, a dangerous supplement that enjoys an originary status.[1] That is, the origin of the 'human' as a species and a *Dasein* is radically aporetic since what lies at the

---

1 As early as 1907, however, Bergson was insisting that mechanical invention, as well as the technics of invention, had to be seen as constitutive of the kind of intelligent life-form we label 'human' since 'from the first' technics has been 'its essential feature' (Bergson 1983: 138). A powerful critique of twentieth-century schools of neo-Hegelian humanism for their forgetting of the techno-genesis of the human, such as Debord's situationism, has recently been evinced by Regis Debray, who argues that these 'essentialist ontologies', which fantasize about a final reconciliation of essence with human existence, are based on delusions of historical transparency and effective historical agency that stem not only from their erasure of technological determination, but from their disclaiming of the 'hard labour of real mediations', such as 'political mediation', conceived as a structuring instantiation of collective existence, and 'technical mediation', conceived as a structuring instantiation of the hominization process'. See Debray 1995: 136–7.

origin of the making of man is the *lack* – or excessiveness, depending on one's perspective – of origin. History appears to have reached the weird point where it is no longer possible to determine whether technology as an extended phenotype is an expression of the desire of our genes or a sign of nature's cultural conspiracy. As Lyotard has put it: the 'truth' of the time of technics is not a 'revelation' but a 'betrayal' (Lyotard 1991: 52). The task of the new technologies is to unblock the 'obstacle' constituted on earth by human life. However, this collapsing of bios and technos into each other is not only politically naive, producing a completely reified grand narrative of technology as the true agent and telos of natural and (in)human history, but also restricts technics to anthropos, binding history to anthropocentrism, and overlooking the simple fact that the genesis of the human is not only a technogenesis but equally, and just as importantly, a *bio-techno*genesis. The phenomenon of symbiosis provides the clearest demonstration of this thesis, presenting a genuine challenge to the entire Occidental tradition of speculative thought and suggesting the urgency of adopting a rhizomatic praxis. The image of the tree has dominated 'all of Western thought from botany to biology and anatomy, but also gnosiology, theology, ontology, all of philosophy . . . ' (Deleuze and Guattari 1988: 18). These new anthropocentric readings of history lead to the entirely spurious claim that with the coming of computers and the arrival of robot intelligence the planet is now entering a 'silicon age'. What this ignores is the fact that metallurgy has an ancient prehuman history, with human metalworking following the bacterial use of magnetite for internal compasses by almost three thousand million years (Margulis and Sagan 1995: 194). Moreover, symbiosis has a filthy lesson to teach us: the human is an integrated colony of amoeboid beings, just as these amoeboid beings (protoctists) are integrated colonies of bacteria. Like it or not, our origins are in *slime*. Biologists have established that the nucleated cell of eukaryotic life evolved by acquisition, not of inherited characteristics à la Lamarck's model of evolution, but of inherited bacterial symbionts, in which 'amid cell gorgings and aborted invasions, merged beings that infected one another were reinvigorated by the incorporation of their permanent "disease"' (ibid.: 90).

The attempt to develop a general theory of evolutionary systems is entirely dependent on the kinds of problems being set up. To consider the nature of species, organisms, and evolution itself, independently of the cognitive framing and mapping of theoretical inquiry – and all theory needs to be understood as a praxis (Reuleaux 1876/1963: introduction) – is to produce nothing but reification. As Bergson pointed out in his thinking of 'creative evolution' in 1907, our science is contingent, relatively both to the variables it selects and to the order in which is successively stages problems (Bergson 1983: 219). Conceptions of 'evolution' only make sense in relation to time-scales within which they are framed. For example, from the perspective of 'universal evolution' species and organisms cannot be treated as fixed or static points of reference or interpreted as the end-points of life's novel activity of invention. The boundaries between species are constantly shifting, mobile, and porous, while geographical landscapes harbour only extrinsic harmonies of an order of ecology in which any equilibrium between populations can only be regarded as temporary. Indeed, on a certain model one could legitimately claim that the 'success' of a species is to be measured by the speed at which it evolves itself out of existence. Deleuze and Guattari's most radical gesture is to suggest that there has never been purely 'biological' evolution, since 'evolution' is technics, nothing but technics: 'There is no biosphere or noosphere, but everywhere the same Mechanosphere' (Deleuze and Guattari 1980: 89; 1988: 69).[2] All systems from the 'biological' to the 'social' and economic are made up of machinic assemblages, complex foldings, and movements of deterritorialization that serve to cut across and derange their stratification. This explains why for them 'pragmatics' (or 'schizoanalysis') becomes the fundamental element upon which everything else depends. Deleuze and Guattari are most keenly interested in the differential rhythms and affective intensities of evolution, the 'invisible' becomings of non-organic life that can only be effectively navigated and mapped when situated on the plane of abstract machines which consists of non-formed matters and non-formal functions (ibid.: 637; 511). In this chapter I want to show how Deleuze and Guattari's mapping of the 'creativity' of machinic life provides a fundamental challenge to both the natural bent of the intellect and to major scientific habits.

---

2 The term 'noosphere' was coined by Bergson's successor at the Collège de France, Edouard Le Roy. It was taken up by Teilhard de Chardin, palaeontologist and priest, as a conscious layer of life superimposed upon the biosphere, and represents the fundamental component in the evolution of the 'human phylum'. See de Chardin 1965: 211ff. In the work of the Russian scientist Vladimir Vernadsky the 'noosphere' is used to account for the emergence of organized matter in terms of an emergent symbiosis between living matter and human technology. For Vernadsky the plastics and metals of industry stem from an ancient life process that co-opts new materials for a surface geological flow that becomes ever more rapid. See Vernadksy 1945: 1–12. For a contemporary version of his position see Margulis and Sagan 1995, who approach 'life' as an autopoietic, photosynthetic planetary phenomenon, and who invoke mystically a 'superhumanity' to account for the 'sentient symphony' of life made up of human beings, transport systems from the energetic to the informational, global markets, and so on (189–95). This 'superhumanity' ingests not only food but also coal, iron, oil, and silicon.

In *Difference and Repetition* Deleuze deploys biological thinking in the service of a philosophy of internal difference. He approaches 'evolution' on the level of a philosophical embryology ('the world is an egg'), insisting that 'Evolution does not take place in the open air' since 'only the involuted evolves' (Deleuze 1994: 118). (Kant speaks of the need to move from a theory of 'evolution' to one of 'involution' in a discussion of 'individual' and 'generic' conceptions of preformationism, while also drawing on a notion of 'virtuality', in 1974/1982: section 81.) Embryology demonstrates, for example, that there are vital movements and torsions that only the embryo is able to sustain, and which would tear apart an adult. This means that there are 'spatio-temporal dynamisms' which can only be experienced at the borders of the liveable: 'Something "passes" between the borders', he writes, 'events explode, phenomena flash, like thunder and lightning' (ibid.). Moreover, in this work Deleuze is already articulating the kind of 'molecular Darwinism' that characterizes Deleuze and Guattari's joint work and their utilization of population thinking in modern biology with its attack on typological essentialism. Deleuze does not read natural selection as a theory about the evolution of 'species'; rather, for him, what is primary is the play of the individual and processes of individuation, in relation to which the evolution of species is only a transcendental 'illusion' (ibid.: 250).[3] In *A Thousand Plateaus* Deleuze and Guattari argue that neo-Darwinism's emphasis on populations over types, and differential rates and relations over degrees, makes for a vital contribution to an understanding of biology as nomadology, steering the logic of life in the direction of a *science of multiplicities*. In the former work Deleuze will reverse the relationship between ontogeny and phylogeny as classically depicted in biological thought, such as Haeckel's famous biogenetic law, insisting that it is the case not that ontogeny simply recapitulates phylogeny but rather that it *creates* it;[4] while in the latter work Deleuze and Guattari make the identical point, speaking of the relationship between embryogenesis and phylogenesis as one that involves the virtual becoming of a creative 'universal

---

3 For Darwin on the importance of 'individual differences' in selection see Darwin (1985: 101ff.). On neo-Darwinism see Mayr (1991), who writes that 'the discovery of the importance of the individual became the cornerstone of Darwin's theory of natural selection' (42); on the move to population genetics within evolutionary theory that characterizes the modern synthesis see Eldredge (1995: 10–30).

4 The inversion of Haeckel's law dates back to work done in the 1920s. For further information see Wolpert (1991: 185), who argues that the 'repetition' taking place in ontogeny is not that of phylogeny but simply of other ontogeny, that is: 'some embryonic features of ancestors are present in embryonic development'. For a comprehensive historical introduction to the problematic see Gould (1977).

evolution': 'the embryo', they write, 'does not testify to an absolute form preestablished in a closed milieu; rather, the phylogenesis of populations has at its disposal, in an open milieu, an entire range of relative forms to select from, none of which is preestablished' (Deleuze and Guattari 1988: 48). One can only insist on the irreducibility of the forms of folding.[5] The antinomies of modern biological thought – individual/species, selector/selectee, organism/environment, variation/selection, and so on – are fully caught up in the antinomies of bourgeois thought and are at play in Deleuze's 'Bergsonism'. In *Difference and Repetition*, I would argue, Deleuze too readily assimilates natural selection into the project of thinking difference and repetition at the level of philosophical embryology and morphology. He claims that selection works in favour of guaranteeing the survival of the most divergent (Deleuze 1994: 248). In this work Deleuze conveniently ignores Nietzsche's critique of Darwin where the critical focus is on the reified notion of 'fitness'. On Nietzsche's understanding, natural selection may well be a machine of evolution, but it functions in accordance with a specific entropic principle, namely, 'survival of the fittest' (see Nietzsche 1968: sections 684 and 685).[6] It can

---

5 Deleuze suggests that the double helix of DNA should be treated in terms of the operations of the 'superfold'. See Deleuze 1988b: 132.

6 Nietzsche felt isolated in his 'contra Darwin' position, in which 'the error of the school of Darwin' became such a 'profound problem' to him. How could one see nature 'so badly'? he asks. In short, Nietzsche is maintaining that Darwinism is a biological theory shot through with assumptions of society and morality. 'I rebel against the translation of reality into a morality', he writes (1968: 685), while insisting that Malthus is not nature (Nietzsche 1979b: 75). Ultimately, the *Auseinandersetzung* becomes for Nietzsche a matter of *transvaluation* of so-called strictly 'biological' values. See, for example, the 'critical' denouement to essay 1 of *On the Genealogy of Morality*. The phrase 'survival of the fittest' appeared in the fifth edition of the *Origin of Species*. It is associated with the work of Herbert Spencer and was adopted by Darwin at the insistence of Alfred Russel Wallace, who considered it a better description of evolution than the misleading 'natural selection', with its anthropomorphic personification of nature. Throughout the *Origin* Darwin speaks of the 'economy' and 'polity' of nature, and there are places where it becomes undecidable whether he is talking of 'nature' or of industrial society. Marx, for one, saw 'civil society', the Hobbesian *bellum omnium contra omnes*, as playing a major role in Darwin's model of 'nature'. One should also note the extent to which a philosophy of 'good and evil' figures in his description of the animal kingdom, and at times he comes dangerously close to reading the text of nature through the lens of an anthropomorphic sentimentalism. The best example of this is his claim that natural selection acts solely for the good of each being, endeavouring to strike a 'fair balance' between the good and evil caused by each organ. It is because selection is not perfect, however, that it is possible to explain a bizarre phenomenon such as the sting of the wasp which when used in attack cannot be withdrawn, so resulting in the wasp's own death through the ripping out of its viscera (Darwin 1985: 230).

thus not be so easily regarded, as it is in Deleuze, as a positive power of differenciation (a 'differenciator of difference'). Indeed, the term 'natural selection' is something of a misnomer since nature does not at all *select*; rather, it operates as an arbitrary force of *extermination*, resulting in the differential loss of differently constituted individuals. Nature does not so much select the fittest as exterminate the ill-fitted, adapting forms of life to the environment slowly and imperceptibly in an entirely mechanistic, algorithmic fashion. Thus, we find in *Difference and Repetition* major tensions emanating from the uneasy alliance Deleuze makes between the competing claims of 'complexity' and 'selection'. In the work with Guattari primacy is clearly given to 'involution' over 'evolution' and to modes of deterritorialization, that is, to the power of endogeny over that of exogeny: 'The more interior milieus an organism has . . . assuring its autonomy and bringing it into a set of aleatory relations with the exterior, the more deterritorialized it is' (Deleuze and Guattari 1988: 53–4). It is precisely the 'creative' reality of deterritorialization that Deleuze was articulating in *Difference and Repetition* in such novel terms and that serves to link the work up with current complexity theory in philosophical biology. For example, in *Difference and Repetition*, the 'formula' for 'evolution' (Deleuze has the word in scare quotes) is given as: 'the more complex a system, the more the *values peculiar to implication* appear within it' (Deleuze 1994: 255).[7] It is the 'centres of envelopment' that function as both a 'judgement' of the complexity of any given system and as the differenciator of difference. For example, we know today that the difference between humans and chimpanzees consists not in their genetic difference, which is minimal anyhow, but in the spatial organization and folding of their cells. Such an insight counters the reductionism of those biologists who place the emphasis on the determination of genes and so erase the trace of genetic indetermination. It is precisely the endogenous powers of spatio-temporal rhythms and intensities that Deleuze is privileging in *Difference and Repetition* as a model of 'evolution' over the strictly exogenous mechanism of selection. This thesis is now supported by leading complexity theorists such as Stuart Kauffman who argue that many of the highly ordered features of ontogeny are not to be regarded as the achievements of selection, but rather as the self-organized behaviours of complex genetic regulatory systems. Moreover, the properties of

---

7 Compare Simondon (1992: 305), whose text on the genesis of the individual, published in France in 1964, exerted a major influence on Deleuze's philosophy of internal difference: 'The living being resolves its problems not only by adapting itself, which is to say, by modifying its relationship to its milieu . . . but by modifying itself through the invention of new internal structures and its complete self-insertion into the axiomatic of organic problems.'

self-organization are so deeply immanent in these complex networks that *'selection cannot avoid that order'* (Kauffman 1993: xvii). On this model selection can in no way be regarded as the sole or primary generator of evolutionary order and composition. When in *Difference and Repetition* Deleuze calls for a 'kinematics of the egg', insisting that what is seminal in embryology is not the division of an egg into parts, but rather the morphogenetic movements, such as the 'augmentation of free surfaces, stretching of cellular layers, invagination by folding', and in which 'transport is Dionysian, divine, and delirious, before it is local transfer' (Deleuze 1994: 214), he is anticipating the turn to questions of embryogenesis and morphogenesis that characterizes current attempts amongst biologists to move beyond the hegemonic neo-Darwinian paradigm. Here the focus is on the production of spatial patterns that are explicable not in terms of the nature of the components involved, such as cells, but rather in terms of the way the molecules interact in time and in space (their relational order). Deleuze goes further in insisting that these processes involve the creation of a space and a time that are *peculiar* to that which is actualized. On this model of a philosophical embryology, time and space are no longer treated simply as universal *a priori* forms of sensible intuition, but rather are understood as components in the *production* of variation and difference. As one eminent neuroscientist who works on embryology has recently put it: 'Diversity must inevitably result from the *dynamic* nature of topobiological events' (Edelman 1994: 64). In short, what Deleuze does not appear to appreciate is that his thinking of difference and repetition, in terms of a thinking of the creation of the new and the different, along the lines of a philosophical embryology and morphology, presents a fundamental challenge to some of the core tenets of the neo-Darwinian synthesis.[8]

---

8 It is interesting to note that the major figure who appears after the cursory treatment of Darwin in *Difference and Repetition* is von Baer. It is the ideas of von Baer that Deleuze utilizes to maintain the highest generalities of life point beyond species and genus in the direction of individual and pre-individual singularities (1994: 249–50). On von Baer's understanding of development as a process of 'individualization' and 'differentiation of the unique' see Gould (1977: 52–9). It is clear that Darwin was unable to take on board the full challenge of von Baer's stress on ontogeny over phylogeny since it would have fundamentally altered his theory of natural selection. At the time of Darwin's writing of the theory of descent embryology was undergoing a significant transformation in its own 'evolution', away from *Naturphilosophie* in the direction of modern epigenetic theory. Darwin's position on embryogenesis – that embryos mirror the history of the race by being similar to adult, though extinct, forms – is the one that Haeckel was later to advance in his biogenetic law, and which stands discredited today. For further insight into this crucial matter see Oppenheimer 1959 and, more recently, Lovtrup 1987: 150–65, who goes so far as to contend that to choose Darwin is to be contra von Baer and vice versa. Deleuze's work is unique

A strand of contemporary biology has sought to move away from the genetic reductionism of ultra-Darwinism — best typified in Richard Dawkins's Schopenhauerean-styled theory of the selfish gene — insisting that questions of form cannot be reduced to those of simple adaptation, since the organism enjoys an integrity and autonomy of its own and has to be treated as a self-organizing structural and functional unity (see Goodwin 1995). But this move from genetic reductionism to organismic holism in complexity theory is by no means a straightforwardly progressive move. The 'organism' is always extracted from the flows, intensities, and pre-vital singularities of pre-stratified, non-organic life in order to produce, through techniques of normalization, hierarchization, and organization, a disciplined body, a controlled subject and a subject 'of' control. The organized body of both biology and sociology is an invention of these techniques of capture and control. It is the judgement of theos: 'You will be organized, you will be an organism, you will articulate your body — otherwise you're just depraved.' (Deleuze and Guattari 1988: 159). This explains why it becomes necessary to think about machines, about the reality of parts and wholes, about machinic modes of 'evolution', and about a 'machinic surplus-value' that produces an excess which cannot be located within a 'subject' since it lies *outside*.

Evolution, like the egg, does not take place in the open air: invention in evolution takes place not simply in terms of a process of complexification, say from a less to a more differentiated state, but rather in terms of a process of what Deleuze and Guattari call 'creative involution'. The word 'involution' should not be confused, as it is in Freud, for example, with regression, but suggests the emergence of a symbiotic field that allows assignable relations between disparate things to come into play. It is this 'block of becoming' that represents the 'transversal communication' between heterogeneous populations, making becoming a rhizome and not a classificatory or genealogical

---

in its suggestion that the work of Darwin and his so-called 'pre-Darwinian' predecessors, such as Cuvier, Geoffroy Saint-Hilaire, and von Baer, can be held together to provide a more complicated conception of 'evolution', one that is not evolutionist. See Deleuze 1988b: 129, where it is argued that the tendency to diverge is produced through endogenous processes of folding. The same shortcoming which contemporary embryologists, such as Lovtrup, find in Darwin, has also been identifed as a major weakness of the modern synthesis (neo-Darwinism). One commentator, for example, has argued that the modern synthesis is unable to generate a theory of ontogeny since it assumes individuality as a basal assumption (Buss 1987: 25). On the significance of von Baer compare in this regard Heidegger, who argues that the significance on his work was impeded and finally buried by Darwinism (1995: 260).

tree.[9] The 'tree' model of evolution is highly ambiguous, being both genealogical (the tree of the family man) and the tree of non-human nature that shows no particular concern for mankind. As one commentator has also noted, it is both an oppressive colonial image and an organic image (Beer 1986: 239). Becoming is to be conceived neither in terms of a correspondence between relations or identities nor in terms of progression or regression along a series. This is to posit evolutionism as linearism (Deleuze and Guattari 1980: 292; 1988: 238–9). It thus becomes necessary to think of a reality that is specific to 'becoming'.

---

9 Evolutionary trees were introduced as the standard iconography for phylogeny in the 1860s by Ernst Haeckel, and have served to buttress an anthropocentric view of life, based on the ladder of progress and a cone of increasing diversity, in which evolution gains a 'moral' meaning as it slowly but surely becomes imbued with consciousness after a history of upward striving and vertical perfection that culminates in 'man'. Stephen Jay Gould has sought to expose the anthropocentric conceits of this tree model of life in his magisterial study of the Burgess Shale dating from the Cambrian period. See Gould 1990: 240ff., especially 263–7.

The word 'involution' to account for distinctive features of 'evolution' is used prominently by de Chardin in his *The Phenomenon of Man* (first published in France in 1955): 'Regarded along its axis of complexity, the universe is, both on the whole and at each of its points, in a continual tension of organic doubling-back upon itself, and thus of interiorization' (de Chardin 1965: 330). De Chardin employs orthogenesis to support a theory of evolution that gives, in quasi-Hegelian fashion, primacy to self-consciousness and spirit (see ibid.: 176). Thus, for him the physico-chemical process of organic involution – an involution of 'complexity' – is 'experimentally bound up with a correlative increase in interiorization, that is to say in the psyche or consciousness' (ibid.: 329). In this schema of, supposedly, 'biological' evolution, in which 'cosmic involution becomes the key perspective through which to grasp its essential dynamic, consciousness is co-extensive with the universe, and the universe 'rests in equilibrium and consistency, in the form of thought, on a supreme pole of interiorization' (ibid.: 338). The 'great human machine' can only 'work', and must work, in terms of the production of 'a super-abundance of mind' (ibid.: 282). Deleuze and Guattari's contention that there is no 'noosphere' or 'biosphere', only the 'mechanosphere', must be seen as being, in part, directed at the overly spiritualist and cosmicist interpretation of 'evolution' and 'involution' advocated by de Chardin. Deleuze and Guattari's conception of evolution as 'creative involution' is radically different from that found in the likes of de Chardin in that it does not in any way privilege mankind as the apex of evolutionary life (in spite of his utilization of involution de Chardin is still reliant on a 'tree' model of life to support his elevation of consciousness and spirit). 'Man' for them is the molar category par excellence; the 'human being' only becomes an interesting phenomenon when it is conceived machinically. In his 1960s study of Bergson, Deleuze cites approvingly Bergson's idea that, in mankind, nature has created a machine that transcends mere machinism: the human condition is to go 'beyond' its condition. 'Man' is capable of scrambing the planes of nature 'in order to finally express naturing Nature' (Deleuze 1991: 107). See Bergson 1983: 264–5.

The important role played by symbiosis in the history of technology, in which previously disjoint and unconnected technologies merge, is widely recognized (Sahal 1981). In biology, however, symbiosis has had a curiously awkward history which reveals much about the anthropocentric determination of the subject and about hominid fears of contamination. It has played, and continues to play, a subversive role in biology since it challenges the boundaries of the organism.[10] Indeed, it has been argued by one commentator that it was not until 1950, when geneticists extended their field of study to micro-organisms, that biology recognized that there were means other than sex for transmitting genes, such as infections and symbiotic complexes. Prior to this it was the institutionalized boundaries of the life sciences themselves, such as zoology, botany, bacteriology, virology, genetics, pathology, etc., which prevented the synthetic studies of symbiosis from being properly assessed (Sapp 1994: 208–9). The importance of symbiotic bacteria in the 'origin of species' – repeated bacterial symbioses result in the emergence of new genes – is now widely appreciated, but must ultimately be disturbing to our anthropocentric claims upon life (and death). The detailed structure of the organelles in eukaryotic cells, such as the mitochondrian, and the composition of the DNA in those organelles show that crucial evolutionary processes were not the result of slow accumulation of random changes (mutations) in the genes of ancestral prokaryotic cells. Rather, it seems highly probable that they were the result of intracellular symbiosis in which some cells incorporated into their own cell contents partner cells of another kind that had different metabolic abilities. Over time the genetic and metabolic organizations of host and guest cells fused to the point where it became impossible to distinguish where one cell began and another finished. The strength of this hypothesis lies in the fact that it offers the most convincing explanation as to why both mitochondria and chloroplasts contain their own ribosomes and DNA. The case of multi-cellular organisms is now part of the 'orthodoxy' of contemporary biology, but there are other more disturbing examples of the transversal character of genetic lineages such as viruses ('poisons'), for example. Modern biology has identified not only 'bacteroids' as playing a crucial role as symbionts in certain metabolic processes,

---

10 The seminal text is Margulis 1970. See also Margulis 1981 and Jacob 1974: 311–12. Margulis has used her work on symbiosis to challenge the view that natural selection provides the prime explanation of evolutionary life. The fossil record and other evidence suggest that evolution from bacterial to nucleated cellular life did not occur by random mutation alone, but rather through ancient motility symbiosis. For an excellent introduction to the extensive use of models of symbiosis to account for a wide range of evolutionary phenomena see the essays in Margulis and Fester 1991.

but also symbiotic 'viroids'. Indeed, a leading researcher in the field in the 1940s postulated the idea of a distinct kingdom for such viroids, the Archetista, arguing that within evolution they have acted, on account of their molecular composition, as highly adaptable intracellular symbionts, so supplying from 'amoeba to man' a virtual 'reservoir' for viruses in the course of evolution (Sapp 1994: 151–2). More recently, Dennett has referred to these pioneers of evolution as 'macros', which is the name given by computer programmers to cobbled-together fragments of coded instructions that perform particular tasks, in order to draw attention to the similarities between the machinery of 'natural' viruses and 'artificial' viruses such as computer viruses. Both are 'bits of *program* or *algorithm*, bare, minimal, self-reproducing mechanisms' (Dennett 1995b: 156–7). Standing as they do at the border between the 'living' and the non-living', and *virtually real*, viruses serve to challenge almost every dogmatic tenet in our thinking about the logic of life, defying any tidy division of the physical, such as we find in Kant, for example, into organisms, the inorganic, and engineered artifacts (for further insight see Eigen 1992: 101–6). Creative evolution on earth would have been impossible without the intervention of the genetic engineering that characterizes viroid life.

The scientific work that was carried out on genetic engineering in the 1950s, which today provides the basis for recombinant DNA technology, derived from observations of the mechanisms of recombination in bacteria. The emphasis was on 'transformations', such as 'conjugation' and 'transduction', which involve the transfer of genetic material from one cell to another by a virus (Sapp 1994: 158). This research, however, must necessarily lead to a fundamental revision of dominant models of evolution. If it is the case that viroid life is one of the key means by which the transferral of genetic information has taken place, then it is necessary to entertain the idea that there are cases where this transfer of information passes from more highly evolved species to ones that are less evolved or which were the progenitors of the more evolved species, with the result that reticular schemas would have to be substituted for the tree schemas that dominate almost all thinking about the logic of life. Transversal communications between different lines serve to 'scramble the genealogical trees' (Deleuze and Guattari 1988: 11). The existence of complex phenotypic traits in organisms has long been recognized as a problem for Darwin's theory of evolution by natural selection, but recent research in biology seeks to show that the paradigm of symbiosis can be used to explain how novel phenotypic traits can come about through the association of organisms of different species. One example given of a symbiotic phenotypic trait, in which these traits only exist by virtue of the association of the partners, is the leghemoglobin protein of the root nodules of legumes, which are coded in part by the *Rhizobium* genome and in part by the leguminous host (Law 1991: 58). The boundaries which ensure the evolution of separate identities begin to collapse and a machinic mode of evolution comes into play. This is a perfect illustration of the rhizomatic evolutionary schema proposed by Deleuze and Guattari, who themselves supply the example of the type C virus with its double connection to baboon DNA and and that of certain domestic cats. Here we have taking place an '*aparallel evolution*' in which there is neither imitation nor resemblance. The becoming-baboon which characterizes the cat does not mean that the cat is imitating the baboon, but rather denotes a rhizomatic becoming which operates in the zone of the heterogeneous (a zone of invention as opposed to imitation) and the connection of already differentiated lines: 'We form a rhizome with our viruses, or rather our viruses cause us to form a rhizome with other animals' (Deleuze and Guattari 1988: 10). Or: *the organism unbound*. Taking machines seriously requires that the autonomy of the machine is de-reified, along with a linear-evolutionary model of machine development, in favour of an analysis of complex machinic becomings.

Like philosophy, the field of biology is full of born Platonists, but symbiosis shows that the delineation of 'organic units', such as genes, plasmids, cells, organisms, and genomes, is a tool of a certain mode of investigation, not at all an absolute or ideal model. It challenges notions of pure autonomous entities and unities, since it functions through assemblages (multiplicities made up of heterogeneous terms) that operate in terms of alliances and not filiations (that is, not successions or lines of descent). The only unity within an assemblage is that of a plural functioning, a symbiosis or 'sympathy' (on the importance of sympathetic relationships in creative evolution see Bergson 1983: 173–4). An animal, for example, can be defined just as productively in terms of the assemblages into which it enters (man–animal symbiosis, animal–animal symbiosis, plant–animal symbiosis) as it can by standard biological classification in terms of genus, species, organs, and so on. When viewed in terms of symbioses a clear establishment of distinct kingdoms is rendered problematic and what becomes important is a 'machinic' phylogenetic becoming. Symbiosis also challenges the notion of informationally closed systems, and corresponds to the function of the idea of the 'rhizome' in the work of Deleuze and Guattari, in which evolution is removed from the limits imposed by filiation. A rhizome operates as an open system, both entropically and informationally, designating, in the words of one commentator, 'a constructive feedback loop between independent information lineages', whether they be cultural, linguistic, or scientific lineages or biological germ lines (Eardley 1995) (an essential part of the history of symbiosis will be to formulate germs not simply as 'disease-causing' but as 'life-giving' entities). As opposed to conventional phyletic lineages, rhizomatic lineages serve to demonstrate the extent to which exclusively filiative models of evolution are dependent on exophysical system descriptions that are simply unable to account for the genuinely creative aspect of evolution (machinic becomings). If the organism is a function of the frame within which the science of biology encodes it, then it is necessary to recognize that the frame captures only a small part of the possible information that assemblages are able to express. A code is inseparable from an intrinsic process of decoding (no genetics without genetic drift, as Deleuze and Guattari pithily express it). Modern work on mutations shows that a code, which is necessarily related to a population, contains a margin of decoding. This decoding takes place not only through the 'supplement' that is capable of free variation, but also within a single segment of code that may be copied twice with the second copy left free for variation. In utilizing the notion of a 'surplus value of code' – codes are always paralogical, always beside – to account for the transferral of fragments of code from the cells of one species to those of another, Deleuze and Guattari insist that this is not to be understood as a process of 'translation' (viruses are not translators), but rather in terms of a singular process of 'side-communication' (*communication d'à-coté*) (Deleuze and Guattari 1980: 70; 1988: 53).

In accordance with this new model of machinic evolution becoming is to be conceived neither along the lines of a correspondence between relations nor in terms of a resemblance or an imitation. This is not to think becoming but to reduce it to the given. There are no series or stages involved in becoming, whether regressive or progressive. What is actual in becoming is the 'block of becoming itself' and not the fixed terms through which becoming passes. This is the force behind Deleuze and Guattari's idea that 'becoming is not an evolution' (ibid.: 291–2; 238). That is, not an evolution if evolution simply denotes descent, heredity, or filiation along an axis of linear or genealogical becoming.[11] The only

---

11 It should be recalled that in the *Origin of Species* Darwin's account of evolution is a theory of 'common descent', what he calls 'descent with modification', which is genealogical identity in difference. The discussion of matters of embryology and morphology in the final chapter of the book, before the 'recapitulation and conclusion', takes place in the context of an examination of 'classification': 'community in embryonic structure reveals community of descent' (Darwin 1985: 427). Darwin does not understand genealogy in linear terms, but rather in terms of a 'branching' in which 'all living and extinct beings are united by complex, radiating, and circuitous lines of affinities into one grand system' (ibid.: 433). Darwin makes it clear, however, that what he is establishing with this model of genealogy are filiations of *blood*, in which the amount or value 'of the differences between organic beings' becomes ever more widely different in the course of evolution, and yet, 'their genealogical *arrangement* remains strictly true' (ibid.: 405).

veritable becomings present in evolution are those produced by symbioses which bring into play new scales and new kingdoms. Only involution breaks with filiative evolution by forming 'blocks' which allow things to pass through and freely become. Involution is difference conceived not on the order of filiation or heredity but excessively in terms of the surplus value of code. Involution is genuine freedom, the rhizome as opposed to the genealogical tree. The model of becoming that the rhizome brings into play has obvious affinities with recent attempts within feminist and postcolonial theorizing to go beyond the genealogical prejudices of an autochthonic politics of identity. Hybridization, however, takes us only so far away from arborescent schemas. Hybrids involve the connection of points, but do not facilitate the passing *between* points. A point remains wedded to a point of *origin*. In rhizomatic-styled becomings becoming denotes the movement by which the line frees itself from the point and renders points indiscernible. *Machinic* 'evolution' refers to the synthesis of heterogeneities, whereas hybridization is still tied to the idea of there being elements that are pure and uncontaminated prior to the mixing they undergo in hybridism. The difference is crucial and enables Deleuze and Guattari to posit 'ethology' as a privileged *molar* domain on account of its demonstration of how the most varied components – from the biochemical, the hereditary and acquired, to the social – are able to crystallize in assemblages that do not respect the distinction between orders. What holds the various components together are 'transversals', in which the 'transversal' itself is to be understood as the *deterritorialized* component within the complex adaptive system, that is, as the non-subject 'agent' of the evolution of complexity (Deleuze and Guattari 1988: 336). In this novel conception of ethology the 'assemblage' is being privileged over the classical emphasis on 'behaviour'. This means that we must arrive at a much more complex understanding of 'evolution' than is facilitated by the Darwinian emphasis on adaptation to external circumstances, which ultimately rests on a reified and unmediated notion of the 'environment'. On Deleuze's ethological model an animal or life-form is never separable from its rapport with the 'world' and its relations with it, but that world is never just 'given' or simply passively adapted to. 'Evolution' involves learning. In nature there is invention (technics): 'Artifice is fully a part of Nature' (Deleuze 1988a: 124). An originary technics thus informs Deleuze's so-called *Naturphilosophie*.

Within philosophy the machine has been classically defined in contradistinction to the organism along the following lines: an organism is a self-organized being in which the parts are reciprocally cause and effect of the whole, forming not just an 'aggregate', or an 'assemblage', but a 'unity'. According to Kant, only organisms display 'finality' (purposiveness), that is, a self-organizing capability (for example, in its genus, *Gattung*); a tree produces nothing other than itself, and so preserves itself 'generically'. By contrast, a machine is entirely lacking in (self-propagating) *formative power (fortpflanzende bildende Kraft)*, and so is unable to self-produce, reproduce, and self-organize. The efficient cause of the machine lies outside the machine in its designer. The only power given to the machine is a 'motive power' *(bewegende Kraft)* (Kant 1974/1982: section 65).[12] On Kant's model an 'organized' being is one in which each part has been trained and disciplined to exist '*for the sake of the other*', so that all the interacting parts exist for the sake of the whole which is ontologically prior and primary (Kant 1995: 60). It cannot be simply a question of inverting the dualism of machine and organism which has structured the history of metaphysics. Rather, the mapping of machines can be constructed in novel ways to the point where the fixity and certainty of techno-ontological boundaries and distinctions begin to de-stabilize and break down in true machinic fashion. The idea that when we speak of living things as machines we are being merely metaphoric also needs to be contested (Emmeche 1994: 50), since again such a view rests on little more than an anthropocentric bias, which itself is not 'natural' but 'artificial', the product of a certain historical formation and deformation of the human animal/machine.

For all its good sense, this philosophical determination of the machine rests on the privileging of notions of unity and finality that then allows for the strict partition between organismic and non-organismic life. Dawkins has conceded that the concept of the organism is of dubious utility precisely because it is so difficult to arrive at a satisfactory definition of it. Much depends on the hierarchy of life which we are seeking to establish. To plant biologists, for example, the leaf may be a more salient 'individual' than the plant, since the plant is a 'straggling, vague entity for whom reproduction may be hard to distinguish from what a zoologist would happily call "growth"' (Dawkins 1982: 253). For Nietzsche, the organism is not to be reified as a monadic entity but to be viewed as a 'complex of systems struggling for an increase in the feeling of power' (Nietzsche 1968: section 703).

---

12 Compare Hegel (1970a: 198–202; 1980: sections 256–60), where the constitution of the organism is compared to the constitution of self-consciousness, as that which 'distinguishes itself from itself without producing any distinction'. This non-machinic conception of the organism as a functional and structural unity resulting from self-organization figures in the work of one eminent contemporary biologist, Brian Goodwin (1995: 182–4). For another account of the difference between machines and living organisms see Serres (1982: 81). For further insight into the relationship between Deleuze's ethology – mediated by the diverse likes of Simondon, Spinoza, Raymond Ruyer, and von Uexküll – and the philosophical tradition (notably Hegel and Heidegger) see Ansell Pearson 1997.

Moreover, there are only 'acentred systems' (ibid.: 488). The 'organism' enjoys a largely semiotic status and cannot be conceived independently of our cognitive mapping of systems and their boundaries. In his 1867 speculations on teleology since Kant, Nietzsche questions the extent to which Kant demonstrates that only organisms can be viewed as ends of nature, arguing that in nature 'a machine would also lead to underlying final causes'. Human thought can only reify the 'eternally becoming' (*ewig Werdende*) of life by grasping living things solely in terms of their forms. In an insight that anticipates the Bergsonian-Deleuzian understanding of creative evolution, he argues:

> our intellect is too dull to perceive continuing transformation: that which it comes to know it names form. In truth no form is given, because in each point sits infinity (*Unendlichkeit*). Every thought unity (point) describes a line. A concept similar to form is that of the individual. We call organisms unities, as centres of purpose (*Zweckcentren*). But unities only exist for our intellect. Each individual has an infinity of living individuals within itself.[13]

In spite of everything Kant seeks to do with the notion of teleology, Nietzsche insists that the standpoint of reflective judgement is utterly whimsical and arbitrary (*willkürlich*). The moves Kant makes, in which the end of the 'real existence' of nature can only be discovered by looking beyond nature, amounts to a violent (moral) subordination of nature to the human reason. Today, he argues, as we undergo the experience of morality's self-overcoming (the self-overcoming of the will to truth), we are compelled to recognize that man has become an animal whose existence in the visible order of things appears as 'arbitrary, beggarly, and quite dispensable' (Nietzsche 1994: II, section 25). It is no wonder that the issue of teleology so often appears as little more than the refractive influence of provincial human interests.

The transhuman imagination does not rest content with anthropocentric prejudices about machines but seeks to devise ways of tapping into their non-human enunciation. A philosophy of the machine begins with the contention that the machine 'is' *not*, since it does not exist in itself but only through alienation. As Deleuze and Guattari point out, an abstract machine is destratified and deterritorialized with no form of its own. An abstract machine in itself, that is, viewed from inside according to its intelligible (virtual) character, is neither

---

13 This passage is taken from Nietzsche's 1867 dissertation outline on *Teleologie seit Kant* (not available in Nietzsche 1987), in Nietzsche 1933–42, volume 3: 371–94. A German original and helpful English translation of this intriguing early piece can be found in the appendix to Crawford 1988: 238–67. In this chapter I have used my own translation, however.

physical nor corporeal. It is not semiotic but *diagrammatic*, operating by matter, not by substance (too hard), and by function, not by form (too unelastic). In other words, the abstract machine is 'pure Matter-Function' that exists independently of the forms and substances it brings into play and distributes. A critique of the machine in terms of a machine's inability to replicate and reproduce itself does not begin to touch on the problematic of machinic heterogenesis. As Butler points out, it is illegitimate to declare that the red clover has no reproductive system simply because the bee must aid and abet it before it can reproduce. He writes: 'Each one of ourselves has sprung from minute animalcules whose entity was entirely distinct from our own, and which acted after their kind with no thought or heed of what we might think about it. These little creatures are part of our own reproductive system' (Butler 1985: 211).[14] The notion of machinic evolution, therefore, does not refer specifically or exclusively to human contrivances, gadgets, or tools, but rather to particular modes of evolution, such as symbiosis and contagion, and is not specific or peculiar to the human–machine relationship, since it also speaks of the machine–machine nexus and alterity. The 'machinic' is the mode of evolution that is specific and peculiar to the 'becoming' of alien life. A machine can only exist through exterior elements. It thus enjoys an existence in terms of being a complementarity, and not simply in terms of its relationship to human design or a designer. A machine lives and dies in connection with other virtual and actual machines, suggesting 'a "non-human" enunciation, a proto-subjective diagram' (Guattari 1992: 59; 1995: 37). An assemblage works through invention, and does not imply a relationship of anastomosis between its components. Rather, it connects and convolutes things in terms of potential fields and virtual elements, crossing ontological thresholds without fidelity to relations of genus and species (Guattari 1992: 56; 1995: 35). The logic of life displays an infinite virtuosity, but, in truth, all that is happening is the transformation of seemingly determinate points into indeterminate lines. In his 'book of machines' Samuel Butler demonstrates, in an unnerving insight into the animal–machine nexus and the human–machine nexus, how it becomes virtually impossible to declare with any ontological certainty who is the host and who is the parasite.

---

14 Even this entrenched thesis on machines has been contested by Richard Laing (1979: 201–15), who has argued that deliberate explicit design is not the sole means by which machines come to exhibit complex behaviour, such as self-replication and self-repair. My aim in this chapter is limited to challenging the way in which we talk about machines and organisms by privileging wholes over parts, unities over multiplicities, and autogenesis over heterogenesis.

In an essay on 'The Organization of the Living' Humberto Maturana and Francisco Varela set out to define, working from within an assumed non-animistic perspective, living systems as machines. They confess that they are attracted to the word 'machine' because of its decisive dynamic connotations. Entities are defined as unities with the power to reproduce and by their autonomy. 'Autonomy' is conceived as the 'self-asserting capacity of living systems to maintain their identity through the active compensation of deformations' (Maturana and Varela 1980: 73). This definition succeeds in capturing the essentially cybernetic nature of self-regulating systems in which feedback plays the crucial role. The question, however, is whether in their conception of the machine Maturana and Varela simply take 'unity' as given, with an underdefined deformation and 'reproduction' being posited in naive and essentialist terms (since things don't just reproduce themselves). In seeking to define a 'living system', Maturana and Varela contend that evolutionary thought has ignored the autonomous nature of living entities. 'Organization' is the principle that is best able to account for the 'unitary character' of living systems. If living systems are 'machines', then they need to be understood in terms of 'relations' and not of component parts. Only in this way is it possible to generate the desired notion of dynamism (*entelecheia*). The usual view of machines is that they are concrete hardware systems, defined by the nature of their components and by the purpose they fulfil in their operations as man-made artifacts. But this view says nothing about how they are constituted. Maturana and Varela are concerned with relations, not components; the latter can be any, so it is the organization which is crucial and constitutive. The organization of machines can then be described as autopoietic. Such machines are homeostatic and all feedback is internal to them. What is peculiar to such machines, however, is not this feature but the fundamental variable which they maintain constant. Such a machine is organized as a network of processes of production (transformation and destruction of components) that produces the components which (a) continuously regenerate and realize the network of processes (relations) that produced them through their interactions and transformation; and (b) constitute the machine as a concrete unity in the space in which the components exist.

An autopoietic machine, therefore, is one which continuously generates and specifies its own organization through its operation as a system of production of its own components. It does this in terms of an endless turnover of components under conditions of continuous perturbations and compensation of perturbations. Organization is the fundamental variable which it maintains constant. In other words an autopoietic machine is defined not in terms of the components or their static relations, but by the particular network of processes (relations) of production. The relations of production of components are given only as *processes*; if the processes 'stop', then the relations vanish. Therefore, machines require regeneration by the components they produce. An autopoietic machine has no inputs and outputs, although it can be 'perturbated' by independent events which cause it to undergo internal structural change. The claim that autopoietic systems are organizationally 'closed' can be misleading if it is taken to imply that these systems do not interact with their environment. Such systems are closed simply in the sense that the product of their organization is the organization itself. Internal changes which take place are always subordinated to the maintenance of the machine organization. A relation between these changes and the course of perturbations which can be pointed to pertain to the domain within which the machine is observed, and not to its organization. An autopoietic machine can be treated as an allopoietic machine, but this will not reveal its particular organization as an autopoietic machine. An autopoietic machine, therefore, is one which maintains as constant certain relations between components that are in continuous flow or change, and it is this which constitutes its modus operandi as one of 'dynamic stability'. The actual manner in which the autopoietic organization is implemented in physical space varies according to the nature, or properties, of the physical materials which embody the structure of the machine in question. Although there are many different kinds of autopoietic machines in physical space, all of them are organized in such a way that any 'interference' with their operation outside their domain of compensations will result in their disintegration. Maturana and Varela reach two principal conclusions concerning the machine: firstly, if living systems are machines (physical autopoietic machines), which transform matter into themselves in a manner such that the product of their operation is always their own organization, then the converse is also true: if it is autopoietic, then a physical system is living; secondly, from this, it follows that the distinction between machine (automaton) and living (spontaneous) becomes untenable and must break down. The classic view is that machines are man-made artifacts with completely deterministic properties and perfectly predictable. Contrariwise, living systems are deemed to be *a priori* autonomous, unpredictable systems. The prejudice is that man could not manufacture a living system but 'only' a machine. As a result of these redefinitions, however, certain distinctions begin to break down and certain prejudices get supplanted.

In spite of the progressive character of the last insight, a fundamental metaphysical opposition operates deep within the so-called machinic thinking of the school of autopoiesis. Maturana and Varela's conception of the machine as a self-referential, self-reproductive monadic entity rests on an opposition between pure autonomy (self-maintenance and self-preservation), on the one hand, and impure heteronomy (invasion) on the other. They do not see that a genuinely machinic thinking of the 'entropy/evolution' problematic must lead to a corrosion of molar-organized unities and identities, leading to the construal of a fluid relationship between 'inner' and 'outer', between autonomy and heteronomy, and between nature and artifice. Autopoiesis cannot allow for transformation except in terms of a highly restricted economy, presenting us with a stark either/or choice: *either* entropy *or* perfect performance. It is guided by a whole conservative metaphysics of living systems, and presupposes a paranoid machine. This is evident in the emphasis it places on systems as closed and recursive unities that are guided by, above all else, the maintenance of stability. To claim, as they do, that organization is an invariant of a component system is to equate change with simple destruction, and to render organization as something 'over' physical reality rather than 'to' it. In contradistinction to Maturana and Varela, Vilmos Csanyi and George Kampis maintain that if new components endowed with new functions come into existence in a system, then the organization of that system cannot remain invariant. Moreover, change in a system's organization, as a result of the emergence of new components, does not result in the disintegration of that system. This must mean that the 'autonomy' of the individual organism is 'always relative' (Csanyi and Kampis 1985: 306). For them the main problem with an autopoietic model of evolution is that it fails to appreciate that if a system were to be driven by the desire for perfect autonomy it would get trapped in an evolutionary deadlock, unable to form further relationships and connections. Exactly the same point was made by Bergson, in the context of a different debate, who argued against a vitalist position which rested on the assumption that nature evolved in terms of a purely internal finality and absolutely distinct individualities (Bergson 1983: 42). It is impossible, he argued, to determine with any degree of fixity where the vital principle of the 'individual', or autonomous machine, begins or ends.

In the three sections of 'The book of the machines' which make up his fiction *Erewhon* of 1872 Samuel Butler challenges the way in which lines are drawn between machinic life and animal life:

Where does consciousness begin, and where end? Who can draw the line? Who can draw any line? Is not everything interwoven with everything? Is not machinery linked with animal life in an infinite variety of ways? The shell of a hen's egg is made up of delicate white ware and is a machine as much as an egg-cup.

(1985: 199)

As Deleuze and Guattari argue, Butler's reflections do not simply contrast two common arguments, one according to which organisms are only more perfect machines, the other according to which machines are never more than extensions of the organism. Butler is not content merely to claim that machines extend the organism (the pre-established unity), or that organisms are machines; rather he wishes to show that (a) the field of evolution is thoroughly machinic from the outset, and (b) organisms can be compared to machines in terms of the sophisticated engineering which integrates their distinct parts (desire is engineering) (Deleuze and Guattari 1972: 337–8; 1983: 284). As a result, Butler destroys the vitalist argument by calling into question the alleged personal unity of the organism, and, by the same token, he undercuts the mechanist position by calling into question the alleged structural unity of the machine. If 'life' can be conceived along the lines of a 'desire-engineering', then there can be no pre-established boundaries and no fixed determination of what constitutes the parameters and identities of individuated entities, such as organisms or machines. The mistake is to view complex machines as single entities whose individuated existence is pre-given. In truth, every complex machine, Butler maintains, is to be regarded as a city or society. Like organisms, machines reproduce themselves through an integrated network of co-evolution (as in the well-known example of the red clover and the bumble bee). Butler's reasoning forces us to question the fixity of Kant's distinction between motive and formative powers. In Deleuze and Guattari's terms the motive power of the technical machine requires the formative power of the social machine for its actualization and reproduction. The human animal enjoys no autonomy from nature and from technics. Like everything else it too is caught up in the 'surplus value of code', which denotes an excess that refers to a process when a part of a machine captures within its 'own' code a code fragment of another machine, and, as a result, owes its reproduction to a part of another machine. It is thus the always excessive desire of machinic becomings that deterritorializes the evolutionary lineages of all phenomena, and which enables us to privilege alliances over filiations, heteronomous assemblages over autonomous entities. It becomes possible to appreciate the compound nature of Deleuze and Guattari's formulation 'desiring-machines', in which the machine passes to the heart of desire and the machine is desiring desire, 'machined': 'Desire is not in the subject, but the machine in desire.' Desiring-machines are truly formative machines, but whose formativity is possible only through functional misfirings; that is, formation requires deformation, and what makes evolution a machinic process is the fact that it takes place through cuttings, breakages, slippages, breakdowns, and so on. Structural unities and mass phenomena (such as molar aggregates) conceal the intrinsic direction of singular multiplicities (interpenetration, direct communication), and force us to lose sight of the multitude of small machines which are dispersed in every organism, which itself is no more than 'a collection of trillions of macromolecular machines' (Dennett 1995b: 206). Ultimately, at the point of 'dispersion', where techno-ontological boundaries break down, it becomes immaterial whether one describes machines as organs or organs as machines: 'A tool or a machine is an organ, and organs are tools or machines' (Canguilhem 1992: 55). Canguilhem also points out that the mechanistic conception of the body posited by Cartesianism is no less anthropomorphic than a teleological conception of the physical world. He shares Nietzsche's view that machines can be considered to be purposive in their endeavour and activity. Indeed, 'man' is only able to make himself the master and proprietor of nature to the extent that he denies any finality or purpose to what lies 'outside' him, such as nature or machines, which are then treated solely as means to serve his hubristic *Zwecken*. Nature and technics take their revenge when the realization dawns that the entire evolution of what we take to be 'spirit' is, in actuality, the becoming of something altogether different than what appears in consciousness and reason, namely, the body: 'In the long run, it is not a question of man at all, for he is to be overcome' (Nietzsche 1968: section 676). So far in this book we have seen the extent to which Nietzsche does not think this overcoming in terms of the abolition of the human but rather only in terms of the destruction of its anthropocentric determination as the superior point of evolution.

If the idea of autopoiesis is to retain any useful function it has to be thought in relation to entities which are evolutive and collective, and which sustain diverse kinds of alterior relations, as opposed to being implacably closed in upon themselves and maintaining their autonomous existence at the expense of casting out and dissipating anything external that would contaminate their inner purity (the machine as beautiful soul). In the case of the machine, entropy and evolution need to be viewed as co-extensive and mutually informative. The 'man–machine alterity' is inextricably linked to a 'machine–machine alterity'. As Guattari points out, machines already 'talk' to each other before they talk to us. The reproducibility of machines is not a pure, programmed repetition, but precisely an evolution. Difference is introduced at this point of breakdown/evolution and is both ontogenetic and phylogenetic. There is no simple or straightforward univocal historical causality since evolutive lineages present themselves as 'rhizomes', meaning that 'datings' are not synchronic but heterochronic (on the crucial role played by heterochrony in the developmental processes of ontogeny, see Raff and Kaufman 1983: 173ff.). The tectonic movements of history have to be understood in terms of singularities which themselves have to be mapped out in terms of a virtual plane of rhizomatic and associative becoming. Such becomings take place 'in' history but are not reducible to, or identical with, it. Guattari has rightly insisted that the question of the ontogenetic evolution of the machine, for example, is not reducible to the 'linear causalities of the capitalistic apprehension of machinic Universes' (1992:79; 1995: 52).

In machinic heterogenesis it is less a question of the identity of a being that retains its heterogeneous texture while traversing different regions, and more of an 'identical processual persistence'. One is speaking neither of a Platonic whole nor of an Aristotelian prime mover, but rather of transversal creatures that 'appear like a machinic hyper-text' (Guattari 1992: 151; 1995: 109). Guattari's insight into this universe of machinic heterogenesis requires a fundamental reconfiguration of ontology. An ontology informed by an appreciation of the machine would not place qualities or attributes as secondary in relation to substance, nor would it conceive of being as a pure and empty container of all possible modalities of coming-into-being. Rather, it would conceive being as first and foremost 'auto-affirmation' and 'auto-consistency' which actualizes itself through virtual and diverse relations of alterity. This would mean that we would cease viewing existence-for-itself and for-others in terms of the privilege of one particular 'species', such as *man*kind, and appreciate that everywhere 'machinic interfaces engender disparity and, in return, are founded by it' (ibid.: 152; 109). 'Being' ceases to be a general ontological equivalent and becomes modelled along the lines of 'generative praxes of heterogeneity and complexity' (ibid.). Evolution by symbiosis – the vitality of viroid life – and rhizomatic becomings constitute an essential part of this heterogeneity and complexity.

In terms of the question of technology, there is no reification of technical machines in the work of Deleuze and Guattari since they readily appreciate that technical machines are only indexes of more complex assemblages that bring into co-evolutionary play material-forces in which the role played by the social machine is decisive. One is not 'oppressed' by a technical machine but by a social machine which determines at any given moment what is the usage, extension, and comprehension of technical elements (compare Braudel 1981: 431: 'there is no technology in itself'). Technical machines are not an economic category but always refer to a socius or social machine that is distinct from them. This is akin to Marx's view that machinery is no more an 'economic' category than is the ox which draws the plough. Deleuze and Guattari insist that assemblages are never purely technological. Tools always presuppose a 'machine', and the machine is always social 'before' it is technical (compare Ellul 1965: 4–5, in which the question of the machine is reduced entirely to a question of mechanized 'technique'). As one commentator has noted, in relation to the new cybernetic machines, in no arena will the technologies themselves be determining (Nichols 1988: 45). In other words, questions concerning cybernetic technology can only be adequately attested to when they are articulated in terms of a social theory of the microphysics of power. One of the reasons given for the primacy of the social machine by Deleuze and Guattari is that technical machines do not contain the conditions for their reproduction, but require the social machine to organize and limit their development. There is no attempt made in their work to crudely biologize the technical-social; both a biological reading of human history and an anthropological reading of natural history must be avoided since the dangers of either strategy are all too obvious. The social is already artificially biologized. The terms of political theory, for example, are terms of capture and regulation, in which the evolution of societies is referred to as 'embryonic', 'nascent', 'underdeveloped', and that of third world societies as 'foetuses' and 'abortions' of culture and civilization. In challenging the reified conception of the organism found within a variety of discursive practices one is not advocating a retreat into a pre-social biosphere, but rather presenting a challenge that operates on myriad fronts. A politics of desire – the machinic assemblage of new solidarities and formations – comes into play when it is recognized that technocracy and bureaucracy (the functioning of the social machine) can never be reduced to being simply the operation of technical machines along the lines of a perfectly run cybernetic machine. In the 1960s Vaneigem argued that, 'by laying the basis for a perfect power structure, the cyberneticians only stimulate the perfection of its refusal. Their programming of techniques will be shattered by the same techniques turned to its own use by another kind of organization' (Vaneigem 1994a: 85). In truth, the situation is now infinitely more complex than the likes of Vaneigem could ever have entertained, since the 'outside' – virtual futures of all kinds – has been captured. Capitalism, having embarked upon a programme of endocolonization, has become a *futures* market on every level one cares to think. 'Nothing is true; everything is permitted' is no longer the slogan of the revolutionary nihilist but that of established powers of capture. The revolution *will* be televised (and already has been). This is the force, for example, behind Umberto Eco's astute insight into (post)modern terrorism: terrorism is not the enemy of the great systems but their natural counterweight, both accepted and programmed (Eco 1986: 116). If the great systems function as headless systems, having no protagonists and not living on individual egoism, then they cannot be struck by killing the king: 'if there exists a completely automated factory, it will not be upset by the death of the owner but rather by erroneous bits of information inserted here and there, making hard work for the computers that run the place' (ibid.: 115). It is no longer sufficient to ponder Marx, he suggests; one must also ponder Norbert Wiener. Capital renders Marx's great insight into history null and void: the history of all hitherto existing society is the history of class struggle *except for the 'history' of (late, always late) capital*! Forever the great cynic, capital cannibalizes all negativity, 'parodistically going beyond its own contradictions' (Baudrillard 1994: 52).

Technology's powerful illusion of independence is part of its immense entropic and imperialistic success: the essence of technology is nothing technological, but it *appears* as if it is.[15] Fetishism of technology is an essential — and *vital* — part of capital's transcendental illusion. But the social definition of what is technologically feasible or desirable is not external to technology but intrinsic to it. A distinction between the 'economic' and the 'technological' is arbitrary and unintelligent (see Hornborg 1992). Capitalism rests on a particular conjunction of technical and social machines. As a distinct social formation it functions by turning the technical machines into constant capital attached to the body of the socius (as opposed to 'human machines', which are made adjacent to the technical machines). The social axiomatic extends its limits through the 'non-technical' means of administration and inscription. Culture works as a mechanism of selection, inventing through inscription and coding the large numbers — organisms and complete whole persons — in whose interests it acts. This explains why 'statistics is not functional but structural', concerning 'chains of phenomena that selection has already placed in a state of partial dependence. . . . This can even be seen in the genetic code' (Deleuze and Guattari 1983: 343). The State exists to regulate the decoded flows unleashed by the schizzo-tendencies of capitalism. While capital melts down everything that is solid and profanes all that is holy, bourgeois society guarantees that the productive forces of change are rendered

---

15 This illusion of the autonomous character of technical development is exposed in an instructive 'critical' fashion by Habermas (1987: 57ff.), who argues that 'technology' — conceived as scientifically rationalized control of objectified processes — be taken to refer to a 'system' in which research and technology are coupled with feedback from both the economy and from modern social administration. As one of the few attempts to develop a 'politics' of technology and a 'democratic' technics, Habermas's inquiry remains an apposite one in the face of the contemporary depoliticization of questions concerning technology and technics. As Habermas notes, one of the ways in which advanced capitalist society 'immunizes' itself against the deterritorializing impact of technical change and the potentiality for free communication about the goals of 'life activity' is through a depoliticization of the mass of the population (120). See also in this regard Winner's helpful historical study (1977).

equilibrial through the territorially fixed and juridically invariant structure of the modern State (Balakrishnan 1995: 56–7) (and news of its death is premature). Moreover, through State regulation and control the decoding practices of science and technics are subjected to a social axiomatic that is more severe than any putative 'scientific' axiomatic. The social and cultural revolution of postmodernity is about the potential liberation of technical machines from monopolistic and scientistic control by the molar forces of capture that characterize the modern capitalist State, a bifurcation point at which capitalism is no longer able to monopolize for itself technical machines as the constant capital attached to its social body. The critical task of an alien thought-praxis, therefore, can only be that of decoding and deterritorializing the prevailing administrative and regulatory machines – in the State, in philosophy, in science, in culture and information – that have defined and restricted the present by despotically blocking the free flow of energy and knowledge throughout the social machine.

Grand narratives, it would seem, are coming back in fashion, and with a vengeance, assuming a distinctly inhuman character, in which we are offered a plethora of apocalyptic scenarios concerning an alleged phase-space transition to a new, 'higher' level of evolution based on machine intelligence, resulting in a genetic take-over of carbon life by soft machines (robots and computers) (for two accounts of our neg-entropic destiny from vastly different thinkers, see Lyotard 1991 and Tipler 1995). But this depiction of neg-entropic destinies, in which the human plays the role of a mere conduit in the inhuman process of complexification, can only provide simple options that are not options at all, such as a retreat into a new ethical purism (mourning the event, bearing testimony to the Event), futile Ludditism, or vacuous cyber-celebrationism. The dangers in conflating biology and technology are immense. Today palaeoanthropologists speak of life on earth taking place in terms of the evolution of techno-organic life that has cultivated positive feedback loops between 'intelligence' and biology resulting in an accelerated evolution, with the increasing hegemony of artificial life over natural life being understood as a Lamarckian invasion and take-over of so-called dumb and blind Darwinian natural selection (see Schick and Toth 1993: 315–16). A new mythology of the machine is emerging and finds expression in current claims that technology is simply the pursuit of life by means other than life.[16] This

---

16 Compare Deleule (1992: 205–6), where he writes: 'Life does not imitate the machine, nor is it reduced to a mechanical construct. It is the machine that actually simulates life. . . . Machines were not built in order to free humans from servile tasks. The function of machines is to increase the power of life itself, to enhance life's capacity for mastery and conquest. The machine does

dubious neo-Lamarckism, which reaches an apogee in Kevin Kelly's assertion that the advantages of a Lamarckian style of evolution are so great that *nature herself* has found ways to make such an evolution possible, is not only philosophical idiocy but also politically naive, resting on a highly vertical and perfectionist model of biotechnical evolution. He constantly speaks of 'what evolution really wants', as if one could easily speak of 'evolution' in terms of a global entity, as in the following gross assertion: 'Evolution daily scrutinizes the world not just for fitter organisms, but to find ways to increase its own ability. . . . Evolution searches the surface of the planet to find ways to speed itself up, to make itself more nimble, more evolvable — not because it is anthropomorphic, but because the speeding up of adaptation is the runaway circuit it rides on' (Kelly 1994: 361). Such 'searching' on the part of evolution, we are told, results in the human brain providing the 'answer' to the problem of how evolution can gain the complexity necessary in order to peer ahead and 'direct evolution's course'. In the process of this ridiculous anthropomorphism questions concerning the utilizations and abuses of A-life and bioengineering for life are rendered completely uninteresting, since, as Bergson would have put it, 'all is given'. In effect, what is happening in this kind of depiction of evolution is a blind, and dumb, reading of the dynamics of contemporary hyper-colonistic capitalism — Kelly's identification of speed with simple acceleration illustrates this — back into the mechanics of the biosphere, resulting in a biological justification of entropic modernization in its most imperialistic guise (speed is irresistible).[17] There are other reactive forces at play in recent paeans to the rise of machine intelligence. As Baudrillard has pointed out, having lost our metaphysical utopias we now build prophylactic ones in which our immortality is guaranteed (you can download your brain!). If in the past it was

---

not in any sense replace life.' This so-called postmodern thesis on the machine was captured in its essential import by Samuel Butler in his strikingly titled essay 'Darwin among the Machines' of 1863, where he poses the question concerning the machine in quasi-Nietzschean terms, posing it as a question about 'the sort of creature' that will succeed man in the supremacy of the earth. His concluding opinion, not surprisingly, was that 'war to the death should be instantly proclaimed against them'. See Butler 1914. What perturbs Butler is the recognition that while machines have proved to be an indispensable aspect of human existence — 'man's very soul is due to the machines; it is a machine-made thing', he writes — in the future hegemonic evolution of machine intelligence the human may prove to be utterly *dispensable* as far as the desires of the machines are concerned (Butler 1985: 207).

17 Of course, the irony of Kelly's position is that he is a control freak. His opposition to natural selection is based on the fact that it takes time, time he does not have, he tells us. 'Who can wait a million years?' he writes (359).

the dead who were embalmed for eternity, today it is the living who are being embalmed alive in a state of survival (life owes me a right *not* to die!) (Baudrillard 1994: 87–8).

At present what we are witnessing within the discernible logic of postmodernity is a transition from the thermodynamic machines of industrial capitalism to the cybernetic machines of contemporary information societies that govern through intelligent control. But this is still a mutation within entropic (post)modernity in which the development of new forces of production outstrips existing relations of production but in no way guarantees their radical transformation or liberation from social control and molarization. Society – and 'we' who exist outside – are becoming more like snakes every day. Did the 'political' die with the collapse of the great empires, including the great empires of thought (-control)? Today the life of the great empires has assumed a retroviral form, fragmented and peripheral, genetically infecting their wastes and by-products, their basic cells and ugly growths, no longer on the order of the political but of the *trans*political whose passion, notes Baudrillard, is that of the interminable work of mourning, lost in 'the melancholy of homeopathic and homeostatic systems', in which evidence for the death of *the* political is impermissible since it would 'reintroduce a fatal virus into the virtual immortality of the transpolitical' (Baudrillard 1994: 51). Postmodernity (human, all too human) spreads the virus of voluntary servitude, an 'ecological micro-servitude, which is everywhere the successor to totalitarian oppression' (and how green were those Nazi valleys). There is only the contagion of technics and the freedom of becoming imperceptible, invisible, and ignoble (learn to growl, burrow, and distort yourself).

# 6

# TIMELY MEDITATIONS ON THE TRANSHUMAN CONDITION

## Nihilism, entropy, and beyond

> In the investigation of nature, human reason is not content to pass from metaphysics to physics; there lies within it an instinct (which, though fruitless, is not inglorious) to transcend even the latter, to fantasize in a hyperphysics.
> (Kant 1995: 17)

> Once more we are seized by a great shudder, but who would feel inclined immediately to deify again after the old manner this monster of an unknown world? . . . Alas, too many *ungodly* possibilities of interpretation are included in the unknown, too much devilry, stupidity, and foolishness of interpretation – even our own human, all too human folly.
> (Nietzsche 1974: section 374)

> It may be that believing in this world, in this life, becomes our most difficult task, or the task of a mode of existence still to be discovered on the plane of immanence today . . . (we have so many reasons not to believe in the human world; we have indeed lost the world . . .). The problem has indeed changed.
> (Deleuze and Guattari 1994: 75)

> History as contingency is a prospect that is more than the human spirit can bear.
> (Heilbroner 1994: 77)

1. Today, one might suppose, it is not so much we who are investigating the future as the future which is investigating us. The future appears to have announced its arrival in a hundred and one signs. If the Messiah arrived he would go unrecognized not simply because his arrival would be belated, but more because the flash of the future is imperceptible. The future seems to have arrived quite a long time ago: a carbon-dating experiment would probably fix its arrival around five hundred and seventy million years ago. Even this dating, however, which refers to the appearance of hard-bodied plants and animals in the

Phanerozoic aeon, suffers from what we might call a Cambrian chauvinism. A less anthropocentric timeline might fix it as one thousand and seven hundred million years ago, during the Proterozoic aeon, with the earliest appearance of eukaryotes and the birth of speciation. No doubt this attempt to determine the future is beside the point. One of the reasons why we are so blinkered about the future and its coming is the fact that we indulge in a highly anthropocentric meditation on the time of technology. When that perennial species, Luddites, declare that they are 'not into' technology, they need to be reminded that it is not so much a question of their personal likes and dislikes, but much more a question of technology being 'into' them. It is necessary to get the question of technology into some kind of perspective. The universe offers a comprehensive system of technics and technology, while humanity has discovered ways of employing and exploiting it. As Ernst Jünger pointed out in his 1932 study of 'The Worker', humanity oscillates between conceiving itself as the apprentice of a sorcerer that has conjured up powers beyond its control and as the creators of an unstoppable progress that hastens towards artificial paradises (Jünger 1982). The human fantasy is to devise a technological system so omniscient that it nullifies the power of the future, transforming the universe into a perfectly administered megamachine of predictable outputs and calculable energies. Technology, we like to think, holds the 'promise' of a life lived in pure immediacy and total transparency. The task is now one of knowing how to cultivate a critique of this hell in which life is being lived 'beyond' illusion. As we continue to labour under what Baudrillard has called the 'subjective illusion of technology', we fail to identify the true ironic character of technology's coming.[1] For Baudrillard such a proposition delivers us from the Heideggerian vision of technology as the final phase of metaphysics, and from any nostalgia for Being and from all unhappy critique based on outmoded notions of alienation and disenchantment (Baudrillard 1996: 83). If it is more a question of technology inventing the human than it is a question of humans inventing technology, then it is necessary to take this *invention* seriously.

2. The time of technics always exceeds itself because it is a time of invention (of the future, of time itself). In raising the question of technology, one wonders whether Heidegger is talking about about the invention 'of' technics at all (in spite of his employing the German *die Technik*), or simply about the human world of

---

1 Baudrillard meditates on the 'irony of technology' in his *The Perfect Crime* (1996: 82–6). Such a condition, however, was already noted and meditated upon by Jacques Ellul in his classic study of *la technique*. See Ellul 1965, and Winner 1977: 61ff.

technology that has become estranged from, and foreign to, mankind and now appears as something that is tremendously inhuman. The question of technology would appear to have little to do with the complex evolution of technics, and more to do with the control and mastery of all kinds of techniques for the purposes of human preservation and the political control of the flow of material-forces. To maintain that technology is making us 'less human' is to suppose that there exists some fixed nature of the human by which one could measure the excesses of technology, and so appraise its inventions in terms of some metaphysical cost-benefits analysis. Heidegger's thesis that in order for the 'truth' of technology to be revealed it is necessary that mankind finds its way back to the full breadth of the space that is proper to its essence (*Wesensraum*) would appear to underestimate massively the extent of technology's invention of the human animal and the nature and extent of its investment in mankind (Heidegger 1991a).[2] Heidegger's own mistake was to argue that the production of machines, which he recognizes is not identical to technics, exists to 'realize' the 'essence of technics in its objective raw material'. The 'essence' of technics here refers to the desire of technology for total mobilization and control. But this desire for control can be recognized as a human, all too human desire, actualized within specific social formations and modes of production. Heidegger's questioning of technology contains its own strange irony. In seeking to invert our instrumentalist and anthropocentric questioning of this event by construing it not as the invention of man but as a gift of Being, he turns the human into little more than an 'instrument', a mere organ of the time of technology, so that mankind is sacrificed on the altar of self-withdrawing Being. 'Being', we are told, 'has sent itself into Enframing.' All the voluntarism that Heidegger takes away from 'man' is now given back to 'Being'. It is not surprising that he should reach the position he did: only a god can save us.

3. Any thinking of the future would seem to be necessarily implicated in questions of theology and teleology, with questions of first and last things. It seems peculiar to our so-called 'postmodern' age, however, that whereas we have abandoned concern with the former (nothing is more intellectually discredited today than the question of origins), it cannot completely eschew the latter. The most radical

---

2 This separation of mankind and technology, which rests on the supposition that mankind stands in some way 'outside' technology, becomes evident in his Messkirch Memorial Address of 1955, where he suggests that the 'proper' relationship to technology is one where we 'can use technical devices as they ought to be used, and also let them alone as something which does not affect our inner and real core' (Heidegger 1966: 54).

embracement of our current inhumanization can thus read like an upturned version of the Hegelian ascent to the Absolute, the absolute knowledge which, ever since Adorno, has proclaimed the horror! the horror!, now screams the delight! the delight! When it confronts the inside that comes from outside and invades its domain – the future – the human goes beyond itself and becomes subject to strange experiences and thoughts of the transhuman. The attempt to map the future is not a pastime peculiar to futurologists. It has been a preoccupation of thinkers ever since nihilism started knocking on the door. In the case of modernity, this can probably be dated back to Kant. Nietzsche's pithy claim that Kant believed in morality not because it is demonstrated in nature and history, but rather in spite of the fact that nature and history continually contradict it remains one of the most disturbing, but perplexing, insights into the character of our modernity. If the morality of a kingdom of ends cannot be located in history – and where else can it materialize? – then it becomes necessary for Kant to show how it is possible to read history as a story of a possible moral progress, an open-ended progression towards morality. All the resources of the human intellect and knowledge are to be garnered to ensure that we do not begin to gloat on the realization that history – the story of the becoming-sick of the human animal – is utterly beyond redemption, that it is the site of ungodliness and immorality.[3] This does not necessarily cancel the moral project, but it does call for its thorough revaluation, especially once the autonomy of the human is called into question.

4. The idea of a 'philosophy of history' is one of the strangest to emerge in modernity, suggesting, as it does, against all evidence to the contrary, that history is not a completely irrational, amoral, and purposeless affair, what Nietzsche calls the gruesome dominion of nonsense and accident, the great 'monstrous fortuity' (Nietzsche 1966: section 203). Rather, nature contains a hidden plan, and reason assumes a cunning disguise in history, working behind humans' backs, deploying evil in the service of the ultimate triumph of good, making humans slaves of history in order finally to make them masters of it, and containing the promise of the ultimate conquest of that senseless beast called history and leading to the constitution

---

3 See Nietzsche 1968: 12A; 1987, volume 13: 46ff.: 'Nihilism, then, is the recognition of the long waste of strength, the agony of the "in vain", insecurity . . . being ashamed in front of oneself, as if one had *deceived* oneself all too long. This meaning could have been the "fulfilment" of some highest ethical canon in all events, the moral world order; or the growth of love and harmony in the intercourse of beings; or the gradual approximation of a state of universal happiness; or even the development toward a state of universal annihilation – any goal at least constitutes some meaning . . . now one realizes that becoming aims at *nothing* and achieves *nothing*.'

of a thoroughly humanized world. Kant's presentation of the 'idea' of a 'Universal History' is deeply paradoxical. The human species likes to think of itself as the superior design of nature. However, Kant concedes that this intelligence is, in fact, thoroughly stupid, and, consequently, all the intelligence guiding history must be ascribed to nature and its hidden plan. If mankind is to become the purpose and goal of history it will only be the as the result of an inhuman force (nature), and not on account of human intentions or designs. In other words, mankind's ultimate humanity can only be actualized through a process of inhumanization (Kant 1991: 41–2). In Kant the emphasis is placed on nature and its concealed plans for man's perfection, which also represents at the same time the perfection of nature. Actual history encourages revulsion and a turning away, while philosophical history may be more than a work of fiction. What is weird about Kant is not his attempt to posit a noumenal reading of history, but rather his belief that the signs of this hidden becoming of history can be interpreted so as to conform to the will and wishes of a moral humanity. Informing his thinking on nature's design for mankind, which partly includes her invention of mankind, is a particular conception of evolution, one which stands at odds with the functional indeterminacy embraced by both Darwin and Nietzsche. Kant insists that an organ 'which is not meant for use or an arrangement which does not fulfil its purpose is a contradiction in the teleological theory of nature'. If this principle is abandoned then we replace not only a law-governed nature but a nature that enjoys and knows purposes, including final ones, with an 'aimless, random process, and the dismal reign of chance replaces the guiding principle of reason' (ibid.: 42).[4] Contingency is simply a truth too awful for the philosopher to bear.

5. It is this moralization and humanization of the forces of life that has characterized the imagination of modernity and that now strikes us as naively critical. The real danger lies in supposing that nihilism can be overcome through the reassertion of human will and autonomy over the recalcitrant heteronomous forces of nature and history. This has been the great myth of much critical modern thought, perhaps nowhere better illustrated than in Raoul Vaneigem's *Revolution of Everyday Life*, in which a total transcendence of nihilism is envisaged in terms of a great refusal that breaks history into two, pogroms before and a new innocence afterwards, leading to the establishment of a non-alienated body and a thoroughly human time and

---

4 Kant also differs radically from Nietzsche in his belief that nature acts prudently and frugally, doing 'nothing unnecessarily' and never being 'extravagant in the means employed to reach its ends' (Kant 1991: 43).

humanized world (Vaneigem 1994a: 179). Speculating on the possibility of investing the cosmos with a human meaning, Vaneigem fantasizes, in a distintly Rousseauesque fashion, about history resulting for the first time in the achievement of a genuine 'people' and a new form of social organization in which 'all the individual creativity will have free rein, so that the world will be shaped by the dreams of each, as harmonized by all' (ibid.: 219). The task now, he claims, is 'to subvert history to subjective ends' (ibid.: 232). History will become authentically lived history when human action becomes transparent to itself. Not only is this so-called libertarian situationist philosophy of life saturated in a vacuous subjectivism, inane demands for absolute inalienable human rights over life, and metaphysical infantilism, but it is destined to result in a highly authoritarian politics, which indeed becomes clear with the publication in the 1980s of Vaneigem's *The Movement of Free Spirit* (1994b: introduction). If Vaneigem's Rousseauian-inspired moralism was concealed in the 'Revolution' book of the late 1960s, which did at least strive towards some dialectical comprehension of the antinomies of the present broken condition, its moral fanaticism is now all too apparent. The thesis of the book is frighteningly simple: the market economy is the evil destroyer of all human value and dignity, and it can only be fought against in terms of an ethics of love. 'I take the demands of love', Vaneigem writes, 'to constitute entirely, at all times and in all places, the sole alternative to market society.' This passage provides unequivocal evidence of the absolutism of Vaneigem's position ('entirely', 'at all times', 'the sole alternative', etc.). He speaks naively of an authentic human species creating, contra the market, conditions favourable to its own harmonious development; and, finally, he advocates his own back to basics programme as a solution to the ills of the market, claiming that beneath the rubble of lies and fraud, late-modern citizens are beginning to re-experience and revalue some 'plain truths of the distant past'. His nostalgia for all things palaeolithic leads him to the claim that economics 'has been the most durable lie of the approximately ten millennia mistakenly accepted as history'. His commitment to harmony and static equilibrium not only belongs to a historically redundant theoretical paradigm – the entropic one of modern critical theory – but also reveals a deep hatred of history, becoming, life, etc. In the face of the marketization of the entire globe, his opposition has about as much practical value and relevance as a recommendation to the Eskimos that, in the face of global warming, they should take up habitation on Venus. The implementation of this green vision of life would require a highly authoritarian politics, a new fascism, of the kind that would forcibly stop the spontaneous emergence of market exchange, resulting in the unleashing of an unimaginable politics not of love but of hate.

6. Viewed from a post-historical perspective, Guy Debord's *Society of the Spectacle* now reads as a paradigmatic example of a classically modernist interpretation of the inhuman time of capital and technology. Looking back in 1988 on this work of 1968, Debord claimed that what he had revealed in his analysis of the spectacle – a kind of Marxian application of Heidegger's thesis on *das Gestell* – was a gradual waning of the sense of history. This concern with the atrophy of historical transcendence has been a common feature of the various strands of critical theory since at least 1945, reaching an apogee in the works of Debord and Marcuse, and present also in the work of Lewis Mumford and his neglected classic of 1957, *The Transformations of Man*.[5] The society of the spectacle denotes the 'autocratic reign' of the market economy which has acceded to an 'irresponsible sovereignty'. In the spectacular society life is no longer lived immediately and resonantly, but has become detached, mediate, and illusory (it has, says Debord, become *philosophical*). Everything which hitherto had been lived directly has now moved into the domain of representation. We now live in a reality that is quickly becoming completely virtualized. As the concrete inversion of life, the spectacle is the 'autonomous movement of the non-living'. In conformity with Marx's analysis of commodity fetishism, Debord maintains that the spectacle does not constitute a collection of images, but rather denotes a social relation between people whose existence is mediated by reified images. Grasped in its totality it is both the result and the project of the current mode of production. It is not to be treated as a supplement to it, which would be to take it as merely decorative, but is to be analysed as the very heart and soul of 'unrealism of the real society'. In its own terms the spectacle represents an 'affirmation of appearance', of all human life as nothing but an appearance, amounting to the end of history as a history of depth. The spectacle is like a virus, spreading everywhere and infecting everyone who becomes contaminated by its illusion, and whose only goal is self-perpetuation. This autonomous self-reproduction of the economy is 'the

---

5 Frederic Jameson defines postmodernism (the cultural logic of late capitalism) as a crisis of historicity in which people's capacity for historical praxis – the activity of being subjects and objects of their own destinal making – has been completely nullified by the world space of multinational capital (Jameson 1991). But post-historic man was already being described as a 'defective monster' in the 1950s by Lewis Mumford. Jameson provides some useful and original cognitive mapping into the realities of our technological futurism in his *tour de force* of an essay on 'Totality and Conspiracy' in Jameson 1995: 9–87. Here he speculates on the extent to which postmodern subjects are no longer able to 'process history' owing to the structural limits of their memory and the fact that the human organism is not able to match the velocities and demographies of the new world system (16).

true reflection of the production of things, and the false objectification of the producers' (Debord 1983: paragraph 16). 'Spectacular technology' does not dispel the religious clouds under which mankind has led an alienated existence, but merely provides it with an earthly cloak. 'The spectacle is the technical realization of the exile of human powers into a beyond; it is separation perfected within the interior of man' (ibid.: 20). The critique which exposes the shallow truth of the spectacle, claims Debord in a moment of privileged insight, reveals itself as the total negation of life. With Debord we find ourselves once again in a Manichean universe, an absolute moralism and humanism confronting an equally absolute immoralism and inhumanism, with history and life posited as unmediated, estranged forces: the demon of history doing battle with the angel of life.

7. It is the forces of production that are responsible for inaugurating the time of history. History has always existed, but not in a historical form. The coming of history amounts to nothing less for Debord than the humanization of time: 'the unconscious movement of time manifests itself and becomes true within historical consciousness' (ibid.: 125). Debord notes that it is the bourgeoisie who perform a revolution of time by subjecting it to a law of perpetual change and innovation (as Marx said, bourgeois society can only exist through the constant revolutionizing of the forces of production). Historical time is not the time of being but the time of auto-production. In an agrarian economy the coalesced forces of tradition which fetter all movement are nourished by a cyclical time. By contrast the irreversible time set into motion by the bourgeois economy eradicates all vestiges of tradition around the entire globe. 'History, which had seemed to be only the movement of individuals of the ruling class, and thus was written as the history of events, is now understood as the *general movement*, and in this relentless movement individuals are sacrificed' (ibid.: 141). The unfolding of economic time means that mankind is subjected to the 'time of things', the mass production of objects produced according to the law of the commodity. The result is a daily invention of history but also of a loss of lived time. However, this history is not historical, merely the repetition of the same, an 'abstract movement of things which dominates all qualitative usage of life'. Debord counters this abstract and inhuman movement of history with the positing of a *subject* of history as the subject 'of' historical time, in which the non-alienated self-constitution and praxial transformation of the worker are pitted against the alienated and automatic objectification of the commodity form (don't you recognize yourself in your alienation, you miserable consciousness?). The subject of history names a living

being which produces itself by becoming 'master and possessor of his world which is history'. The tale being told is one of progress in which the proletariat seizes control of the forces of history, and in the process transforms the invention of history brought into being by the bourgeoisie. If it was the destiny of the bourgeois class to unleash historical time into the rhythms of material existence, it is now the destiny of the working class to humanize this inhuman unleashing by assuming its rightful ownership of, and control over, it.

8. This thinking on time and history is suffused with a metaphysics of authenticity and inauthenticity. The worker, according to Debord, desires not only to make or produce historical time, to be immanent in himself, but to live the time it makes and produces. The 'particular' time of the bourgeoisie, which masquerades as the 'universal' time of the globe, will be replaced by the genuinely authentic time of the worker (echoes of Jünger in Debord – as in Heidegger, Marcuse, and so on). Spectacular time is inauthentic, the time of the commodity that exists in a consumable pseudo-cyclical time of repetition. Authentic time denotes the time in which, or 'of' which, history is simultaneously made and lived (it is not alienated history). The existence of the spectacle serves to remind us of the false consciousness of time, of a time that is not immediate and transparent to the subject who makes history. Debord writes poetically of the prospects for a new proletarian dwelling in which communism offers the promise of the 'total realization' of human time. The ruse of history is that that which threatens this 'twilight world' is also 'the force which could subject space to lived time' (ibid.: 178). Debord ends his anthropocentric speculations on the fate of history and geography by speaking of the 'historical mission of installing truth in the world', a truth that can only be fulfilled when individuals link themselves up with the progressive forces of history. God may have been dead for Debord, but he was keen to resurrect his bloody spirit in the guise of a lordly humanity ruling over not only history but the entire evolution of life.

9. In a recent incisive analysis Regis Debray has compared Debord's manifesto on the society of the spectacle to the posture of the Young Hegelians. He persuasively brings out the striking parallels between Debord's depiction of the spectacle and Feuerbach's critique of religious illusion in his *Essence of Christianity* of 1841, showing that, other than for the detail of phrasing, the discourse of Situationism follows word for word a Hegelian track of alienation, objectification, negation, and reversal, culminating in a reversal of the reversal. In the hands of Debord, Debray notes, the tradition is kept safe. Following a 'recognition', a reversal of the reversal, humans will come back down to earth from their estranged heaven,

overturn their love of God, of ideology, of the State, of the spectacle, into 'a love of active and sentient humanity' (Debray 1995: 136). Debray astutely attributes to Debord a singular failure – a failure he has in common with the broad current of humanist Marxism – to grasp the 'technogenesis of the human' (it is the lack of origin that lies at the origin of mankind's making). The theological postulate of a human essence continues to inform the atheist humanism of neo-Hegelians like Debord that dreams of a final reconciliation of existence with human essence. As a result, essentialist ontologies like Debord's erase the trace of everything that has been discovered about the human animal and evolution since the middle of the nineteenth century, as if Darwin, Freud, Leri-Gourhan, and Simondon had never existed. Debord's essentializing of the transhuman condition can be located within the very terms in which he chooses to 'frame' his analysis: *the* society of *the* spectacle. This is to erase all social, historical, and technological determination, with the result that an analysis is offered which disclaims all mediation, whether 'political' mediation in the form of the structuring instantiation of collective existence, or 'technical' mediation in the form of the structuring instantiation of the hominization process (ibid.: 136–7). The issue confronting critical theory is no longer one of political 'correctness', but that of intellectual anachronism. In an ironic condition of technology it is necessary to recognize that the 'dialectic has indeed fulfilled itself . . . not at all by taking in the negative, as in the dream of critical thought, but in a total, irrevocable positivity' (Baudrillard 1996: 75). It is no longer one's alienation one is fighting aginst, but rather one's transparency.

10. The thesis of the end of history which now dominates the postmodern *Stimmung* was, in fact, a common one in the sensibility of the 1950s. In the work of Maurice Blanchot it is specifically linked to the time of technology. As Blanchot notes, it is not that history comes to an end, but rather that certain principles, questions, and formulations stop making sense. Once the idea of a singular and unique origin, and the idea of a universal historical narrative that accompanies it, is given up on, then we no longer enjoy the right to a language in which the categories that have supported it up to now have become invalidated (categories such as unity, identity, primacy of the Same, the exigency of the self-Subject, etc.) (Blanchot 1993: 272). The time of technology does not mean the end of everything since, as Blanchot notes, the end of everything doesn't amount to much. An apocalyptic declaration of the collapse of the world through the dominance of technology and the erasure of mankind doesn't say a great deal since it belongs to a language of eschatology wholly out of tune with the mood generated by the plural event of nihilism. As Hans Magnus Enzensberger has noted, in a post-

modern, posthistoire world the apocalypse ceases to be a unique, singular event, becoming a regular, almost daily, occurrence (Enzensberger 1990: 151–60). The danger for thinking now, Blanchot holds, is that in taking note of the immense changes taking place as a result of the coming of modern technology, the philosopher will concoct a horrible mix of vague science, confused vision, and dubious theology. While speaking in the name of science he writes as an author of science fiction. This contains a healthy warning against superficial attempts to map inhuman futures and indulge in premature ejaculations celebrating the death of the human (an anthropomorphic declaration if ever there was one). One might begin to locate a way out of the impasse of the 'end' by recognizing nihilism as an inevitable feature of the transhuman condition. The question is whether one has the capacity and resources to emerge from the experience of *Untergang* free of anthropocentric conceits.

11. What takes place when nature is unhumanized and mankind is artificialized? Does nihilism not start knocking on the door as the uncanniest of all guests? While nihilism may not be quite the *a priori* of universal history – or maybe it is as a parody of history that makes buffoons of humans – it can be recognized as the virtual truth of all human history to date. It is for this reason that Nietzsche claims that the causes of nihilism lie in our faith in the categories of reason by which we have measured the value of the world in accordance with categories that refer to a purely fictitious world. Considered psychologically – that is, from the perspective of a psychological *a priori* – human values are the result of utilitarian perspectives that have been designed to enhance human control and mastery over nature and the external world but which in the process have been falsely projected into the essence of things (Nietzsche 1968: section 12B). The positing of themselves as the meaning and measure of evolution is the anthropocentric conceit of humans that is exposed with the advent of nihilism. Now humans feel very small, dwarfed, as if their entire horizon of meaning had been wiped away, with the earth unchained from its sun, the so-called pinnacle of life on earth finds its world growing colder by the day, moving away from all suns, plunging backwards, sideways, forwards, in all directions (Nietzsche 1974: section 125). It is not simply a question of humans recuperating from the illness of nihilism, since their adaptive capacities are severely tested by it. Their hardware and software have been assaulted and invaded by the future. One solution to the problem of humans and their sick becoming is to envision the overhuman as the vision of a non-anthropocentric future of the human. This would be to conceive of the 'human/transhuman' as neither a predicate nor a property that belongs uniquely

to a ready-made subject (such as 'man'). This is a 'subject' best grasped as a 'free, anonymous, and nomadic singularity which traverses men as well as plants and animals independently of the matter of their individuation and the forms of their personality' (Deleuze 1990: 107). This requires a fundamental reconceptualization of the 'value' of evolution. For Nietzsche we lack the right to posit consciousness as the aim and wherefore of the total phenomenon of life. Becoming conscious is simply one means by which the powers of life unfold and extend. It is no more than an anthropocentric prejudice to posit spirituality or morality, or any other sphere of consciousness, as the highest value and seek to justify the world by means of this (Nietzsche 1968: section 707). The objection to be placed against all cosmic theodicies to date, to all the highest values in theology and philosophy (it is theological prejudice that has dominated in philosophy), is that one kind of means – consciousness and human existence – has been misunderstood as the end, with the result that life and the enhancement of its powers are reduced to a mere means. Our logic of means and ends is based on a perverse misunderstanding of the processes of life. It is this reified logic of life that can explain all human philosophies of pessimism and nihilism, such as that which we find in Schopenhauer, where the *denial* of life is posited as the aim of evolution. If life does not conform to the will and wishes of human needs and desires then it is to be denied and calumniated! Such a 'lunatic interpretation', Nietzsche says, is only possible because life is being measured by aspects of consciousness. In this case the means of inhuman life are made to stand against the wished-for human end. The mistake is that instead of a purpose being identified which might explain such a means, a goal that actually excludes such a means is presupposed and posited in advance. Nietzsche identifies the error of Kant's thinking on technics and teleology, for example, as follows: we take a desideratum in respect of certain means as a norm – namely, pleasant, rational, and virtuous ones – on the basis of which is then posited the general purpose of what would be desirable. Kant's ultimate solution is to posit God (theological prejudice), but it is precisely God who turns life into a monstrosity. The greatest reproach against the existence of God is the existence of God. Liberation from pessimism about the human condition and lot is possible once the total consciousness that posits means and ends is eliminated. It is unwise to posit a conception of becoming which appeals to necessity in the shape of an overreaching and dominating total force acting as a kind of prime mover: 'There is no total consciousness of becoming' (ibid.: section 708). If the total value of the world cannot be evaluated, such as its ultimate purpose, then pessimism belongs among comical things. There is no 'in-itself' behind evolution (evolution is not 'spirit') (ibid.: section 709). The world is not an 'organism' but in all respects 'chaos' (ibid.: section 711). The standpoint of overhuman value, if one is to be articulated, would be that concerning the conditions 'of the preservation and enhancement for complex forms of relative life-duration within the flux of becoming' (ibid.: section 715: 1987, volume 13: 36–7). This is not to deny that Nietzsche is not caught up in the net of anthropomorphism. The paradoxes which afflict the doctrine of eternal return are sure evidence that Nietzsche is ensnared in naiveties and conceits like any other modern philosopher. It is, to give just one example, a massive contradiction on his part to urge us to *will* eternal meaninglessness as a way of embracing an eternal nihilism (Nietzsche 1968: section 55; 1987, volume 12: 212ff.).[6]

12. The transhuman condition is not about the transcendence of the human being, but concerns its non-teleological becoming in an immanent process of 'anthropological deregulation'.[7] When Nietzsche asks his 'great' question, what may still become of man?, he is speaking of a future that does not cancel or abort the human, but one which is necessarily bound up with the inhuman and the transhuman. What will become of the human – including its meaning and application as a technical and ontological category – is a question 'of' the future. We children of the future can lend our weight to Nietzsche's essential insight into 'this fragile, broken time of transition (*Übergangszeit*)': the ice that supports people today becomes thinner with each passing day, so that 'we ourselves who are homeless constitute a force that breaks open ice and other all too thin "realities"' (Nietzsche 1974: section 377).

13. Nietzsche maps the arrival of the future, therefore, in terms of an inexorable logic of nihilism, an event which can no longer come differently since it represents the logical conclusion of our great values and ideal so far (Nietzsche 1968: preface, section 4). It is this insight into the logical inevitabilty of nihilism's opening that enables Nietzsche to declare that it is the future which regulates our today. With the advent of this event of nihilism the present becomes a fractured time, a time of splitting, in which the very question of 'man' and the future of the human is called into suspicion and undergoes critical treatment. Nihilism arrives

---

6 The passage I am referring to reads: 'Let us think this thought in its most terrible form: existence as it is, without meaning or aim. . . . This is the most extreme form of nihilism: the nothing (the "meaningless"), eternally!'.
7 I owe this wonderful phrase to Baudrillard (1994: 97), who, unnecessarily and somewhat myopically, restricts its meaning to the genetic transmutation currently underway in the human engineering of genes.

to scramble the codes of the present and to undermine mankind's anthropocentric claim on history. Why, Nietzsche asks, is it necessary to ascribe to everything that happens in nature and history a moral meaning and purpose, such as, he mentions, technology? The task is to become superficial about nihilism by exploring its depths, transmuting oneself into a perfect nihilist who has left the experience 'behind' oneself. An economic, and economical, reading of nihilism is called for. One should not give excessive weight to social distress or suffering in general, since every exaggeration of a narrow point of view is itself already a sign of sickness, like the preponderance of every 'no' over the 'yes'. The 'active negation', the decisive 'no', arises out of the tremendous strength and tension of the affirmative 'yes' (Nietzsche 1968: section 1020). In exposing the transcendental illusion – showing that nihilism canot account for its own creative conditions of possibility and excessive becoming, or the fact that it is always 'beyond' itself – Nietzsche frees the time of nihilism from any passive movement and from any entropic conception of becoming.[8] The danger does not lie in the failure to defeat or conquer nihilism, but rather in the insistence that it should not happen and should not be 'allowed' to happen. Nihilism always speaks of the future, heralding the arrival of something other than itself, and without its event growth would be impossible. Nihilism arrives for us as a necessary learning experience which has been implicit in our positing of values all along. Is nihilism, therefore, solely a problem peculiar to man? 'The most universal sign of the modern age', Nietzsche writes, is the fact that 'man has lost dignity in his own eyes to an incredible extent' (Nietzsche 1968: section 18). Losing the centre of gravity by virtue of which we have lived, and doing penance for having been Christians for two thousand years, we abruptly plunge into opposite valuations 'with all the energy that such an extreme overvaluation of man has generated in man' (ibid.: section 30). Nihilism on this level of extremes is a pathological condition: from the realization that mankind enjoys no ultimate purpose in the evolution of life the inference is drawn that there is no meaning at all. As such, nihilism assumes the guise of a 'monstrous event' (*ungeheure Ereigniss*) that is 'on its way and wanders' (Nietzsche 1974: 125).

---

8 Nietzsche's construal of the arrival of nihilism in terms of the 'uncanniest of all guests' finds an echo in the literature of biology, where entropy is often perceived as the 'uninvited guest' that signals death, decay, and degeneration. A great deal of social and cultural thought from the late nineteenth century onwards has construed nihilism as an entropic force, corrosive in its effects, and damaging to the endurance and performance of social structures and institutions. The only way to critically affirm nihilism and entropy is by exposing the transcendental illusion of both: 'I seek a conception of the world that takes this fact into account – Becoming must be explained without recourse to final intentions . . . ' (Nietzsche 1968: section 708).

As a sign from the future — and the past — of imminent collapse, decay, and transformation, the event of nihilism is monstrous in two senses: firstly, in the sense of scale, as something so tremendous that 'man' may not prove equal to it and will have to undergo a process of self-overcoming in order to endure it; secondly, in the sense of excess, the excessive time of its event which establishes new horizons of meaning: the horizon has become 'free again' (ibid.: 343). The geanealogy of morals establishes a new pathology of life.

14. Not only is it futile, but it is also deeply unintelligent to lament the loss of a centre of gravity, including the alleged corrosion in late modernity of an effective historical agency. Would not the praxis of such a historical agency ironically signal the death of any genuinely interesting becoming? A machinic philosophy of history, which displaces man as the phallogocentric object and goal of history, does not claim that it is machines as opposed to men that make history, since there is no subject or agent of history. To say that machines are inventions of humanity is to utter a truism. To say that the time of their invention is inhuman because it follows a logic of excess is to begin to think extra-morally beyond good and evil (which also includes the affirmation of good and evil). The end of history as conceived by critical modernity enables one to conceive of a more radical notion of becoming which does full justice to its complexity. The notion of the 'rhizome', for example, serves to demonstrate that there is no central controlling agent, or overarching self-positing subject, in a process of complex evolution. Thus, it is no longer possible to conceive of evolution, whether of nature or of industry, in terms of isolated and individual dynamic regimes. The rhizome enables one to conceive of evolution in terms of an intricate, interweaving web of regimes and adaptive systems. The rhizome cuts across linear historical time, both heralding the future (which can come from anywhere), and warning of a scrambling of codes of life that rapidly approach ossification and petrification. So far as the question of technology is concerned, a rhizomatic mapping of our evolution would suggest the necessity of moving away from a Faustian conception of technology — what Toffler has called a 'macho-materialism' (Toffler 1990: 69–84) — with its predilection for total control over nature, over machines, and over techniques of life of all kinds, to one in which the 'undecidability' (in the sense deployed by Deleuze and Guattari) and non-calculability of our 'machinic enslavement' and involvement with the becoming of technics are affirmed and engaged with.

15. At present we are witnessing in a wide range of discourses, including cyber-theory, strands of continental philosophy, and the new biology, a renaissance of grand narratives in which pre-Darwinian notions of evolution are making a rapid

come-back. Our objection to this come-back is partly a matter of taste – they smell offensively of a popular Hegelianism – and partly a matter of intellectual conscience. As Stephen Jay Gould has noted, all classic forms of evolutionary spin doctoring, now revamped in the guise of a techno-Lamarckism, are designed to avoid the unwanted consequences of the Darwinian de-anthropocentrization of evolution, namely, the fact that human beings are not the result of predictable evolutionary progress, but simply a 'fortuitous cosmic afterthought' (Gould 1996: 327). Spin doctoring revolves around two different subjects: the first is the 'process' of evolution considered as a theory and a mechanism; the second is the 'pathway' of evolution considered as a description of the history of life. In the former subject spin doctoring is evident in the attempt to construe evolution as inherently progressive, and as working towards some higher good (the species, for example), producing better-designed organisms in terms of some linear progression; in the second subject spin doctoring is evident in the attempt to read life in terms of a continuous flux displaying directionality towards more and more complex entities, such as beings with large brains. Both of these expressions of spin doctoring are present in the techno-Lamarckism which characterizes many postmodern conceptions of evolution, in which the elevation formerly and anthropocentrically assigned to humans as their rightful privilege over nature is now bestowed on machines as theirs. But here there is an interesting story to tell about the coming of machines, a story of entropy and negentropy.

16. In a novel reworking of the philosophy of history, Richard Blackburn has argued that it is entropy and the destructive forces of nature, such as microparasitism, which serve to corrode the human species and its artificial environment. That which gives rise to humans' invention of an artificial evolution is also that which compels them to enhance their artificiality continually: it is, ironically, both the *producer* and *consumer* of humanity and its distinctive artificial habitat (Blackburn 1990: 20). Our entire civilization has evolved, therefore, in accordance with thermodynamic instability, transforming stable systems into unstable ones in order to release free energy. The cunning of unreason – reason's vampire – exists in symbiotic relationship with the human animal, with the destructive forces absorbing human action and sucking human blood dry. As the rational species which cultivates an intelligence through trial and error in order to devise increasingly superior means to attain its ends, homo sapiens 'is persistently assailed by vampirish objects and agencies whose collective negativity can be designated as the predatory enemy of this rationality, the vampire of reason' (ibid.: 22). This is where speculation on the coming of the machines enters the picture. It

is machines that can now be read as an essential part of the biological ruse of reason. Recent scientific studies, including one on robotics by Hans Moravec, and another by the eminent mathematical physicist Frank Tipler, seek to demonstrate that what is driving the evolutionary push into a machine-dominated and controlled future, including the colonization of the universe, is the problem given to life by entropy, the 'gift' of ultimate and final heat-death (Moravec 1988: 147ff.; Tipler 1995: 109ff.). Tipler, who writes as a self-confessed anti-Heideggerian cybernetician, argues that the colonization of the universe by intelligent self-reproducing machines is the biosphere's only chance of surviving the inevitable demise of our solar system at the grim hands of the second law of thermodynamics. He resurrects de Chardin's notion of the 'Omega Point' to support his neg-entropic promise of guaranteed immortality for all in the future (see de Chardin 1965: 283ff.).[9] The Omega Point refers to the point at which the noosphere coalesces into a supersapient being. Tipler does not deny that the second law is operative in the universe's final meltdown, but maintains that the 'energy of the gravitational shear near the Omega Point is sufficient to avoid Heat Death' (Tipler 1995: 109). As the Omega Point is approached a free energy source – the differential collapse of the universe – diverges to infinity, so escaping the moment of final death.

17. If this vision of the future sounds like a horrible concoction of science, science fiction and highly dubious theology, it is even more disturbing than appears at first sight. This vision of neg-entropic futures ultimately rests on a biologistic legitimation of capital and universal imperialism. This comes out clearly in Lyotard's depiction of the monster of the future in his thinking of the time of the inhuman. In an essay entitled 'Time Today' Lyotard tells an uncomfortable – and, one might think, irrelevant – story about the next few billion years. While you read this book the sun gets older and older. In 4.5 billion years, though it is not necessary to fix an exact date, it will explode in a truly earth-shattering

---

9 In the perspective of 'noogenesis' the aim, de Chardin says, is not to 'humanize' time and space but rather to *super-humanize* them. Far from being mutually exclusive, the 'universal' and the 'personal' (the centred) can be posited as growing in the same direction and culminating simultaneously in one another. Thus, 'The Future-Universal could not be anything else but the Hyper-Personal – at the Omega Point' (de Chardin 1965: 285–6).

It should also be noted, as not incidental to his conception of the neg-entropic future, that de Chardin advocated the utilization in the coming centuries of a 'noble human form of eugenics' in order that moral and medical factors can replace 'the crude forces of natural selection' (ibid.: 310).

display of fireworks. At the moment the earth is just a little beyond the halfway point of its expected lifetime, a life devoted to death, no doubt casting life on earth into a mid-life crisis. The only future one can be certain of is that of arrangements of matter and energy facing constant self-creation and self-destruction. At the limit point of the death of the sun – a death which will dwarf that of God's in comparison – history will truly end and our insoluble questioning will matter no more, existing beyond piety. Of course, the limit spoken of only makes sense in a human context. Once the sun explodes there will no longer be such a limit since the human will no longer be 'there' to experience either side of it. Only matter will remain, but, as we *Daseins* know, matter does not matter.

18. According to Lyotard, we are witnessing in the age of hyper endo- and exo-colonistic capital the gathering of forces in a process of neg-entropy that has been underway since life first began on earth.[10] The problem – same as it ever was, and it was – is that of time, or rather to be more precise, the fact that the universe is running out of it. Moravec puts it like this: in a continually expanding universe time is cheap but energy has to be carefully husbanded, while in a collapsing universe, such as the one we unfortunately occupy, energy is cheap but there is no time to waste. All life-forms, Lyotard suggests, can be regarded as technical devices for filtering information useful to an organism's survival and for processing this information in self-regulating terms. Now, the human being can be broken into its hardware and software aspects. The body is the hardware of the complex technical device we call 'thought'. The software is the symbolic and recursive power of human language. The fate of technology is being decided by the attempt to provide the human software with a hardware that is independent of the entropic conditions of life on planet earth. The new computer technologies are making possible the programming and control of information, such as its memorization, less and less dependent on earth-bound conditions. The human race thus finds itself pulled forwards – but not upwards – by this time of information at an ever-increasing velocity, experiencing more and more 'future shock', such is the race against time. Time is not, and never has been, on our side. The human brain can now be depicted as the midwife that services this cosmic

---

10 See Margulis and Sagan 1995: 23: 'One should not assume that only humans are future-oriented. Our own frenetic attempts (and those of the rest of life) to survive and prosper may be a special, four billion-year old way the universe has organized itself "to" obey the second law of thermodynamics.'

process of complexification.[11] Cybernetics appears as the (in)human science of control and communication which freely places itself in the service of the neg-entropic evolution of the great cosmic mind, confirming Heidegger's prophetic insight into the take-over of the heritage of philosophy by the new science of cybernetics (Heidegger 1972: 58). In this autonomous process of complexification the aim is to stock more and more information, to improve competence, and to make efficiency gains (such as the junking of the outlived human body), and in this way to maximize performance and increase our chances of success against the demonic powers of the future. When seen in this context, Lyotard's argument goes, capital can be seen for what it is, not so much a figure in or of human history, but more the effect of an ancient cosmic destiny. Human beings have never been the subjects of this process, even though they have been ironic agents of it, witless collaborators in the making of their own redundancy (the irony of technology would appear to be a lethal one).

19. It is in the context of these paradoxical – human or inhuman? – reflections on the time of the future that Lyotard reconsiders his definition of the postmodern condition as signalling the end of grand narratives of emancipation and enlightenment.[12] He now suggests that we think of it in terms of a split between two pro's, on the one hand the project of enlightenment modernity and its dream of self-transparency and social immanence, and on the other, the 'programme' of inhuman neg-entropic postmodernity. The modern project of emancipation through the maturity of enlightenment was novel in not being governed by the past, being in essence futural. In this way it has served the process of complexification, the process which ironically leads to its own demise. The illusion it endures, however, is believing that the entropy of time and its neg-entropic evolution can be made subject to human history. Unfortunately, at least from the perspective of our existence as humanoids, it is the 'programme' that is proving better able to meet the challenges thrown down to life by entropy. As Lyotard sees it, the dominance of the programme brings with it the attempt to neutralize as far as possible the unpredictable effects engendered by the freedom and contingency that belong uniquely to the human project. The reign of bodiless information means nothing less than the end of the event (of time). The task of philosophy

---

11 One of the earliest accounts of this phenomenon can be found in de Chardin 1965: 53, who speaks of the 'law of complexification' as the 'great law of biology'.
12 See Lyotard 1989, where he writes: 'This is what the postmodern world is all about. Most people have lost the nostalgia for the lost narrative. It in no way follows that they are reduced to barbarity. Science . . . has taught them the harsh austerity of realism' (41).

today is simply that of bearing testimony to the non-event of the event. If in *The Postmodern Condition* Lyotard had sought to live beyond nostalgia and mourning, he is now firmly entrenched in such a condition, devotionally mourning the event of lost time for the rest of time.

20. Unknown to himself, Lyotard has in fact resurrected in this grand narrative of the time of the inhuman an old theory of technics that characterized a strand of thought in the late nineteenth century, notably in the writings of Henry Adams, which was taken up again in more recent times by Jacques Ellul in the 1950s. Adams, for example, believed that history was governed by a law of acceleration which involved a process of increasing energy, organization, and complexity that defied all attempts at either conscious direction or opposition. When the machines land we humans simply become the carriers of their will: 'A law of acceleration', he wrote, 'cannot be supposed to relax its energy to suit the convenience of man' (Adams 1931: 493). On this model of the time of the inhuman, history is reduced to physics in which historical development is to be accounted for in terms of the government of thermodynamics, the science of the relationship of heat and mechanical energy. The increase in energy and organized complexity is what constitutes the anti-entropic becoming of material reality (Winner 1977: 48–9). There are a number of problems afflicting this well-worn depiction of evolution by neg-entropy (there is nothing postmodern about it). For all its talk of complexity, or complexification, it rests on a dubious linear, rational, additive accumulation (see ibid.: 63), with the result that on this model technics does become *Geist*, nothing but *Geist*. As one commentator on the phenomenon has noted, entropy and the laws of thermodynamics, like all scientific constructs, can be deployed to secure an anthropocentric conception of life's evolution (Rifkin 1981: 260) (on the human organism conceived as 'the perfect animal', on account of its being a 'spontaneously, self-producing' neg-entropic 'end', and hence the apotheosis of nature in spirit, see Hegel 1970b: 108–9). Jameson is simply wrong when he suggests that within postmodernity we witness the emergence of a new kind of narrative that is more consistent with the dynamics of the world system than the older anthropomorphic or humanist kind which centred on notions of personal agency (1995: 56). The new grand narratives are as anthropormorphic as hell. The danger of this anthropocentric utilization of entropy thinking is that the phenomena of instrumental rationality and technological mastery are provided with a biologistic reasoning and the evolution of technics is unproblematically compared to the process of natural selection selecting ever more complex forms of life. This, for example, is the position of Blackburn, who mistakenly attributes

to Darwinism a teleological drive in favour of the selection of complexity (1990: 211). But natural selection contains no inbuilt tendency in favour of complexity (indeed, it has real difficulties in explaining it). There is no 'law' within the theory of natural selection that would enable one to claim that evolution displays any kind of teleological progressivism, including a drive towards complexity. To propose otherwise, and to apply such a model to human technical evolution, is to naturalize and reify the contingent, non-linear, and rhizomatic character of our technological becoming.[13] It is also to give the evolution of technology the status of social Darwinism, which rests on a highly crude conception of 'fitness'. Indeed, this was precisely how Samuel Butler conceived of the coming of machines as far back as the 1860s as the next line of the fittest. Such a view necessarily results from any attempt to place 'Darwin among the machines' (and, one might add, the humans). Instead of recognizing the challenge Darwinism presents for the philosophy of history, Blackburn identifies Kantian and Hegelian speculations with natural selection.[14] The problem with current theorizing on our inhuman futures is that it ends up reifying the demonic powers it sets out to demystify. In the case of Lyotard's thinking on time today, the monstrous logic of capitalism is granted a logic of autonomy which in reality it does not enjoy. His presentation of the inhuman time of our neg-entropic destiny results in an abstract and ahistorical opposition between a pure ethicism on the one hand and the unstoppable – because cosmic – accumulation process on the other. Is this not to be seduced by capital's own desire to construct itself as the transcendental ground of all change and innovation?[15] Capital enjoys a monopoly on neither entropy nor neg-entropy.

---

13 One will find little evidence in Darwinian theory for Blackburn's contention that nature manifests a tendency towards an ever more complex and expansive order, an order, he claims, which has been 'promoted in the case of living things by natural selection and in the case of human beings by means of the higher forms of existence' (1990: 160). Of course, the positing of a drive for complexity is entirely intelligible within a Lamarckian schema of evolution. For more on this see Burkhardt 1995: 151ff.

14 'The cunning of reason in human history for Hegel and the cunning of nature in political history for Kant can be seen as intimating the operation of progressive forms of natural selection' (Blackburn 1990: 161). The only problem here is that it is not 'natural' selection that is being identified but an entirely different process.

15 There is little that is 'empirical' about the claims of our current 'capital-logicians', as Jameson has called this new species of idol worshippers. On the contrary, their claims are purely 'philosophical': 'what Hegel . . . called Absolute Spirit, is now from our perspective rather to be identified as Capital itself, whose study is now our true ontology . . . for us the absent totality, Spinoza's God or Nature, the ultimate (indeed perhaps the only) referent, the true ground of being of our own time' (Jameson 1995: 82).

As Deleuze and Guattari argue, capitalism can be treated as an 'axiomatic' precisely because it operates immanently. In other words, it has no laws of development other than immanent ones, which is why when it confronts limits these prove to be nothing other than its own limits (Deleuze and Guattari 1980: 579; 1988: 463).[16] Lyotard has, in key respects, provided a postmodern update of Marcuse's well-known and untenable thesis on one-dimensionality advanced with a degree of historical acuity in the 1960s. One-dimensionality in Lyotard's schema is part of life's long battle with entropy. The real problem with Lyotard's fantastical account is that it ascribes to capital a vitalism and a teleology. He thus ends up, ironically, offering us the kind of meta-narrative which he had sought to show in the earlier essay on the postmodern condition was now discredited. Grand narratives concerning a neg-entropic future end up being complicit with the image that the system of control likes to project of itself, that is, portraying advanced technological life as if it were simply a mere continuation of natural history. The cybernetic dream of a virtually instinctive machine of self-regulation is, as Habermas has noted, equivalent to the 'biological base value of survival at any cost, that is, ultrastability' (Habermas 1987: 60). It is precisely for this reason that one must demand a continual *politicization* (and artificialization) of evolution.

21. The thesis on the autonomous character of technical development ignores not only the crucial mediating role played by the social machine, but also the origins of self-regulating capital in specific relations of production, such as private property. No matter how much cybernetic capital assumes a monstrous, reified form, abstractly and inhumanly pursuing its own logic of autonomy, this does not mean that it has transcended its origins in specific social relations of production. It simply gives the appearance or illusion of such transcendence. To propose the end of politics as far as the question of technology is concerned – on the basis of the intellectually lazy claim that technology is getting 'out of control' – is simply to become seduced by capitalism's effective depoliticization of the matter of planetary evolution. Certain power interests are nicely served by such

---

16 The difference Deleuze and Guattari are referring to here is that between an 'axiomatic' and a 'code'. The former operates immanently in the sense that it deals directly with functional elements and relations, the nature of which is 'indeterminate', while the latter works transcendentally and expresses specific and determinate relations between elements that cannot be subsumed by a higher formal unity *except* by means of transcendence (1980: 567; 1988: 454). The passage from political obligation by (transcendent) divine right to obligation by (immanent) rational self-determining agency (contract by consent) illustrates the difference on the level of the transition to political modernity.

depoliticization. Taken in themselves machines explain nothing since they are always part of apparatuses and assemblages that are as much social as they are technical. Moreover, the evolution of technology does not take place in terms of some rational teleology, and in its concrete details its history cannot be said to be either linear or a matter of destiny. Rather, the development of technical machines, including technology as a global system, is the story of contingencies and situations of historical lock-in. For example, the utilization and exploitation of certain energy resources and fuels is the result of such historical contingency and lock-in, in which the 'decisions' of the social machine of a capitalist world economy are crucial. Today new lessons about economics and politics can be learned from the biology of distributed control in fields of self-organization and in processes of emergent 'informal' order in complex systems, in which the role of central control is positively disastrous and simply unintelligent. On the level of global culture and politics the imperialist-entropic logic of 'development' needs to be contested in the light of knowledge gained from observation of these phenomena. The dominant mono-agricultural policies imposed upon third world farming practices is just one example of this entropic logic of development pursued by technologies whose evolution is driven by capital's logic of accumulation. The farming techniques of these local cultures already contain their own highly sophisticated and intelligent mechanisms and systems of feedback in which learning and adaptation take place and in which innovations are tried and tested. 'Third world' economists and others have effectively challenged the widespread view prevalent among Western 'experts' that farming practices based on biodiversity enjoy only low productivity (see Goodwin 1995: 213ff.). New developments in genetically engineered agriculture are a prime example of entropic development, the product of a monocultural mind-frame that ignores the qualitative fertility of species diversity in favour of quantitative reductionism, in which variety and diversity are sacrificed in favour of the cultivation of specific species' traits that are maximized in order to give a high yield of certain products, such as milk from cows, seed from grain, and so on. This is not an argument against engineering and artifice in favour of some questionable return to nature; rather, it is an argument about types of engineering and modes of agriculture. Legitimations of the economic forces of entropic capital are based on the application of crude Darwinian models of survival of the fittest, but in such accounts the 'test' of fitness is naturalized and depoliticized. The issue of 'development' is not an issue of nature but one about politics. To account for the apparent universal triumph of capitalist development by appealing to the lesson of entropy, as Lyotard does, is simply to evade the task of thinking about political options, opportunities, and struggles. It provide us with a debilitating vision of our future inhumanity which, through the biologization of the forces of evolution, spuriously takes on the appearance of a destiny that is judged to be beyond 'human' influence.

22. There is much that is apposite in Lyotard's reflections on time today. He is correct to claim that capital is a far greater inhuman force than we dare admit to ourselves. As he notes, capitalism is only the name given to a socio-economic process of development of which no one is master (Lyotard 1993: 96). However, this insight opens up spaces of resistance as much as it encourages acquiescence in an evolutionary system alleged to be 'out of control'. Here it is necessary to divorce a speculative comprehension of capital from conventional fascist-paranoid images of it. As Baudrillard has noted, capital is a 'sorcery' of the social relation, a challenge to society that needs to be responded to as such, not denounced according to some ahistorical criterion of morality or economic rationality (Baudrillard 1992: 174). Capital operates as a virtual machine trapped within a productionist logic of eternal repetition. As Brian Massumi has argued, capital operates virtually in the sense that it transforms production into futural processuality in which activity is fundamentally energetic rather than object-oriented. It is not, for example, simply a question of late-modern society capitalizing on life-forms in terms of imposing upon them an external mechanism of capture and putting them up for sale. Rather, life-forms that have never existed, being solely the product of an artificial manufacturing, are commercialized at the point of their emergence. Within postmodern capital, human life exists within a virtual modality and from the angle of its mutational aptitude (Massumi 1992: 135): 'The capitalist machine has developed perceptual abilities that enable it to penetrate life and direct its unfolding. It can go straight to the code of its molarity, resolve it into its constituent part-objects (in this case genes), recombine them to yield a special-order product (adult individuals) and market the final product – or the transformational *process* itself, at any one of its steps' (ibid.: 133–4). Deleuze and Guattari have noted that as the molar mode of organization characteristic of the modern social machine becomes 'stronger', it reveals a tendency to effect a molecularization of its elements and relations. Such a process of miniaturization defines the existence of the human 'mass' individual within late-modern capitalism, which in order to perfect its exploitation of the human has learned how to molecularize the individual and introduce a whole micro-management of petty fears, so creating a macro-politics of society that is governed by a micro-politics of insecurity (Deleuze and Guattari 1988: 216). If it is the case that politics has been rendered superfluous in the face of the economism of capitalist deterritorialization, becoming little more than the effectuation of a programme

of administration and management, that is, a system of anti-production soaking up machinic surplus value, then a significant refusal consists in not granting capital the first and last word as the 'subject' and goal-less goal of evolution (goal-less because it is motored by cybernetic self-stabilization, the eternal return of entropic death cultivated as a living system). Capital is a certain type of machinic assemblage, a particular social machine which operates on the machinic phylum but which neither controls nor steers machinic evolution. With the advent of the modern State a mutation takes place in which the regime of 'machinic enslavement' that charaterized the imperial Signifier is replaced by a regime of 'social subjection'. The condition of the modern/postmodern is an ambiguous one because under capital decoded flows of energy and matter do not cease to flow or cease to engender new flows. The difference between enslavement and subjection can be understood along the following lines: in the former, pre-capitalist condition human beings exist as constituent pieces of a machine which they form among themselves and with other things, such as animals and tools, under the direction of a higher unity (a megamachine) (Mumford 1966: 1–15). In the latter, capitalist condition, however, human beings are no longer simply components of the great machine, but workers and users socially subjected and mediated rather than enslaved. Capitalism brings with it the triumph of motorized machines and the deterritorialization of technical machines, as Marx recognized, arguing that it is not machines that create capital but capital that creates machines (Marx 1976: 492ff.). It would be a mistake to view our modern condition as simply a novel form of ancient enslavement to the megamachine, since what is distinctly modern about it is that it takes place on the level of the immanence of an axiomatic, and not under the transcendence of a formal unity. Moreover, the rise of cybernetic and informational machines implements a more generalized and insidious mode of subjection: 'recurrent and reversible "humans–machines systems" replace the old nonrecurrent and nonreversible relations of subjection between the two elements; the relation between human and machine is based on internal, mutual communication, and no longer usage or action' (Deleuze and Guattari 1980: 572; 1988: 458). With the evolution of late-modern capital any distinction between the organic composition of capital (the source of human surplus value) and the machinic composition of capital becomes blurred and actually breaks down as a tenable or useful distinction (compare Marcuse 1968: 27–37).[17]

---

17 For further insight into the development of human and machinic surplus value see the important analysis in Deleuze and Guattari 1984: 232ff. As they note, the flows of code liberated in science and technics by the capitalist mode of production engender a machinic surplus value, in which

23. The 'evolution' of the system of capitalism can be de-reified by exposing, through a machinic analysis, the illusion of total control it inevitably gives rise to. It has to be seen as a system of production that is subject to a complex evolution which proceeds by way of experimentation and testing, utilizing a pragmatic adaptiveness in the face of an ever-changing 'environment' that it itself has immanently and artificially produced. The function of an axiomatic – whether one is speaking of politics, morality, science, or technology – is to put a stoppage on decoded flows, to arrest their movement, so as to ensure that they do not break out in all directions and lead into uncontrollable and unpredictable trajectories. Deleuze and Guattari list four main flows that persist in tormenting the centralized powers of the world economy: the flows of matter-energy, the flow of population, the flow of food, and urban flow (Deleuze and Guattari 1980: 584–5; 1988: 468). The problems associated with these flows are generated by the axiomatic but are not resolvable by it (an obvious example is the circulation and distribution that would make it possible to feed the entire population of the world). It thus becomes necessary to speak on behalf of life in all its immorality so as to give expression to all the other sonorous machines which fill up the messy universe. As Deleuze and Guattari argue, the very conditions that make the State and its capture of the war machine possible, namely, constant capital (tools, techniques, and equipment) and variable capital (human invention and ingenuity), also continually re-create unexpected possibilities for 'counterattack, unforeseen initiatives determining revolutionary, popular, minority, mutant machines', and for the creation of new non-organic social relations (ibid.: 1980: 526–7; 1988: 422–3). It is not a question of a (post-)historic creature – the human animal – facing inevitable and tragic death at the hands of a monster from outer space (neg-entropic capital). It now becomes a matter of affirming our involvement in a machinic becoming and actively participating in our inhumanization, as opposed to thinking that the human being stands outside the machine with the power to negate abstractly its own machinic conditions of existence.

---

knowledge, information, and specialized education are as much parts of capital ('knowledge capital') as is the most elementary labour of the worker. Toffler calls this the 'Global K-Factor', which he regards as decisive for an understanding of the economic and political dynamics of 'third wave' societies (Toffler 1990: 391ff.). Indeed, Toffler goes so far as to claim that the K-factor poses a far greater long-term threat to the power of organized finance than organized labour and anti-capitalist political interest groups and parties (ibid.: 89). Such an insight also informed Lyotard's conception of the 'postmodern condition', in which it was noted that in the age of computerized machines 'the question of knowledge is now more than ever a question of government' (Lyotard 1989: 9).

24. As Immanuel Wallerstein has pointed out, the crisis of capitalism as a geopolitical world economic system is not 'moral' but 'structural' (Wallerstein 1991a: 111). By 'crisis' he means something quite specific, referring to the situation in which a complex historical system evolves to a point at which the cumulative effects of its internal contradictions means that it is no longer possible for the system to resolve its dilemmas through adjustments in its 'ongoing institutional patterns'. The capitalist world economy constitutes a 'historical' system with a historical life – a genesis, cyclical rhythms, and secular trends – and a set of contradictions that ultimately signal its demise. Contradictions, Wallerstein maintains, are not to be viewed simply as conflicts but rather denote a special case of transition. The latter always exist in a system, whereas the former emerge at crystallized points of transformation and are specific to singularities or phase transitions. Contradictions refer to 'structural pressures' which compel groups to move in opposite directions at the same time. They do so, not because of some natural schizophrenia, but because their immediate interests conflict with their long-term interests. As a result, social groups engage in behaviour designed to resolve these dilemmas which then creates secular trends that serve to undermine the viability of the historical system. Organized opposition, he insists, is endogenous to the evolution of the system, that is, it can be viewed as part of the same secular development that characterizes the system's structures. Wallerstein argues that short-term contradictions lead to middle-term solutions which translate into long-term linear curves that then approach asymptotes (ibid.: 14). As these asymptotes are approached the pressures to return to an equilibrial condition diminish, leading to increasing oscillations and bifurcation in the system. The result is not a small change in a curve emerging from large random fluctuations, but large changes resulting from small fluctuations. This condition of 'complexity' in an adaptive system such as late capitalism can serve to explain why the sense of crisis has become so endemic to the system on every level from the economic to the moral, political, and cultural. On the economic level, the crisis is generated by, firstly, the secular trend of complete commodification (now widely accepted as the standard definition of the postmodern condition), and, secondly, the political trend to a squeeze on long-term profit margins. It does not matter if this economic and structural crisis manifests itself most visibly on the level of a cultural politics. As Wallerstein notes, the worldwide assemblage of antisystemic movements has, from 1968 onwards, grown stronger, bolder, and more diverse and difficult to contain and manage. The sense of crisis reflects a general, pervasive dismay at 'this flowering of tendencies which seem on the point of getting out of control' (ibid.: 110). However, if birfurcation points are

unpredictable in their outcomes it is impossible to locate any inevitable secular line of human history that would enable one to speak securely of 'progress'. Like all great historical systems, capitalism will perish more as a result of its successes than its failures. Wallerstein thus suggests, as did Deleuze and Guattari in the infamous analysis of capitalism 'and' schizophrenia in *Anti-Oedipus*, that it is only in the acceleration of the decadence of the present system, and not in its controlled transformation, that the prospects lie for creating a new world-historical system (Wallerstein 1991b: 36).[18]

25. Deleuze and Guattari themselves offer a politics of multiplicities which contends the power of that which cannot be calculated by the prevailing axiomatic. The becoming-minoritarian to be affirmed does not simply refer to a small number but to that which escapes statistical capture and regulation, speaking of things which do not admit of 'resolution'. They insist that this is not to denigrate the struggle and resistance that take place on the level of hegemonic axioms, such as the struggles of the third world, the struggle for women's rights, the struggle for abortion, and so on. The emphasis is on these struggles as indexes of another becoming, one whose aims and objectives cannot be assimilated or co-opted by the axiomatic. It is not a question of the 'minority' entering and taking over the majority system; rather, the task is one of bringing to bear the force of the non-denumerable. The issue is badly considered if it is posed in terms of anarchy versus organized molar politics, or decentralization versus centralism. Rather, it is a matter of a calculus of difference which cannot be calculated in terms of the logic of an identity politics. The contention of the non-denumerable is not, it should be stressed, the expression of a political idealism or an abstract moralism. To claim that it is, is to ignore everything Deleuze and Guattari say about capitalism and its outside or other. They rightly warn against reifying politics either by treating its theory as an apodictic science or treating its praxis in terms of a world super-government that makes all the final, one-dimensional decisions. As they point out, no one is in a position to control the money supply, let alone control once and for all the molecular flows and machinic transformations produced within the schizzo-logic of the capitalist machine. They clarify the politics of the undecidable as follows:

---

18 'So what is the solution? Which is the revolutionary path? . . . To withdraw from the world market . . . in a curious revival of the fascist "economic" solution? Or might it be to go in the opposite direction? To go still further, that is, in the movement of the market, of decoding and deterritorialization?' (Deleuze and Guattari 1984: 239)

when we talk about 'undecidable propositions' we are not referring to the uncertainty of resolutions, which is a necessary feature of every system. We are referring, on the contrary, to the coexistence and inseparability of that which the system conjugates, and that which never ceases to escape it following lines of flight that are themselves connectable. The undecidable is the germ and locus par excellence of revolutionary decisions. Some people invoke the high technology of the world system of enslavement; but even, and especially, this machinic enslavement abounds in undecidable propositions and movements that far from belonging to a domain of knowledge reserved for sworn specialists, provides so many weapons for the becoming of everybody/everything, becoming-radio, becoming-electronic, becoming-molecular.

(Deleuze and Guattari 1980: 590–1; 1988: 473)

26. Almost all modern thought has privileged an equilibrial model of reality. This is true of both positivist and German idealist traditions of thought in the nineteenth century. Classical economics, for example, in spite of its early appreciation of self-regulatory systems through bottom-up emergence, and the free play of market forces, rests on the assumption that stable and harmonious order is generated through the power of the invisible hand. In short, classical economics, like classical social theory, has no conception of positive feedback and the role it plays in social-technical evolution. In idealist philosophy the classic example of an equilibrial model is Hegel's speculative dialectic, which gives expression to a cognitive faith in the power of the mind to triumph over the complex, chaotic, and unpredictable forces of evolution. In spite of his recognition of the role of discord, disharmony, and inequality in the generation of life, Hegel's holism is one which can only construe the functioning of the whole in terms of 'stable equilibrium of all the parts', evolving in terms of the 'alienation of opposites', with 'each part a Spirit at home in this whole' (Hegel 1980: sections 462 and 486). On this model all 'negativity' (what is alien or outside) only exists to confirm the immense self-recuperative powers of Reason, which can even look into 'the entrails of things and open every vein in them' and still find itself at home in the universe (Hegel 1970a: 186). Today, the sciences of chaos and complexity theory are exposing the extent to which the real is no longer 'rational', and vice versa, but rather the most probable, giving priority to chance, to singularity and phase-space transition, and to non-linear dynamical systems which thrive on positive feedback: 'All knowledge is bordered by that about which we have no information' (Serres 1982: 83). Around the time that Hegel was seeking to deify history (the story of God's marching on earth) with his speculative propositions, a little-known French army engineer by the name of Sadi Carnot was carrying out work on steam engines which would launch the science of thermodynamics and blast apart the equilibrial assumptions of the new idealism. In his *Reflections on the*

*Motive Power of Fire* Carnot stressed the extent to which in the steam engine heat – what, following Lavoisier, he called 'caloric' – flowed from a high-temperature region (the boiler) to a low-temperature one (the condenser). Carnot incorrectly concluded that no energy is lost from the system, but nevertheless realized that the more efficient the system the less energy it needed to run on, and that what produced the energy was the difference between the boiler and the condenser (Carnot 1960: 50). Carnot enthusiastically drew analogies between natural heat engines and synthetic ones, insisting that it was to heat that the motive power of life owed its origins and evolution. What Carnot enables us to see is that human technology is basically a species of neg-entropic capture designed to ward off catastrophism, but whose invention always exceeds its own constructed apparatuses of capture on account of its deterritorializing character.[19] It was Rudolf Clausius who coined the term 'entropy' in 1865 to account for the heat lost from any mechanical system. In the Newtonian model no energy is lost in the system, with the result that all processes are reversible and chance has no role to play. In the new thermodynamic model, however, energy is no longer conceived mechanistically and irreversibility becomes the principal directional 'law' of time, serving to introduce randomness and disorder into any system from the unstable borders of a cloud to the movement of tides and a jagged shoreline. Michel Serres has drawn a useful distinction between the two models by describing mechanical systems as 'statutes' that are based on fixity and equilibrium, and post-Carnot systems as 'motors' that create movement (dynamics) and that go beyond the simple relations of forces through the creation of innovative energy (Serres 1982: 71). It is thus only on the basis of the second law that we can begin to conceive the dynamics of multi-temporal living systems, including the drift of irreversible thermal flow, the quasi-stability of eddies, the conservative inheritance of genetic nuclei, the erratic blinking of aleatory mutations, and the upstream flows of neg-entropic islands such as recycling, refuse, memory, growth in complexity, etc. (ibid.). Entropy thus becomes the 'marker' of evolution in a system, its 'arrow of time'. Moreover, increasing entropy points towards the spontaneous evolution of that system. The achievement of Boltzman lay in showing that irreversible

---

19 Manuel de Landa provides a helpful account of Carnot's invention of 'abstract machines' (1991: 141–2). Carnot's abstract depiction of the heat engine is abstract enough for its terms to be reversed so that it could be used to build a refrigerator. Once an abstract mechanism is dissociated from its physical materiality, it enters the lineages of other technologies. For further insight into Carnot see Serres 1982: 54–65. On computers as the 'realization' of *plastic* 'abstract machines' see Langton 1988: 11.

increases in entropy are expressions of growing molecular disorder and of the gradual erosion of initial states of dissymetry.

27. Prigogine has argued that life expresses in specific ways the conditions in which the biosphere is embedded, 'incorporating the nonlinearities of chemical reactions and far-from equilibrium conditions imposed on the biosphere by solar radiation' (Prigogine and Stengers 1985: 14). The 'rediscovery of time' within science – by which is meant the primacy of irreversible processes – takes place within a new model of 'evolution' that conceives of non-equilibrium, the flow of matter and energy, as generative of special and complex kinds of order, for example, 'dissipative structures' which are dissipative because their inner organization is capable of upholding a minimum entropy production (the excess of entropy is passed on to the environment). Vilmos Csanyi has argued that the laws of thermodynamics, of the conservation and dissipation of energy, only stipulate the general conditions necessary for a living system to exist, and on their own are insufficient for explaining the functioning, complexity, and structure of biological systems. In other words, there is a fundamental difference between the complexity of a living cell and the orderliness of a simple chemical reaction (Csanyi 1989: 31). Brooks and Wiley lend support to this view when they argue that if living organisms 'obey' the second law, just as steam engines do, then strictly thermodynamic considerations are unlikely to explain the diversification of organisms compared to the lack of diversity among steam engines (Brooks and Wiley 1988: 33). Csanyi insists upon a qualitative distinction between order and organization. It is the self-organizing phenomenon of replication that is able to account for the complexity of organization. An individual bacterial cell is able to spread its mode of organization by producing its own components in a large number of copies at the expense of the system's energy resources. The bacterial cells can be viewed as a 'system precursor', defined as a 'minimal network of components that is able to maintain its own organization and also to transform an unorganized system into one of similar organization' (Csanyi 1989: 47). Csanyi's work is successful in exposing the transcendental illusion of entropy, but it remains stuck within an autopoietic, or autogenetic, model of evolution, and so is unable to account for the machinic character of the complex, implicated becoming of living systems.

28. What are the implications of this paradigm-shift in the natural sciences, away from static and equilibrial models to non-linear and dynamical ones, for an understanding of social and historical reality? The best way to think this is by way of a contrast between modern and postmodern models of science. Classical science pictures a world in which every event is determined by initial conditions which

are, in principle, determinable with absolute precision. This science emphasizes stability, order, harmony, uniformity, etc., and concerns itself with closed systems and linear relations in which small inputs uniformly yield small results. Its hubristic nature is best captured in the image of Laplace's well-known demon, which, equipped with Newton's laws of motion and gravity and knowledge of the position of every particle of matter, believes itself able to predict the future of the entire universe (it is reported that Metternich always went into battle with a copy of Laplace stuffed in his uniform). The new paradigm, however, concentrates attention on open systems (such as the earth in relation to the cosmos) and non-linear relations in which small inputs are capable of triggering tremendous change and innovation. A chaotic system is simply defined as one which shows a sensitivity to initial conditions. This goes completely against the grain of classical science, since it is based on the insight that any uncertainty in the initial state of a system, no matter how seemingly small or trivial, will lead to growing errors in any attempt to predict its future behaviour. Complexity theory recognizes that there are closed systems, but insists that these constitute only a small part of the physical universe. Most biological and social systems are open systems, exchanging energy or matter and information with their environment, and enjoying potentialities for evolution (precisely what 'evolution' means in complexity will be addressed shortly) that are not susceptible to simple mechanical equations and predictability. All systems contains sub-systems which experience constant fluctuation. At times a single fluctuation, or a combination of fluctuations, may become so powerful that, as a result of positive feedback, the existing or prevailing structure and organization are shattered. This can be defined as the moment of 'revolution' in a system, a point of singularity and bifurcation. In recent decades molecular biologists have found that positive feedback loops – what chemists call auto-catalysis – constitute the very stuff of dynamic life, showing that self-organization emerges spontaneously under conditions that are far from equilibrium and that produce dramatic reorganizations of matter. It is this emphasis on non-linear processes that reach points of bifurcation, in which slight fluctuations or deviations can have massive consequences, that Wallerstein has deployed to fruitful effect in his treatment of historical systems as complex systems. For him the fact that the 'solution' of a bifurcation is indeterminate does not mean that it is beyond the reach of serious research or speculative inquiry. By clarifying the network of forces at work, and elaborating possible vectors, it ought to become possible, he suggests, to cast light on 'real historical choices' (Wallerstein 1991b: 270).

29. Developments in artificial life, such as genetic algorithms, biomorphs, and neural networks, are affording a better understanding of the non-linear dynamics of evolutionary life, with computer models demonstrating the actual process of spontaneous emergence and self-organization. 'Human' evolution is fast becoming susceptible to, and manipulable by, synthetic engineering. Indeed, engineering can no longer be restricted to electrical and mechanical models, since it is becoming increasingly open knowledge that engineering models can be applied with far-reaching results to the domains of historical change and cultural politics. Systems, including human social and technical systems, are exchangers and connectors of energy and information. It is these complex adaptive systems that have shaped human history and knowledge. Intelligent life is both assembled from, and the assembler of, information-evolution. This is to speak of an inescapable neg-entropic loop but one which, contra Lyotard, is not governed by a single theo-logic. Life's self-comprehension and engineering are best carried out not through top-down philosophical determination (and obfuscation), but rather through the technical (diagrammatic) study of its actual and specific engineerings and bottom-up processes of spontaneous self-organization. What the new praxis of A-life has shown is that the dominant (Darwinian) biologies have failed to tell the full story of evolution. The problem with the hegemonic models is that change is viewed in terms of fixed and mechanistic processes taking place in a closed universe. In its concreteness and simplicity evolution by selection of the 'fittest' is analogous to classical statistical mechanics and an outgrowth of the political economy of English liberalism in which the competition of units of production was seen as bringing progress to the whole. The union of natural selection with Mendelian genetics simply carried forward the tradition of classical mechanics that merged with statistical dynamics at the end of the nineteenth century (Wesson 1991: 35). Population genetics, however, which construes the gene as the basic atom of evolution, is unable to account for complex evolution grasped as the 'ability to make transitions' since it neglects self-organizing and self-regulating systems which function in conditions of uncertainty and instability in a universe that is open and unbounded (ibid.: 36). On the model of complexity organisms have to be conceived as open systems that undergo constant flux and that self-generate internally as well as externally, evolving interactively within an ecological and ethological context, in which any change is irreversible simply because there is no stable equilibrium to which they can return. Simondon proposed the idea of a 'metastable equlibrium' as a way of thinking the 'becoming' of a living system. For him, a being does not possess a 'unity in its identity', which would be that of a stable state in which transformation is not possible, but rather

it enjoys a *'transductive unity'*, meaning that it is able to 'pass out of phase with itself'. On this understanding, becoming is a dimension of the being and not simply something that happens to it following a succession of events that affect a being which is already given and established (Simondon 1992: 301–2, 311). This is to speak of complex 'evolution' as a vital and dynamic process. Simondon was convinced that all processes of 'invention', whether in the domain of biology or that of 'epistemology' (knowledge), can be understood as 'transductive', as opposed to being either inductive or deductive, since what is of primary importance in invention is the 'discovery of the dimensions according to which a problematic can be defined' (ibid.: 313). In other words, transduction is nothing other than the process of ontogenesis itself. This means for Simondon, in a powerful argument he uses against the dialectic, that 'time' is also invented in accordance with the 'becoming' of this ontogenesis (the dialectic presupposes a previous time period in which the activity of auto-genesis unfolds) (ibid.: 315).

30. The construction of the steam engine was the culmination of theoretical work dealing with a specific technological problem (how to pump water out of mines), which unpredictably led to a whole new science and thought-paradigm, namely, thermodynamics. It is a classic instance of the feedback loop that exists between technics and theory. The steam engine is a good example in the history of human technics of technology both evolving in accordance with the 'law' of path-dependency and illustrating the phenomenon of 'punctuated equilibrium', which serves to account for innovation on the level of both biological (natural) and human (artificial) evolution. Contingency in this context refers to the fact that a historical event is contingent when it takes place as the result of a long string of unpredictable antecedents, as opposed to the outcome of nature's so-called fixed laws (Gould 1991: 69). Contingent events are dependent upon choices from a past that seemed tiny and trivial at the time, with the result that 'Minor perturbations early in the game nudge a process into a new pathway, with cascading consequences that produce an outcome vastly different from any alternative' (ibid.). This is true of both the rise of mammals (biology) and the dominance of the qwerty typewriter system (technology). In an analysis of 'fitness landscapes', in which 'adaptation' is construed as an attempt to optimize systems that are riddled with conflicting constraints, Stuart Kauffman has followed Gould in maintaining that the increasing diversity of the biosphere and technosphere, or meat and metal, are informed by the same or similar fundamental 'laws' (Kauffman 1989 and 1995). Gould, however, emphasizes the extent to which the impact of accident and chance in evolution results in non-adaptive and pre-adaptive effects.

A classic example is the human brain, but the history of technics is littered with examples of non-adaptation or pre-adaptation where many major inventions were designed to solve small local problems but then mushroomed into something entirely different.

31. A number of theorists associated with complexity have seen in it the chance to reconcile Clausius and Darwin, or entropy and evolution (the one spearheading in the direction of total dissipation, the other revealing ever-increasing novel and creative adaptations). Prigogine is perhaps the best-known exponent of this reconciliation whose notion of 'dissipative structures' gives expression to complex adaptive systems which maintain themselves at the cost of energy. On this model entropy acts as a progenitor of complexity, of order out of chaos. It is developments in the new geology, however, which pose the greatest challenge to the gradualist ethic of classical Darwinism, placing at the centre of our understanding of the evolution of the earth a truly radical notion of contingency, one which makes it even more alien than the de-anthropocentrization performed by Darwin. As one of today's leading lunar and terrestrial geochemists has noted, if the asteroid which impacted on earth 65 million years ago, removing the giant reptiles in a global catastrophe, had missed, it is highly unlikely that species of humans like us would have evolved at all (Ross Taylor 1992: 294). A notion of discontinuity or punctuation is crucial to any radical conception of chaotic, complex, non-linear evolution. The thesis of 'punctuated equilibrium' (PE) associated with the work of Stephen Jay Gould and Niles Eldredge has dramatically remodelled the notion of 'evolution' bequeathed to us by Darwin (who spoke of a gradualist 'descent with modification') (Eldredge and Gould 1972; Eldredge 1985). On this model species and individuals are construed as homoeostatic systems in which a gradualist phyletic evolution is disturbed rarely, but profoundly, by rapid and episodic events of speciation. In fact, the 'material theory of evolution' put forward by the maligned geneticist and student of embryology Richard Goldschmidt in 1940 anticipated the thesis of PE by several decades. Goldschmidt put forward the notion of 'macromutations' in arguing for a leaps and bounds theory of evolution in which life on planet earth is characterized by long periods of stasis followed by abrupt periods of explosive change (the time-scale is a geological one). On this model there are two types of speciation, one that is continuous, cumulative, and adaptive, and one that is discontinuous and non-adaptive. The effects in embryology of the macro-mutations are to be understood as 'cascading'. A parallel can be found in the philosophy of technology in which a gradualist model has dominated until quite recently. Even though

classical economists, such as Steuart and Smith, distinguished between a sudden and a gradual introduction of new machines, the overriding conception in their appreciation of technological change is one of gradual applications of new methods of production with technology understood as evolving in terms of small, incremental steps. The emphasis has been, therefore, on downplaying the role of major innovations and conceiving change as a process involving the steady accumulation of minor improvements and modifications. Mokyr has proposed that a parallel process of macro-mutation can be seen to be at work in the evolution of technology, or what he calls 'macroinventions' (Mokyr 1990: 291). Although they may constitute a minority of all inventions ever made, it is not numbers which are important but 'cascading effects'. His claim is that it is the emergence of new ideas and macro-inventions, such as the screw propeller, chemical fertilizers, and the Bessemer process, that prevent the drift of cumulative small inventions swimming into the law of diminishing returns. A condition of positive feedback – irreversible and drastic technological take-off – is arrived at through the 'wave-effect' of macro-invention. The 'cascading effect' of technological innovation would thus appear to conform to a chaotic model (on the distinction between innovation and invention see Schumpeter 1976). Such a model can even be found in Marx's analysis of capital, in which he traces the evolution of technics back to small, revolutionary changes through an appreciation of the physical characteristics of mechanical equipment (tools, the slide rule, automated machinery systems, and so on) and of capital as effecting an integrated system of machines. It is for this reason that Marx maintains not that it was the steam engine taken as an isolated technology which created the Industrial Revolution, but rather that it was the invention of machines which made a revolution in the form of the steam engine necessary (Marx 1976: 496–7).

32. In short, the Darwinian conception of evolution is stuck within a Newtonian and mechanistic paradigm. In a recent article Mike Davis has sought to show that natural selection conceives evolution in terms of a well-regulated mechanical system, and that in this regard it is the influence of Lyell's *Principles of Geology* that proved decisive in Darwin's formation and articulation of gradualist evolution in the theory of selection. Lyell's uniformitarian geology expels catastrophe and chaos from the the non-linear and contingent evolution of the earth in several ways. Firstly, it construed tectonic change as taking place gradually over vast periods; secondly, it sought to expose a steady-state system in the evolution of the planet by maintaining that any cross-section of geological time would reveal the same processes and land form; and thirdly, it necessarily draws the 'evolutionist'

conclusion that the present is an analogue for the past. In Darwin's theory of biological evolution this results in an expelling of saltation, an emphasis on extinction and speciation as merely the result of uniformitarian scales and rates in which adaptation is constantly fine-tuned by natural selection, and in which evolution, therefore, proceeds in terms of a subtle and progressivist logic (Davis 1996: 54). By contrast, the new geology of 'bolide impact' construes the evolution of the earth as an open system in which the major events of evolutionary change are events of punctuation and, moreover, not simply the result of plate tectonics but of extra-terrestrial impact. On this model, therefore, the solar system is fundamentally 'historical' (as outlined in Gould's sense above), a 'bricolage of unique events and assemblages', and open to galactic perturbations; catastrophic and uniformitarian processes are seen as interwoven on all temporal levels, and the past can be treated as only a partial analogue for the future (Davis 1996: 61). Furthermore, the new geology, which is inspired by chaos and complexity theory, lends support to the thesis of punctuated equilibrium as the real 'agent' of evolutionary change. As Davis puts it: 'Mass extinction events are non-Darwinian factories of natural selection. At its extremes, evolution is a punctuated equilibrium between autonomous dynamics of environmental and genetic change' (ibid.). The dogma of gradualist evolution by natural selection as the dominant, albeit not exclusive, agent of evolutionary change is seriously shaken.[20] As Davis notes, it is difficult to reconcile the irrefutable evidence of mass extinctions – such as the Permian one, which extinguished 96 per cent of the earth's marine species and 84 per cent of all genera 245 million years ago – with the thin wedge and

---

20 No doubt Davis exaggerates the rivalry between the thesis of PE and natural selection, and no doubt orthodox Darwinists would have no major difficulty in reconciling the phenomenon of regular extinctions with the step-by-step gradualism of natural selection. They do not necessarily amount to an incompatible theory of evolution once it is appreciated that natural selection works in terms of the short-term selection of short-term advantage (any 'progress' will last for only a short time and be short-lived). We need to allow for a plurality of *tempos* and *modes* of 'evolution'. The thesis of PE, for example, works best as a novel account of *speciation*. What is needed is a comprehensive and multi-dimensional appreciation of contingent 'evolution' which would take seriously the existence of historical lock-in, as well as geological catastrophism, and deprive selection of any residual linear and (ultimate) teleological prejudices. Although a rigid distinction between 'extra-terrestrial' and 'terrestrial' would be an arbitrary one, it can be argued that even on the level of terrestrial development the geography of the earth is subject to constant and dramatic change on account of a number of major factors, such as the inconstancy of the magnetic field (which may be directly caused by impacts from space), continental drift, and tectonic and volcanic activity. In the latter case the effects are unpredictable since the earth

fine-tuning which characterize evolution on the model of natural selection. In short, the history of the planet is the story of 'irreversible and unpredictable contingency' (ibid.), in which innumerable possible evolutionary pathways can be prescribed out of the same initial conditions (ibid.: 70), and in which catastrophe 'replaces the linear temporal creep of microevolution with nonlinear bursts of macroevolution' (ibid.: 75). On this new model terrestrial events are inseparable from their continuum with extra-terrestrial processes. Comet bombardments act as 'superchargers' of geological and biological evolution. History meets its other and is overtaken by becomings on account of the fact that not only is it marked by fault lines but it is also ruled by the contingency of catastrophe in which explosions fuel innovation (for an application of PE to the evolution of the 'human' from the long stability of homo erectus to the sudden explosion of new 'human' types, see Eldredge 1985: 125ff.). This is the domain of 'evolution', not normal, gradualist adaptation, but a wild and untamed proliferation of monstrous variety and diversity. Natural history and human history come together on the level of the new 'impact' theory, guaranteeing that the future will be deviant, degenerate, and monstrous. Or, as one of the first philosophers of punctuated equilibrium wrote:

---

can either be chilled by volcanic activity, through dust being poured out into the stratosphere, or warmed by such activity through the pouring out of carbon dioxide. Thus even the 'explosions' of evolution have to be seen as taking place, when situated on an appropriate geological time-scale, against a background of constant change. It is within such an 'environment' of geological change that ultra-Darwinists (non-progressivists) see natural selection operating. However, on the level of macro-evolution, a major revision of a central tenet of Darwinism is undoubtedly called for. On the model of catastrophic contingency, offered by the application of non-linear dynamics to the domain of geology, 'evolution' is a story of the survival not of the 'fittest' but of the 'luckiest'. To give an example cited by Davis (1996: 75), the adaptive advantage enjoyed by mammals during the extinction of the dinosaurs 65 million years ago may simply have been the result of the fact that they were concentrated in circum-polar regions that were least affected by the low-latitude Chicxulub impact which led to the dinosaurs being wiped out. In his unconvincing, and at times silly, attack on Gould, Dennett singularly fails to grasp the *historico-geological* nature of Gould's thesis on contingency with its claim that if the tape of life were wound back and allowed to play again from an identical starting point it would not produce the same phenomena, such as the Cambrian explosion (Dennett 1995b: 299–312). Concerning the evolution of life on earth Gould rightly insists: 'Little quirks at the outset . . . unleash cascades of consequences that make a particular future seem inevitable in retrospect. But the slightest early nudge contacts a different groove, and history veers into another plausible channel, diverging continually from its original pathway. The end results are so different, the initial perturbations so apparently trivial' (Gould 1990: 320–1).

At these turning points of history we behold beside one another, and often mutually involved and entangled, a splendid, manifold, junglelike growth . . . a tremendous ruin and self-ruination, as the savage egoisms that have turned, and almost exploded, against one another wrestle for 'sun and light'. . . . All sorts of new what-fors and wherewithals . . . decay, corruption, and the highest desires gruesomely entangled.

(Nietzsche 1966: section 262)

33. 'Evolution' of the earth, and of the life and death on it, can be configured in terms of a theatre of cruelty. The only teaching that is faithful to life's betrayal of itself, to its complexity and contingency, to its desire for creative destruction, is one of evil. 'Just like the plague there is an evil time, the victory of dark powers, a higher power nourishing them until they have died out' (Artaud 1993: 21). In the theatre of cruelty, as in the plague, there appears a strange sun, 'an unusually bright light by which the difficult, even the impossible suddenly appears to be our natural medium' (ibid.). For 'us' the effect of this theatre of life and death is not simply a 'contagion' but, like the event of the plague, a 'revelation' which urges forward the exteriorization of a latent undercurrent of cruelty and perversity. The 'poison' of the theatre destroys when injected, but it works like a plague, containing a 'redeeming epidemic', speaking of a 'superior disease' since it is nothing other than an 'absolute crisis' in which matters of life and death are played out (again and again). Energy is intensified and life driven into delirium. Life as a good or bad infection, gasping for its resurrection: I am the future, I am tomorrow, I am the end.

Nothing distinguishes me ontologically from a crystal, a plant, an animal . . . we are drifting together toward the noise and black depths of the universe, and our diverse systemic complexions are flowing up the entropic stream, toward the solar origin, itself adrift. Knowledge is at most the reversal of drifting, that strange conversion of times, always paid for by additional drift; but this is complexity itself, which was once called being. . . . To be or to know from now on will be translated by: see the islands, rare or fortunate, the work of chance or of necessity.

(Serres 1982: 83)

# BIBLIOGRAPHY

Adams, H. (1931), *The Education of Henry Adams*, New York, Modern Library.

Ansell Pearson, K. (1991/1996), *Nietzsche contra Rousseau*, Cambridge, Cambridge University Press.

Ansell Pearson, K. (1992), 'Who is the Übermensch? Time, Truth, and Woman in Nietzsche', *Journal of the History of Ideas*, 53, pp. 309–33.

Ansell Pearson, K. (1997), 'Life Becoming Body: On the "Meaning" of Post Human Evolution', *Cultural Values*, vol. 1, no. 2

Ansell Pearson, K. (forthcoming), 'Nature as Music: Animal Becoming Art/Art Becoming Animal. On Deleuze and von Uexküll', in C. Boundas (ed.), *Deleuze's Becomings*, New York, Routledge.

Arendt, H. (1958), *The Human Condition*, Chicago, University of Chicago Press.

Artaud, A. (1993), *The Theatre and its Double*, trans. V. Corti, London, Calder.

Balakrishnan, G. (1995), 'The National Imagination', *New Left Review*, no. 211, pp. 56–69.

Ballard, J. G. (1987), *The Drowned World*, New York, Carroll & Graff.

Bataille, G. (1985), *Visions of Excess: Selected Writings 1927–39*, trans. A. Stoekl, Minneapolis, University of Minnesota Press.

Bateson, G. (1978), *Mind and Nature*, London, Fontana Collins.

Baudrillard, J. (1992), *Selected Writings*, ed. M. Poster, Oxford, Basil Blackwell.

Baudrillard, J. (1993), *The Transparency of Evil: Essays on Extreme Phenomena*, trans. J. Benedict, London, Verso.

Baudrillard, J. (1994), *The Illusion of the End*, trans. C. Turner, Oxford, Polity Press.

Baudrillard, J. (1996), *The Perfect Crime*, trans. C. Turner, London, Verso.

Beer, G. (1986), '"The Face of Nature": Anthropomorphic Elements in the Language of *The Origin of Species*', in L. J. Jordonova (ed.), *Languages of Nature*, London, Free Association Books, pp. 207–44.

Benjamin, W. (1979), *Illuminations*, trans. H. Zohn, London, Collins.

Bergson, H. (1960), *Time and Free Will*, trans. F. L. Pogson, New York, Harper Torchbooks.

Bergson, H. (1983), *Creative Evolution*, trans. A. Mitchell, Lanham, University Press of America.

Bergson, H. (1990), *Matter and Memory*, trans. N. M. Paul and W. S. Palmer, New York, Zone Books.

Blackburn, R. J. (1990), *The Vampire of Reason: An Essay in the Philosophy of History*, London, Verso.

Blanchot, M. (1993), *The Infinite Conversation*, trans. S. Hanson, Minneapolis, University of Minnesota Press.

Boothby, R. (1991), *Death and Desire: Psychoanalytic Theory in Lacan's Return to Freud*, London, Routledge.

Bowler, P. J. (1992), 'Lamarckism', in E. F. Keller and E. A. Lloyd (eds), *Keywords in Evolutionary Biology*, Cambridge, Mass., Harvard University Press, pp. 188–94.

Braudel, F. (1981), *The Structures of Everyday Life: The Limits of the Possible*, London, HarperCollins.

Brooks, D. R. and Wiley, E. O. (1988), *Evolution as Entropy: Toward a Unified Theory of Biology*, Chicago, University of Chicago Press.

Burian, R. M. (1992), 'Adaptation: Historical Perspectives', in E. F. Keller and E. Lloyd (eds), *Keywords in Evolutionary Biology*, Cambridge, Mass., Harvard University Press, pp. 7–13.

Burkhardt, R. W. (1995), *The Spirit of System: Lamarck and Evolutionary Biology*, Cambridge, Mass., Harvard University Press.

Buss, L. W. (1987), *The Evolution of Individuality*, New Jersey, Princeton University Press.

Butler, S. (1914), 'Darwin among the Machines', *A First Year in Canterbury Settlement*, London, A. C. Fifield, pp. 179–85.

Butler, S. (1985), *Erewhon*, Harmondsworth, Middlesex, Penguin.

Butler, S. (1922), *Unconscious Memory*, London, Jonathan Cape.

Canguilhem, G. (1992), 'Machine and Organism', in J. Crary and S. Kwinter (eds), *Incorporations*, New York, Zone Books, pp. 44–70.

Carnot, S. (1960), *Reflections on the Motive Power of Fire*, ed. E. Mendoza, New York, Dover Publications.

Caygill, H. (1991), 'Affirmation and Eternal Return in the Free-Spirit Trilogy', in K. Ansell Pearson (ed.), *Nietzsche and Modern German Thought*, London, Routledge, pp. 216–40.

Chardin, T. de (1965), *The Phenomenon of Man*, London, Fontana.

Clarke, A. C. (1964), *Profiles of the Future*, New York, Bantam Books.

Conway, D. W. (1989), 'Overcoming the *Übermensch*: Nietzsche's Revaluation of Values', *Journal of the British Society for Phenomenology*, 20 (3), pp. 211–24.

Cornell, J. F. (1984), 'Analogy and Technology in Darwin's Vision of Nature', *Journal of the History of Biology*, 17 (3), pp. 303–44.

Crawford, C. (1988), *The Beginnings of Nietzsche's Theory of Language*, Berlin and New York, Walter de Gruyter.

Cronin, H. (1991), *The Ant and the Peacock: Altruism and Sexual Selection from Darwin to Today*, Cambridge, Cambridge University Press.

Csanyi, V. (1989), *Evolutionary Systems and Society: A General Theory of Life, Mind, and Culture*, Durham, Duke University Press.

Csanyi, V. and Kampis, G. (1985), 'Autogenesis: The Evolution of Replicative Systems', *Journal of Theoretical Biology*, 114, pp. 303–21.

Darwin, C. (1985), *The Origin of Species*, Harmondsworth, Middlesex, Penguin.

Davis, M. (1996), 'Cosmic Dancers on History's Stage: The Permanent Revolution in the Earth Sciences', *New Left Review*, 217, pp. 48–85.

Dawkins, R. (1976, revised edition 1989), *The Selfish Gene*, Oxford, Oxford University Press.

Dawkins, R. (1982), *The Extended Phenotype*, Oxford, Oxford University Press.

Dawkins, R. (1991), *The Blind Watchmaker*, London, Penguin.

Debord, G. (1983), *The Society of the Spectacle*, Detroit, Black and Red.

Debray, R. (1995), 'Remarks on the Spectacle', *New Left Review*, no. 214, pp. 134–42.

Deleule, D. (1992), 'The Living Machine: Psychology as Organology', in J. Crary and S. Kwinter, *Incorporations*, New York, Zone Books, pp. 203–33.

Deleuze, G. (1966/1991), *Le Bergsonisme*, Paris, PUF; *Bergsonism*, trans. H. Tomlinson and B. Habberjam, New York, Zone Books.

Deleuze, G. (1968/1994), *Différence et répétition*, Paris, PUF; *Difference and Repetition*, trans. Paul Patton, London, Athlone Press.

Deleuze, G. (1973), *Proust and Signs*, trans. R. Howard, London, Allen Lane.

Deleuze, G. (1983), *Nietzsche and Philosophy*, trans. H. Tomlinson, London, Athlone Press.

Deleuze, G. (1984), *Kant's Critical Philosophy*, trans. H. Tomlinson and B. Habberjam, London, Athlone Press.

Deleuze, G. (1987), *Dialogues: Gilles Deleuze and Claire Parnet*, trans. H. Tomlinson and B. Habberjam, London, Ahtlone Press.

Deleuze, G. (1988a), *Spinoza: Practical Philosophy*, trans. R. Hurley, San Francisco, City Light Books.

Deleuze, G. (1988b), *Foucault*, trans. S. Hand, London, Athlone Press.

Deleuze, G. (1989a) *Cinema 2: The Time-Image*, trans. H. Tomlinson and R. Galeta, London, Athlone Press.

Deleuze, G. (1989b), *Masochism: Coldness and Cruelty*, trans. J. McNeill, New York, Zone Books.

Deleuze, G. (1990), *Logic of Sense*, trans. M. Lester with C. Stivale, London, Athlone Press.

Deleuze, G. (1993), *The Fold: Leibniz and the Baroque*, trans. T. Conley, London, Athlone Press.

Deleuze, G. and Guattari, F. (1972/1983), *L'Anti-Oedipe*, Paris: PUF; *Anti-Oedipus*, trans. R. Hurley et al., London, Athlone Press.

Deleuze, G. and Guattari, F. (1980/1988), *Mille Plateaux*, Paris, PUF; *A Thousand Plateaus*, trans. B. Massumi, London, Athlone Press.

Deleuze, G. and Guattari, F. (1994), *What is Philosophy?*, trans. G. Burchell and H. Tomlinson, London, Verso.

Dennett, D. C. (1995a), 'Evolution, Error, and Intentionality', in P. K. Moser and J. D. Trout (eds.), *Contemporary Materialism: A Reader*, London, Routledge, pp. 245–75.

Dennett, D. C. (1995b), *Darwin's Dangerous Idea: Evolution and the Meanings of Life*, London, Allen Lane.

Derrida, J. (1973), *Writing and Difference*, trans. A. Bass, London, Routledge.

Derrida J. (1982), *Margins of Philosophy*, trans. A. Bass, Hemel Hempstead, Harvester Wheatsheaf.

Derrida, J. (1992), *Acts of Literature*, ed. D. Attridge, London, Routledge.

Desmond, A. and Moore, J. (1992), *Darwin*, London, Penguin.

Diderot, D. (1963), *Diderot. Interpreter of Nature: Selected Writings*, trans. J. Stewart and J. Kemp, London, Lawrence & Wishart.

Eardley, M. (1995), 'Deleuze and the Nonformal Function', unpublished dissertation, University of Warwick.

Eco, U. (1986), 'Striking at the Heart of the State', in *Travels in Hyper-reality*, trans. W. Weaver, London, Pan.

Edelman, G. (1994), *Bright Air, Brilliant Fire: On the Matter of the Mind*, Harmondsworth, Middlesex, Penguin.

Eigen, M. (1992), *Steps Towards Life: A Perspective on Evolution*, Oxford, Oxford University Press.

Eldredge, N. (1985), *Time Frames: The Rethinking of Darwinian Evolution and the Theory of Punctuated Equilibria*, London, Heinemann.

Eldredge, N. (1995), *Reinventing Darwin: The Great Evolutionary Debate*, London, Weidenfeld & Nicolson.

Eldredge, N. and Gould, S. J. (1972), 'Punctuated Equilibria: An Alternative to

Phyletic Gradualism', in T. J. M. Schopf (ed.), *Models of Paleobiology*, San Francisco, Freeman, Cooper.

Ellul, J. (1965), *The Technological Society*, trans. J. Wilkinson, London, Jonathan Cape.

Emmeche, C. (1994), *The Garden in the Machine: The Emerging Science of Artificial Life*, trans. S. Sampson, New Jersey, Princeton University Press.

Enzensberger, H. M. (1990), *Political Crumbs*, trans. M. Chalmers, London, Verso.

Foucault, M. (1977), 'Nietzsche, Genealogy, History', in Foucault, *Language, Counter-Memory, Practice*, Oxford, Basil Blackwell.

Foucault, M. (1990), 'The Thought from Outside', in M. Foucault and M. Blanchot, *Foucault/Blanchot*, trans. J. Mehlman, New York, Zone Books.

Freud, S. (1990), *The Origins of Religion*, Harmondsworth, Middlesex, Penguin.

Freud, S. (1991), *On Metapsychology*, Harmondsworth, Middlesex, Penguin.

Georgescu-Roegen, N. (1971), *Entropy and the Economic Process*, Cambridge, Mass., Harvard University Press.

Goodwin, B. (1995), *How the Leopard Changed its Spots: The Evolution of Complexity*, London, Phoenix.

Gould, S. J. (1977), *Ontogeny and Phylogeny*, Cambridge, Mass., Harvard University Press.

Gould, S. J. (1983), *The Panda's Thumb*, London, Penguin.

Gould, S. J. (1989), *Wonderful Life: The Burgess Shale and the Nature of History*, London, Hutchinson Radius.

Gould, S. J. (1991), *Bully for Brontosaurus*, London, Hutchinson Radius.

Gould, S. J. (1995), *The Individual in Darwin's World*, London, Weidenfeld & Nicolson.

Gould, S. J. (1996), *Dinosaur in a Haystack*, London, Jonathan Cape.

Guattari, F. (1992/1995), *Chaosmose*, Paris, Galilée; *Chaosmosis: An Ethico-aesthetic Paradigm*, trans. P. Bains and J. Pefanis, Sydney, Power Publications.

Haas, L. (1929), *Der Darwinismus bei Nietzsche*, Giessen.

Habermas, J. (1987), *Toward a Rational Society*, trans. J. J. Shapiro, Oxford, Polity Press.

Hegel, G. W. F. (1970a/1980), *Phaenomenologie des Geistes*, Frankfurt, Suhrkamp; *Phenomenology of Spirit*, trans. A. V. Miller, Oxford, Oxford University Press.

Hegel, G. W. F. (1970b), *Hegel's Philosophy of Nature* (volume 3), ed. and trans. M. J. Petry, London, Allen and Unwin.

Heidegger, M. (1961), *Nietzsche* (in 2 volumes), Pfullingen, Gunther Neske.

Heidegger, M. (1966), *Discourse on Thinking*, trans. J. M. Anderson and E. Hans Freund, New York, Harper Torchbooks.

Heidegger, M. (1968), *What Is called Thinking?*, trans. J. Glenn Gray, New York, Harper Torchbooks.

Heidegger, M. (1972), 'The End of Philosophy and the Task of Thinking', in Heidegger, *On Time and Being*, trans. J. Stambaugh, New York, Harper Torchbooks, pp. 55–74.

Heidegger, M. (1979), *Nietzsche: The Will to Power as Art*, trans. D. F. Krell, London, Routledge.

Heidegger, M. (1987), *Nietzsche: The Will to Power as Knowledge and Metaphysics*, trans. D. F. Krell et. al., San Francisco, Harper and Row.

Heidegger, M. (1991a), *Die Technik und die Kehre*, Pfullingen, Neske.

Heidegger, M. (1991b), *The Principle of Reason*, trans. R. Lilly, Bloomington, Indiana University Press.

Heidegger, M. (1995), *The Fundamental Concepts of Metaphysics: World, Finitude, Solitude*, trans. W. McNeill and N. Walker, Bloomington, Ind., Indiana University Press.

Heilbroner, R. L. (1994), 'Technological Determinism Revisited', in M. R. Smith and L. Marx (eds), *Does Technology Drive*

*History?*, Cambridge, Mass., MIT Press, pp. 67–79.

Hornborg, A. (1992), 'Machine Fetishism, Value, and the Image of Unlimited Good: Towards a Thermodynamics of Imperialism', *Man*, 27, pp. 1–18.

Howard, J. (1992), *Darwin*, Oxford, Oxford University Press.

Huxley, J. (1953), *Evolution in Action*, London, Chatto & Windus.

Jacob, F. (1974), *The Logic of Living Systems*, trans. B. E. Spillman, London, Allen Lane.

Jameson, F. (1991), *Postmodernism, or the Cultural Logic of Late Capitalism*, Verso, London.

Jameson, F. (1995), *The Geopolitical Aesthetic: Cinema and Space in the World System*, London, BFI Publishing.

Jünger, E. (1982), *Der Arbeiter: Herrschaft und Gestalt*, Stuttgart, Klett Cotta.

Kampis, G. (1991), *Self-Modifying Systems in Biology and Cognitive Science: A New Framework for Dynamics, Information, and Complexity*, Oxford, Pergamon Press.

Kant, I. (1974/1982), *Kritik der Urteilskraft*, Frankfurt, Suhrkamp; *Critique of Judgement*, trans. J. C. Meredith, Oxford, Oxford University Press.

Kant, I. (1991), *Political Writings*, trans. H. B. Nisbet, Cambridge, Cambridge University Press.

Kant, I. (1995), *Opus postumum*, trans. E. Forster and M. Rosen, Cambridge, Cambridge University Press.

Kauffman, S. A. (1989), 'Cambrian Explosion and Permian Quiescence: Implications of Rugged Fitness Landscapes', *Evolutionary Ecology*, 3, pp. 274–81.

Kauffman, S. A. (1993), *The Origins of Order: Self-Organization and Selection in Evolution*.

Kauffman, S. A. (1995), 'Technology and Evolution: Escaping the Red Queen Effect', *The McKinsey Quarterly*, 1, pp. 119–29.

Kaufmann, W. (1974), *Nietzsche: Philosopher, Psychologist, and Antichrist*, 4th edn, New Jersey, Princeton University Press.

Kelly, A. (1981), *The Descent of Darwin: The Popularization of Darwinism in Germany 1860–1914*, Chapel Hill, University of North Carolina Press.

Kelly, K. (1994), *Out of Control: The New Biology of Machines*, London, Fourth Estate.

Klossowski, P. (1985), 'Nietzsche's Experience of Eternal Return', in D. B. Allison (ed.), *The New Nietzsche*, Cambridge, Mass., MIT Press, pp. 107–21.

Krell, D. F. (1992), *Daimon Life: Heidegger and Life-Philosophy*, Bloomington, Ind., Indiana University Press.

Laing, R. (1979), 'Machines as Organisms: An Exploration of the Relevance of Recent Results', *Biosystems*, 11, pp. 201–15.

Lampert, L. (1987), *Nietzsche's Teaching*, New Haven, Yale University Press.

Lampert, L. (1993), *Nietzsche and Modern Times*, New Haven, Yale University Press.

Landa, M. de (1991), *War in the Age of Intelligent Machines*, New York, Zone Books.

Langton, C. G. (1988), 'Artificial Life', in *Artificial Life: SFI Studies in the Sciences of Complexity*, Reading, Mass., Addison-Wesley, pp. 1–46.

Law, R. (1991), 'The Symbiotic Phenotype: Origins and Evolution', in L. Margulis and R. Fester (eds), *Symbiosis as a Source of Evolutionary Innovation*, Cambridge, Mass., MIT Press.

Leroi-Gourhan, A. (1993), *Speech and Gesture*, trans. A. Bostock, Cambridge, Mass., MIT Press.

Lovtrup, S. (1987), *Darwinism: The Refutation of a Myth*, London, Croom Helm.

Lyotard, J. F. (1989), *The Postmodern Condition: A Report on Knowledge*, Manchester, Manchester University Press.

Lyotard, J. F. (1991), *The Inhuman: Reflections on Time*, trans. G. Bennington and R. Bowlby, Oxford, Polity Press.

Lyotard, J. F. (1993), *Political Writings*, trans. B. Readings and K. P. Geiman, London, UCL Press.

McHale, J. (1969), *The Future of the Future*, New York, Ballantine Books.

Malthus, T. (1798/1992), *Essay on the Principle of Population*, ed. G. Gilbert, Oxford, Oxford University Press.

Marcuse, H. (1968), *One Dimensional Man*, London, Abacus.

Marcuse, H. (1987), *Eros and Civilization*, London, Ark.

Margulis, L. (1970), *The Origin of Eukaryotic Cells*, New Haven, Yale University Press.

Margulis, L. (1981), *Symbiosis in Cell Evolution*, San Francisco, W. H. Freeman.

Margulis, L. and Fester, R. (1991), *Symbiosis as a Source of Evolutionary Innovation*, Cambridge, Mass., MIT Press.

Margulis, L. and Sagan, D. (1995), *What is Life?*, London, Weidenfeld and Nicolson.

Marx, K. (1976), *Capital: volume one*, trans. B. Fowkes, Harmondsworth, Middlesex, Penguin.

Massumi, B. (1992), *A User's Guide to Capitalism and Schizophrenia*, Cambridge, Mass., MIT Press.

Maturana, H. and Varela, F. (1980), *Autopoiesis and Cognition: The Realization of the Living*, London and Dordrecht, D. Riedel.

Mayr, E. (1982), *The Growth of Biological Thought: Diversity, Evolution, and Inheritance*, Cambridge, Mass., Harvard University Press.

Mayr, E. (1991), *One Long Argument: Charles Darwin and the Genesis of Modern Evolutionary Thought*, Harmondsworth, Middlesex, Penguin.

Mokyr, J. (1990), *The Lever of Riches: Technological Creativity and Economic Progress*, New York, Oxford University Press.

Moravec, H. (1988), *Mind Children*, Cambridge, Mass., Harvard University Press.

Morton, P. (1984), *The Vital Science: Biology and the Literary Imagination 1860–1900*, London, Allen & Unwin.

Müller-Lauter, W. (1978), 'Der Organismus als innerer Kampf', *Nietzsche-Studien*, 7, pp. 189–223.

Mumford, L. (1957), *The Transformations of Man*, London, Allen and Unwin.

Mumford, L. (1966), 'The First Megamachine', *Diogenes*, 55 (July–September), pp. 1–15.

Nageli, C. von (1898), *A Mechanico-Physiological Theory of Organic Evolution*, trans. V. A. Clarke and F. A. Waugh, Chicago, Open Court.

Nichols, B. (1988), 'The Work of Culture in the Age of Cybernetic Systems', *Screen*, 29, pp. 22–47.

Nietzsche, F. (1933–42), *Historisch-Kritische Gesamtausgabe*, Munich.

Nietzsche, F. (1966), *Beyond Good and Evil*, trans. W. Kaufmann, New York, Random House.

Nietzsche, F. (1967), *The Birth of Tragedy*, trans. W. Kaufmann, New York, Random House.

Nietzsche, F. (1968), *The Will To Power*, trans. W. Kaufmann and R. J. Hollingdale, New York, Random House.

Nietzsche, F. (1969), *Thus Spoke Zarathustra*, trans. R. J. Hollingdale, Harmondsworth, Middlesex, Penguin.

Nietzsche, F. (1974), *The Gay Science*, trans. W. Kaufmann, New York, Random House.

Nietzsche, F. (1979a), *Ecce Homo*, trans. R. J. Hollingdale, Harmondsworth, Middlesex, Penguin.

Nietzsche, F. (1979b), *Twilight of the Idols*, trans. R. J. Hollingdale, Harmondsworth, Middlesex, Penguin.

Nietzsche, F. (1982), *Daybreak: Thoughts on the Prejudices of Morality*, trans. R. J. Hollingdale, Cambridge, Cambridge University Press.

Nietzsche, F. (1983), *Untimely Meditations*, trans. R. J. Hollingdale, Cambridge, Cambridge University Press.

Nietzsche, F. (1984), *Dithyrambs of Dionysus*, bilingual edition, trans. R. J. Hollingdale, London, Anvil Press.

Nietzsche, F. (1986), *Human, All Too Human*, trans. R. J. Hollingdale, Cambridge, Cambridge University Press.

Nietzsche, F. (1987), *Nietzsche Sämtliche Werke: Kritische Studienausgabe* (in 15 volumes), ed. G. Colli and M. Montinari, Berlin and New York, Walter de Gruyter.

Nietzsche, F. (1994), *On the Genealogy of Morality*, trans. C. Diethe, Cambridge, Cambridge University Press.

Oppenheimer, J. (1959), 'An Embryological Enigma in the *Origin of Species*', in B. Glass et al., *Forerunners of Darwin: 1745–1859*, Baltimore, Johns Hopkins University Press, pp. 292–323.

Orsucci, A. (1993), 'Beiträge zur Quellenforschung', *Nietzsche-Studien*, 22, pp. 371–88.

Orsucci, A. (1996), *Orient-Okzident: Nietzsches Versuch einer Loslösung vom europäischen Weltbild*, Berlin and New York, Walter de Gruyter.

Paul, D. B. (1988), 'The Selection of the "Survival of the Fittest"', *Journal of the History of Biology*, 21 (3), pp. 411–24.

Pippin, R. B. (1988), 'Irony and Affirmation in Nietzsche's *Thus Spoke Zarathustra*', in M. A. Gillespie and T. B. Strong (eds.), *Nietzsche's New Seas*, Chicago, University of Chicago Press, pp. 45–71.

Plotkin, H. (1995), *Darwin Machines and the Nature of Knowledge*, London, Penguin.

Prigogine, I. and Stengers, I. (1985), *Order out of Chaos*, London, Fontana.

Raff, R. A. and Kaufman, T. C. (1983), *Embryos, Genes, and Evolution*, New York, Macmillan.

Regis, E. (1992), *Great Mambo Chicken and the Transhuman Condition: Science Slightly Over the Edge*, Harmondsworth, Middlesex, Penguin.

Reuleaux, F. (1876/1963), *The Kinematics of Machinery: Outlines of a Theory of Machines*, trans. A. B. W. Kennedy, New York, Dover.

Rifkin, J. (1981), *Entropy: A New World View*, New York, Bantam Press.

Rose, S. (1992), *The Making of Memory: From Molecules to Mind*, London, Bantam Press.

Ross Taylor, S. (1992), *Solar System Evolution: A New Perspective*, Cambridge, Cambridge University Press.

Rousseau, J. J. (1990), *Judge of Jean-Jacques: Dialogues*, trans. J. R. Bush et al., Hanover and London, University Press of New England.

Sahal, D. (1981), *Patterns of Technological Innovation*, Reading, Mass., Addison-Wesley.

Sapp, J. (1994), *Evolution by Association: A History of Symbiosis*, Oxford, Oxford University Press.

Saunders, P. T. and Ho, M. W. (1976), 'On the Increase in Complexity in Evolution', *Journal of Theoretical Biology*, 63, pp. 375–84.

Saunders, P. T. and Ho, M. W. (1981), 'On the Increase in Complexity in Evolution II', *Journal of Theoretical Biology*, 90, pp. 515–30.

Schick, K. D. and Toth, N. (1993), *Making Silent Stones Speak: Human Evolution and the Dawn of Technology*, London, Weidenfeld & Nicolson.

Schumpeter, J. (1976), *Capitalism, Socialism, and Democracy*, London, Allen and Unwin.

Serres, M. (1982), *Hermes: Literature, Science, and Philosophy*, Baltimore, Johns Hopkins University Press.

Sigmund, K. (1995), *Games of Life: Explorations in Ecology, Evolution, and Behaviour*, London, Penguin.

Simondon, G. (1992), 'The Genesis of the Individual', in J. Crary and S. Kwinter (eds), *Incorporations*, New York, Zone, pp. 297–319.

Spencer, H. (n.d.), *The Data of Ethics*, New York, Crowell & Company Publishers.

Spinoza, B. (1955), *The Ethics*, trans. R. H. M. Elwes, New York, Dover Publications.

Stallabrass, J. (1995), 'Empowering Technology: The Exploration of Cyberspace', *New Left Review*, 211, pp. 3–33.

Stegmaier, W. (1987), 'Darwin, Darwinismus, Nietzsche: Zur Problem der Evolution', *Nietzsche-Studien*, 16, pp. 264–88.

Stock, G. (1993), *Metaman: Humans, Machines, and the Birth of a Global Superorganism*, London, Bantam Press.

Stonier, T. (1992), *Beyond Information: The Natural History of Intelligence*, London, Springer-Verlag.

Theweleit, K. (1992), 'Circles, Lines, and Bits', in J. Crary and S. Kwinter (eds), *Incorporations*, New York, Zone Books, pp. 256–64.

Tipler, F. (1995), *The Physics of Immortality: Modern Cosmology, God, and the Resurrection of the Dead*, London, Pan.

Toffler, A. (1990), *Powershift: Knowledge, Wealth, and Violence at the Edge of the 21st Century*, London & New York, Bantam Books.

Tudge, C. (1995), *The Day Before Yesterday: Five Million Years of Human History*, London, Cape.

Uexküll, J. von (1934/1992), 'A Stroll Through the Worlds of Animals and Men: A Picture Book of Invisible Worlds', *Semiotica*, 89 (4), pp. 319–91.

Vaneigem, R. (1994a), *The Revolution of Everyday Life*, trans. D. Nicholson-Smith, London, Rebel Press.

Vaneigem, R. (1994b), *The Movement of Free Spirit*, New York, Zone Books.

Vernadsky, V. (1945) 'The Biosphere and the Noosphere', *American Scientist*, 33, pp. 1–12.

Vorzimmer, P. J. (1970), *Charles Darwin: The Years of Controversy*, Philadelphia, Temple University Press.

Wallace, A. R. (1891), *Natural Selection and Tropical Nature: Essays on Descriptive and Theoretical Biology*, London, Macmillan.

Wallace, A. R. (1958, reprinted 1971), 'On The Tendency of Varieties to Depart indefinitely from the Original Type', in C. Darwin and A. R. Wallace, *Evolution by Natural Selection*, London, Cambridge University Press, pp. 268–80.

Wallerstein, I. (1991a), *Geopolitics and Geoculture: Essays on the Changing World-System*, Cambridge, Cambridge University Press.

Wallerstein, I. (1991b), *Unthinking Social Science: The Limits of Nineteenth-Century Paradigms*, Oxford, Polity Press.

Wesson, R. (1991), *Beyond Natural Selection*, Cambridge, Mass., MIT Press.

Wheelwright, P. (ed.) (1966), *The Presocratics*, New York, The Odyssey Press.

Wicken, J. S. (1987), *Evolution, Thermodynamics, and Information: Extending the Darwinian Paradigm*, Oxford, Oxford University Press.

Williams, J. (1996), 'Narrative and Time', *Proceedings of the Aristotelian Society*, 47–61.

Williams, R. (1994), 'The Political and Feminist Dimensions of Technological Determinism', in M. R. Smith and L. Marx (eds.), *Does Technology Drive History?*, pp. 217–35.

Winner, L. (1977), *Autonomous Technology: Technics-out-of-Control as a Theme in Western Political Thought*, Cambridge, Mass., MIT Press.

Wolpert, L. (1991), *The Triumph of the Embryo*, Oxford, Oxford University Press.

Yates, F. (1966), *The Art of Memory*, London, Routledge & Kegan Paul.

Young, R. M. (1985), *Darwin's Metaphor: Nature's Place in Victorian Culture*, Cambridge, Cambridge University Press.

# INDEX

abstract machine(s) 125, 138–9, 180 n. 19
Adams, H. 170
adaptation 4–5, 30, 33, 88, 90–92, 99, 107, 117, 130, 136, 149, 174, 184–5, 187; and exaptation 88; gradualist 188
Adorno, T.W. 36, 154
anthropocentrism 2, 6, 11, 13, 24 n. 12, 115–17, 119, 124, 132, 137–8, 152–3, 159, 161–2, 164, 170; *see also* de-anthropocentrization
anthropomorphism 5, 7–8, 11, 29, 32, 59, 62, 86, 90, 105–7, 109–15, 122, 144, 149, 161, 170; and Darwin 127 n. 6; and Darwinism 110; Deleuze and Guattari on 119; and Nietzsche 163; and Nietzscheanism 110
Apollonian 120
Arendt, H. 20 n. 10
aristocratic radicalism 106
Artaud, A. 82–3, 189
artificial life (A-Life) 4, 34, 148–9, 183
ascetic ideal 33, 37–9, 47, 54–5
assemblage(s) 71, 120, 134–6, 139, 145, 174; technological 145; *see also* machinic
auto-catalysis 182
autopoiesis 117, 122, 125 n. 2, 140–2, 144
autopoietic machine 140–1

bacteria and origin of species 132
Baer, K.E. von 129–30 n. 8

Bagehot, W. 87
Bataille, G. 69–70
Bateson, G. 88–9 n. 9
Baudrillard, J. 2, 29, 29 n. 21, 34–5, 147, 149, 152, 174; on the subjective illusion of technology 152
becoming(s) 5–8, 11–12, 15–16, 19–20, 25, 27–8, 43–5, 47–51, 58, 61–3, 73, 77, 80, 83, 92–4, 99, 107–8, 111, 116–21, 125–6, 131, 135–6, 138, 150, 154 n. 3, 156, 162–5, 183–4, 188; of alien life 139; of the animal 118, 120; anti-entropic 170; block of 130, 135; and evolution 135; and history 23; and memory 14 n. 4, 23–4, 24 n. 12, 28; -minoritarian 178; -molecular 179; rhizomatic 134, 145; and technology 171
Benjamin, W. 24, 26 n. 17, 28 n. 20
Bergson, H. 6–7, 27 n. 19, 62, 92–3 n. 13, 117–18, 123 n. 1, 124–5, 125 n. 2, 131 n. 9, 134, 142, 149–50
biologism 12, 109–12, 114–15
Blackburn, R. 166, 170–1
Blanchot, M. 63, 66, 78 n. 10; on technology 160
Boltzmann, L. 180
Braudel, F. 145
Brooks, D.R. 181
Bruno, G. 24
Butler, S. 2, 139, 142–3, 149 n. 16, 171

Cambrian explosion 188 n. 20
Canguilhem, G. 144
capitalism 2, 145–50, 171–2, 174–8; see also late-modern capital
Carnot, S. 179–80, 180 n. 19
categorical imperative 46, 66
Chardin, T. de 31, 125 n. 2, 131 n. 9, 167, 167 n. 9
Christianity 2
Clausius, R. 180, 185
complexity theory 93, 122, 128, 179, 182–3, 185, 187
Conway, D.W. 38
Copernicus, 55
Csanyi, V. 142, 181
cyberspace 2–3, 33

Darwin, C. 2, 4, 11–12, 13 n. 3, 17–18, 29 n. 21, 34, 44, 85–113, 115, 117, 127, 127 n. 6, 129 n. 8, 133, 148, 155, 160, 171, 185–7; and complexity 171; and genealogy 135 n. 11; and gradualism 185, 187; and A.R. Wallace 30 n. 21; see also Nietzsche
Davis, M. 186–7, 187–8 n. 20
Dawkins, R. 12–13 n. 3, 130, 137
de-anthropocentrization 116, 185
death-drive 7, 58, 60, 63, 63 n. 3, 64, 71–6, 80, 82
Debord, G. 3, 123 n. 1, 157–60
Debray, R. 123 n. 1, 159–60
Deleuze, G.: on active and reactive 16 n. 7, 21 n. 11, 43–5; his Bergsonism 127; on the body 119; and complexity 128–9, 136; *Difference and Repetition* 58, 77, 126–9; on eternal return 15 n. 7, 42–6, 65–6; on ethology 117, 136, 137 n. 12; contra Freud 59; on *Matter and Memory* 27 n. 19; on memory 24–7; and molecular Darwinism 126; on natural selection 104; and so-called *Naturphilosophie* 136; *Nietzsche and Philosophy* 21, 24, 42, 79–80; on Nietzsche's superman 12; on reactive force 88 n. 8; on selection 43–5, 76, 127–9, 147

Deleuze, G. and Guattari, F.: 7, 14 n. 4, 23, 46, 67–8, 77, 82, 104, 118 n. 35, 119, 122, 126, 130, 131 n. 9, 134–6, 138, 143, 145–6, 165, 172, 172 n. 16, 174, 176, 178; *Anti-Oedipus* 104, 178; on the death-drive 71; on mimicry 103 n. 26; on non-organic life 120, 125, 130; on politics 178; on social and technical machines 143, 145–8, 174–5; *A Thousand Plateaus* 22, 67, 71, 118 n. 35, 126; on undecidable propositions 178–9; *What is Philosophy?* 7, 23 n. 12
Dennett, D.C. 133; on S.J. Gould 188 n. 20
Derrida, J. 11, 48
desiring-machines 143
Dionysian 17, 62, 120, 129
Dionysus 74

Eardley, M. 134
Eco, U. 146
Eigen, M. 89 n. 9
Eldredge, N. 185
Ellul, J. 4, 10 n. 1, 145, 152 n. 1, 170
embryogenesis and morphogenesis 129; and phylogenesis 126–7
Empedocles 86 n. 2
engineering 4, 34, 91, 114, 143, 173, 183; bio- 149; desire- 143; genetic 34, 133, 173
entropy 4, 7, 63–5, 73, 80, 82–3, 88, 93, 122, 127, 134, 142, 147, 149–50, 156, 164, 166–70, 172–3, 175; as co-extensive with evolution 144; and development 173; and negentropy 166, 171; and nihilism 164 n. 8; see also negentropy
Enzensberger, H.M. 160
Eros 83; and Thanatos 64
eternal return 8, 14, 38, 42, 44–6, 54, 57–83, 101–2, 108, 163, 175; as an alternative principle of selection 101; as counter-entropic principle 77; and overman 78, 78 n. 10; as selective thought 44; and thermodynamics 62, 80
ethology 117, 136; see also Deleuze
eugenics 14, 34, 167 n. 9

feedback 15, 29, 62, 88–9, 97 n. 22, 102, 134, 140, 147 n. 15, 148, 174, 179, 182, 184, 186
Feuerbach, L. von 159
Foucault, M. 16 n. 8
Freud, S. 24, 26, 58–61, 63–4, 71–6, 83, 160; and involution 130

Galileo 24
*Geist* 18, 99, 102–3 n. 26, 170; *see also* technics
God 7, 41, 123, 160, 162, 179; death of 12, 37, 68, 159, 168
Goldschmidt, R. 185
Goodwin, B.C. 13 n. 3
Gould, S.J. 166, 184–5, 187, 188 n. 20
grand narratives 2–4, 124, 148, 165, 169, 170, 172
Guattari, F. 6, 76 n. 9, 128, 144–5; on complexity 145; *see also* Deleuze

Habermas, J. 172; on technology 147 n. 15
Haeckel, E. 87, 126, 129 n. 8, 131 n. 9
Hegel, G.W.F. 96 n. 21, 115–16, 137 n. 12, 179
Heidegger, M. 11–12, 16 n. 8, 33, 38, 114–15, 117, 118 n. 35, 119, 122, 157, 159, 169; on von Baer 130 n. 8; on Nietzsche's biologism 109–12; on the organism 115–16; on technology 152–3, 153 n. 2
Hering, E. 28 n. 20
Hobbes, T. 98, 127 n. 6
Huxley, J. 111
Huxley, T.H. 87
hybridization 136
hylomorphism 120

involution 19, 34, 118, 130, 136; creative 130, 131 n. 9; and evolution 126, 128, 131 n. 9; technics of 13

James, W. 87
Jameson, F. 3, 157 n. 5, 170, 171 n. 15

Jünger, E. 152, 159

Kampis, G. 142
Kant, I. 27 n. 18, 29, 32, 32 n. 23, 66, 86 n. 2, 113, 115, 126, 133, 138, 143, 154; on the organism 136–7; on universal history 155; *see also* Nietzsche
Kauffman, S.A. 128, 184
Kelly, K. 32, 149, 149 n. 17
Klossowski, P. 45 n. 2, 46 n. 3

Lamarck, J.B. 4, 25, 28 n. 20, 61, 87, 124, 148–9; *see also* neo-Lamarckism
Lampert, L. 38
Laplace, Marquis Pierre Simon 182
late-capital 5, 147, 174–5; and complexity 177
Lavoisier, A.L. 180
Leroi-Gourhan, A. 29–31, 160
Lyell, C. 186
Lyotard, J.F. 3, 124, 167–9, 169 n. 12, 170–4, 176 n. 17, 183

machinic 5, 114–17, 122, 130, 134, 136–7, 139, 141–3, 176, 178; assemblages 125, 146, 175; becomings 134–5, 143, 176; death 82; enslavement 165, 175, 179; heterogenesis 139, 145; hyper-text 145; philosophy of history 165; phylogenesis 6; phylum 175; surplus-value 130, 175, 175–6 n. 17; unconscious 74
Malthus, T. 96, 96 n. 20, 96 n. 21, 100
Marcuse, H. 3–4, 28 n. 20, 74 n. 7, 159, 172
Margulis, L. 125 n. 2, 132 n. 10
Marx, K. 32, 127 n. 6, 145, 147, 157, 175, 186
Massumi, B. 6, 174
Maturana, H. 140–2
Mechanosphere 120, 125, 131 n. 9
memes 1, 13
memory 14, 17, 20, 22, 24–8, 30–1, 36, 61, 66, 111, 121; organic 94 n. 15; technics of 23–4, 27–8
Mendelian genetics 183
metallurgy 124

Metternich, F. von 182
Mill, J.S. 34, 92
mnemotechnics 6, 23–4
Mokyr, J. 186
molar 5, 23, 27, 102–4, 104 n. 30, 116, 136, 142–3, 148, 174; politics 178
molecular 5, 23, 102, 104, 104 n. 30, 116–17, 174
Moravec, H. 33, 167–8
Mumford, L. 4, 157

Nageli, C. von 93, 93 n. 14
negentropy 148, 167, 167 n. 9, 168–72, 176, 180, 183; *see also* entropy
neo-Darwinism 126, 129; *see also* ultra-Darwinism
neo-Lamarckism 1, 149; techno-Lamarckism 166
Newton, I. 182
Nietzsche, F.: on the animal 120–2; on art 121–2; *Anti-Christ* 38; and bad conscience 19–20; *Beyond Good and Evil* 106; *The Birth of Tragedy* 47; on complexity 100–1; on critique 16, 19, 40, 43; contra Darwin 86, 93, 101, 105–6, 108–9, 127; on Darwin's error 104, 127 n. 6; *Daybreak* 51; and death of God 12; *Ecce Homo* 15; and ecology 14; and the future 10–11, 39–40, 46–7, 49, 163–4; on gay science 51–6; *The Gay Science* 51, 53, 57, 66, 105; *On the Genealogy of Morality* 12, 24, 38, 85, 87, 90, 92–3, 102, 106; *Human, All Too Human* 40, 46–7, 86, 97 n. 22; on justice 103; and Kant 66, 138, 154, 155 n. 4, 162; on mimicry 103 n. 26; on proud death 72; contra Rousseau 18, 48–50; *Schopenhauer as Educator* 87; on science 55–6; and selection 8, 41–2, 44–5, 47, 53, 101–2, 105, 108; *Thus Spoke Zarathustra* 38, 77, 80; *Twilight of the Idols* 106; *see also* nihilism
nihilism 7, 21, 35, 27, 62, 72, 154–5, 160–2, 164–5; Nietzsche on 154 n. 3, 161, 163–4; as pathological 164

Omega Point 167
ontogeny 128, 144; and phylogeny 126, 144
order-word 68–9
overhuman 10–11, 14–17, 20, 24 n. 12, 28, 40, 82, 91, 111, 161, 163; *see also* posthuman and transhuman
overman 14–15, 21, 37–41, 50, 54, 56, 68, 78–80, 91, 101; *see also* Übermensch

perfect nihilist 164
Permian extinction 187
perspectivism 42, 47
philosophy of history 154–5, 166, 171; *see also* machinic
Pippin, R.B. 38
plane of immanence 46, 120, 151
political, death of 150
political theory 146
politics of desire 146
possessive individualism 6
posthuman 2–3, 5, 33–5; *see also* overhuman and transhuman
postmodern(ity) 2–5, 7, 33, 148, 150, 153, 157 n. 5, 160, 166, 169–70, 172, 175, 177; capital 174; science 181; terrorism 146
preformationism 126
Prigogine, I. 181, 185
Proust, M. 26, 28 n. 20
punctuated equilibrium 21, 184–5, 187, 187 n. 20, 188

Red Queen hypothesis 89
Rée, P. 17
repetition 38, 58, 60–1, 65–6, 69, 73–7, 79, 158–9, 174; as demonic power 76; of the same 158
rhizomatic/rhizome 6, 14 n. 4, 24 n. 12, 124, 130, 134–6, 144–5, 165, 171
Rousseau, J.J. 18, 48–50
Roux, W. 93, 98, 98 n. 23, 99, 106
Roy, E. Le 125 n. 2

Sagan, D. 125 n. 2

schizoanalysis 125
Schopenhauer, A. 61, 162
self-overcoming 2, 17, 26, 29, 33, 39, 47, 50–1, 73, 89, 108, 110, 165; Nietzsche's 50–1; of the will to truth 138
Serres, M. 179, 180 n. 19
Simondon, G. 128 n. 7, 160, 183–4; on ontogenesis 184
situationism 123 n. 1, 156, 159
Smith, A. 98, 186
soul 13, 28, 31
Spencer, H. 34, 87, 87 n. 6, 92, 106 n. 33
Spinoza, B. 95, 98
spirit: *see* Geist
State 147–8, 160, 175–6
Strauss, D. F. 29, 106
suicide 71–2
superman 12, 14, 38
surplus value of code 135–6, 143
symbiosis 91, 124, 130, 132–4, 136, 139, 145, 166; bacterial 132

technics 4, 11, 29–31, 113–14, 120, 123–4, 136, 143–4, 148, 150, 152–3, 162, 165, 185–6; and evolution 125; as *Geist* 170; and theory 184
technology 4–5, 10 n. 1, 11, 25, 31, 114, 123, 132, 147–8, 152, 157, 160, 164–5, 168, 173–4, 176, 179, 184, 186; cybernetic 146; and entropy 147; as extended phenotype 124; fetishism of 147; as grand narrative 124; irony of 169; and natural selection 112; as neg-entropic capture 180; philosophy of 185; question of 4, 145, 152–3, 172; recombinant DNA 133; as social Darwinism 171; 'spectacular' 158; subjective illusion of 152
Tipler, F. 167

Toffler, A. 165, 175 n. 17
transcendental illusions 7, 26, 60, 126; of capital 7, 147; of entropy 7, 181; of nihilism 7, 164, 164 n. 8
transference 76
transhuman 1–4, 6–8, 10, 32–3, 35–6, 39, 105, 108, 122, 138, 154, 160–1, 163
transversal communication 23, 130, 133, 136

*Übermensch* 14, 85, 91; *see also* overman
ultra-Darwinism 130
utility 6, 94–5, 97, 113; Darwin/ism and 95, 95 n. 18
Uexküll, J. von 118, 118 n. 35, 119

Vaneigem, R. 3, 146, 155–6
Varela, F. 140–2
Vernadsky, V. 125 n. 2
Virilio, P. 71
viroids 133
virtual 2, 5–6, 68, 97 n. 21, 126, 133, 139, 145, 150, 157, 161, 174; futures 146
vitalism 2, 34, 117, 119, 142–3, 172, 184

Wallace, A.R. 29 n. 21, 88 n. 9, 90 n. 12, 111–12
Wallerstein, I. 177–8, 182; on the crisis of capitalism 177
war machine 72, 72 n. 6, 176
Weismann, A. 64
Wiener, N. 147
Wiley, E.O. 181
will-to-power 8, 12, 21, 90, 92–4, 97–8, 105–9, 117, 120; and survival of the fittest 102

Zarathustra 37–8, 58, 67, 70–1, 76–7, 79, 80–1; becoming of 58; death of 77; *Zarathustra-Nachlass* 77–8